# Oxford Tactic for the TOEIC® test

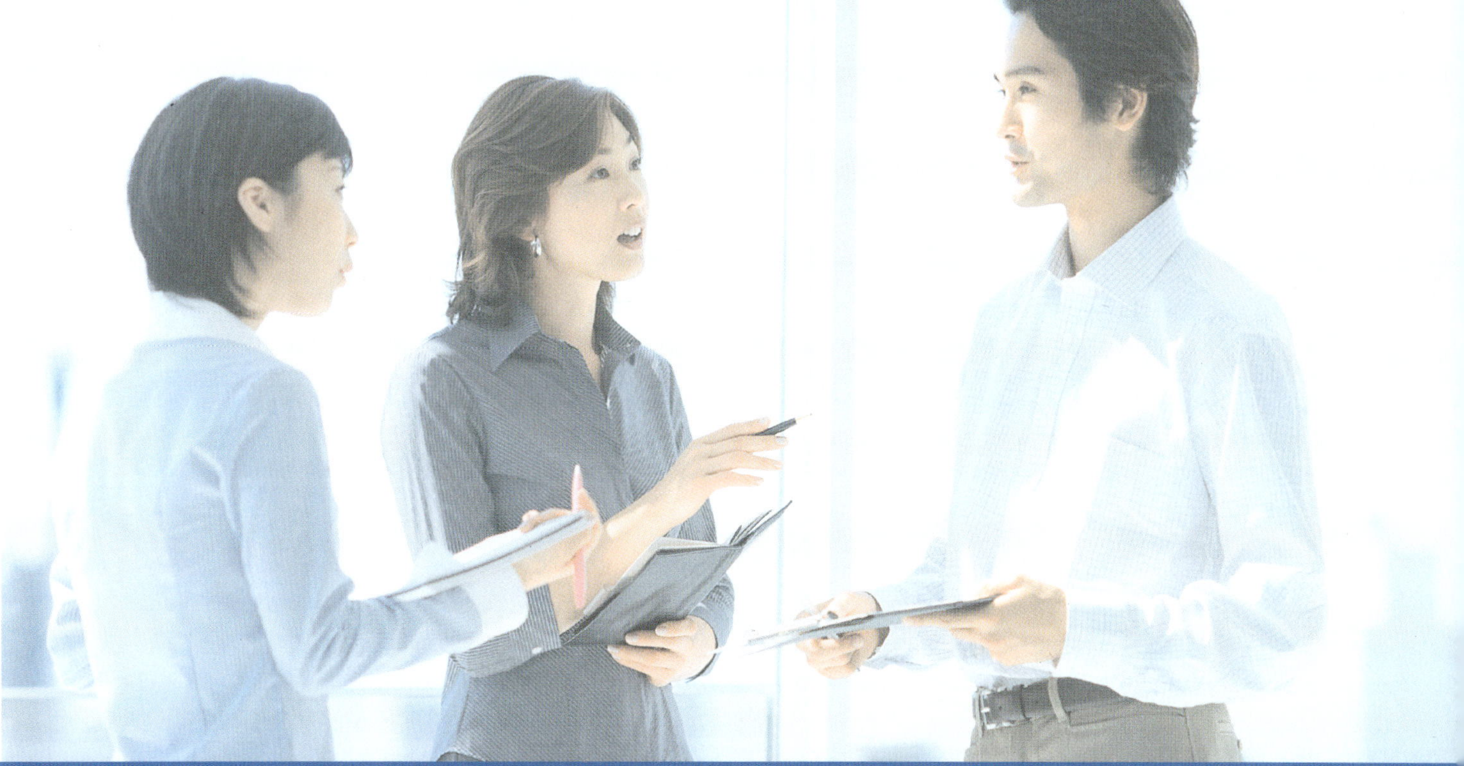

## Contents

OXFORD
UNIVERSITY PRESS

# Overview of the new TOEIC® test

The Test of Englisih for International Communication (TOEIC®) is a multiple-choice test used to measure the English proficiency of non-native English speakers.
With more than 4.5 million people taking the test each year it is an increasingly relevant standard for institutions, companies, and government agencies worldwide.

The TOEIC test is scored from 10–990 points. The chart below shows an approximation of how the scores relate to actual proficiency.

| | |
|---|---|
| over 960 points | Higher general professional level |
| 900 – 955 points | General professional level |
| 785 – 900 points | Advanced working proficiency |
| 605 – 780 points | Basic working proficiency |
| 405 – 600 points | Intermediate proficiency |
| 255 – 400 points | Elementary proficiency |
| 010 – 250 points | Novice |

## Test format and changes to the TOEIC Test

The material in this book reflects the changes made to the test as of May 2006. These changes are intended to make the test a more effective tool to assess actual ability to use English.
Although the overall timing and number of test parts and questions remains unchanged, some significant alterations have been made to the individual test parts. These changes are as follows:

| Part | Old name | New name | Old Q's | New Q's | Changes |
|---|---|---|---|---|---|
| **Listening (45 minutes)** | | | | | |
| 1 | Photos | Photos | 20 | 10 | Half the number of questions |
| 2 | Question-Response | Question-Response | 30 | 30 | No change |
| 3 | Short Conversations | Short Conversations | 30 | 30 | Conversations are longer and each features 3 questions rather than one |
| 4 | Short Talks | Short Talks | 20 | 30 | Talks are longer |
| **Reading (75 minutes)** | | | | | |
| 5 | Incomplete Sentences | Incomplete Sentences | 40 | 40 | No change |
| 6 | Error Recognition | Text Completion | 20 | 12 | New part features questions similar to Part 5, but within a context. |
| 7 | Reading Comprehension | Reading Comprehension | 40 | 28 single 20 double | New questions based upon double passages. Many texts are longer. |

# How to score highly on the TOEIC test

The TOEIC test is a challenging test for speakers of English at all levels due to its tight time limits, large amounts of information to process, and use of carefully selected distractor choices.
Even native speakers of English rarely get a perfect score! There are a number of skills (both test-related and linguistic) you will need in order to do well on the new TOEIC test.

**Key test-taking skills:**
- Familiarity with the test format, instructions and question types – Although all the instructions are printed and exemplified at the start of each test part, knowing these before you go into the test will save you a lot of time and confusion on the actual day.

- Time management – You must plan your time in order to allow yourself more time in the places it will have the greatest effect.
- Efficiency of information processing – You must deal with the lengthy texts and extended listenings in the quickest and most effective manner.
- Awareness of features that can make incorrect answer choices attractive – Being aware of the common forms these 'distractors' take will enable you to avoid them and choose the right answer.

**Linguistic skills**
- Familiarity with the different native speaker accents – Unlike previous forms of the test, the new TOEIC test uses a variety of different accents of English. Being familiar with the speech patterns of North American, Canadian, British and Australian speakers will help you deal with the listening section.
- Awareness of the sound changes that occur in natural English speech – The sound of words spoken in natural conversation can differ dramatically to when they are said in isolation. Being aware of the ways that sounds are combined, dropped and changed in natural speech (e.g. 'going to' often sounds more like 'gonna') can significantly improve your listening comprehension.
- Understanding language in use (conversational English) – The English used in the TOEIC test reflects everyday usage as encountered in offices, shops and on the street, in English-speaking environments all around the world. In order to do well on the test, you must have a clear understanding of how the language is actually used in the real world.
- Vocabulary and grammatical understanding – Last, but certainly not least, success in the TOEIC test requires an extensive range of vocabulary, and knowledge of how these words change and are organized grammatically.

# About this course

The **Oxford Tactics for the TOEIC Test** was specifically designed to develop each of the test-taking and linguistic skills noted above.
The text is divided up into four cycles of seven units – each unit covering one part of the test. Within each unit you will find a series of activities that will focus on each of the key test-taking and linguistic skills noted above.

## Unit outline
Each of the 28 units in the course follows a consistent and easy to follow format and timing. The main sections of each unit, and the key test-taking and linguistic skills it develops, are shown below:

## A Strategy (25–40 mins)

This section provides language and test-taking input that will help you get a higher score in the test. It features a number of "Test tips" that provide important information on the conventions and challenges found in the test, and advice on how to handle them.
Accompanying these are three activities that exemplify and give direct practice on these key points. The activities are broken down as follows:

**1. Language building** –This includes a variety of different tasks aimed at building vocabulary and grammatical knowledge that is relevant to the section and the test as a whole.

- Vocabulary and grammatical understanding
- Understanding language in use (conversational English)

**2. Test tactic** – These activities relate directly to one or more of the unit's "Test tips", and give immediate practice and reinforcement related to test-taking skills such as time management and dealing with the listenings more efficiently and effectively.
(Note – Part 7 features an additional Test tactic instead of a Language building for the first activity)

- Time management
- Efficiency of information processing
- Awareness of features that can make incorrect answer choices attractive

**3. Tactic practice** – These focus directly on the Tactics and/or Language building tactics covered in the unit. They aim to further contextualize and reinforce the tactics introduced in the unit. Unlike activities 1 and 2, these always appear in the same format as found on the actual test.

- All skills noted for activities 1 and 2, plus:
- Familiarity with the test format, instructions and question types

### Understanding natural English

This feature, which appears just before the Mini-tests, focuses on two main challenges students face in the listening section. First of all, it aims to draw attention to one of the main factors that hinders students from understanding natural speech – the fact that in natural conversation sounds change or are dropped altogether, and words can sound completely different to how they are spelled. The short gap-fill listening activities will exemplify and explain these common changes. Secondly, the new TOEIC test features speakers from the United States, Canada, Britain, and Australia. In order to help students become familiar with these different accents, each of the sentences in this section will be spoken by three speakers from different countries.

- Awareness of the sound changes that occur in natural English speech
- Familiarity with the different native speaker accents

## B Mini-Test (10–20 minutes)

These aim to give practice of each part of the test under timings similar to what will actually be faced on the TOEIC Test.
Roughly half of the questions will focus on the tactics covered in the unit, while the rest are a random selection of question types appropriate to the test part.
The Tapescripts and Answer Key booklet in the pack allows for analysis and feedback.

- Familiarity with the test format, instructions and question types
- Time management skills
- Awareness of features that can make incorrect answer choices attractive (by looking at the explanatory answers in the Tapescripts and Answer Key.)
- Reinforcement and further practice (under test-condition timing) of the language and tactics covered in the lesson

## C Learn by doing/Grammar practice/Reading in action

In different parts of the test covered in the course, this section has a slightly different form and name, although the overall purpose is the same – to extend the language beyond the test context and show how it may be applied in different contexts and/or used in the real world. The increased understanding this brings makes the language more memorable, and gives a broader understanding of how it is actually used and the different ways it may appear on the test.
The communicative activities included in this section are often accompanied by "Activity Files" at the back of the book that provide additional language and information used to complete the task.

### Listening Parts 1–4: Learn by doing (20–30 minutes)

These activities aim to provide further practice which is relevant to the test part and unit focus, and make the student more familiar with the language through a variety of communicative oral tasks. These include pair conversations, role plays, short presentations and communicative games.

- Understanding language in use

### Reading Parts 5 and 6: Grammar/vocabulary practice (10–15 minutes)

These tasks aim to reinforce and recycle the grammar/vocabulary point covered in the unit. Areas covered include phrasal verbs, adjectives, adverbs, etc.

### Reading Part 7: Reading in action (20–30 minutes)

These activities aim to reinforce the types of reading tasks found in Part 7 (dealing with forms, letters, emails, etc.) However, they aim to take them a step further by adding a task in which the information gained is used to create some sort or response, e.g. completing a letter or orally checking a schedule, etc.

- Understanding language in use
- Vocabulary and grammatical understanding
- These sections will also provide useful practice for the Speaking and Writing elements that will become part of the TOEIC test in the future.

## D Further practice (Homework for Parts 1–4)

These provide additional focused practice on the given test part. They typically involve the student writing test questions or texts similar to the ones found in the test part based upon English newspapers, magazines or their own ideas.

- Vocabulary and grammar building and reinforcement

## Additional features

### Word lists and accompanying quizzes

Building an extensive vocabulary is one of the key ways to improve your score on the TOEIC test. To help you accomplish this, the most challenging vocabulary from each unit is listed, defined and exemplified at the back of the book. These words are organized by unit to allow for easy after-class review, or they may be studied in advance to prepare for a lesson. Furthermore, to help ensure that these words are understood and remembered, the word list for each unit includes one or two quiz exercises for students to test themselves. All the words from the word list are also included in an alphabetical list at the back of the book for easy study reference.

### Two practice tests

In addition to the 28 units of the course, two complete practice tests are also available in the pack. These can be used as presented as pre and post tests for the course. Alternatively, individual test parts or blocks of questions can be used as additional practice material during the course. These tests are accompanied by audio CDs, explanatory answer keys and tapescripts, and a score conversion chart to allow test takers to get an estimated TOEIC test score.

## Suggested study approaches

The text was specifically written to suit a variety of course lengths and styles. Two of these are shown below.

Approach 1: Fixed courses
(Courses of 40–45 hours in length) – Go through each cycle of the units in the order presented.
(~30 hour courses) Do Parts 1–4 and 7 as presented, assign Parts 5 and 6 for homework.
(~20 hour courses) Do sections A and B only of Parts 1–4 and 7, assign Parts 5 and 6 for homework.

Approach 2: Short/Flexible courses
Courses may be custom-designed for shorter/non-fixed study durations, or ones which aim to target only specific test parts. In this case, it is recommended that teachers do all the chosen test parts of the first cycle of units before moving on to the next. The reason for this is that the tactics and language foci of the earlier units tend to be more general and applicable between test parts.

# TOEIC® test general strategies

This course has been designed to provide you with specific tactics to deal with each individual part of the test. In addition to these there are a number of general things you should remember about taking and preparing for the test.

## Overall test strategies

### Don't leave any questions unanswered – make your "best guess"

If you aren't sure of the correct answer, eliminate any answers you think are wrong, then choose the answer that looks best from the remaining choices. Wrong answers are not penalized, and even a blind guess gives you a 25–33% chance of getting the right answer. If you can eliminate even one wrong answer, your odds of success go up as high as 50%!

### Don't listen to/read the instructions for each part of the test

Be familiar with the test format so you can use this time to start previewing the questions.

### Use the order of the questions as a guide.

Except for general situation or main idea questions, the answers in the reading or listening will be presented in the same order as the questions. This means the answer to the first question will appear early in the passage, the next question will come after that, etc.

## Listening strategies

### Do not wait for all answer choices to be read before answering.

If you think you know the answer, mark it immediately. Then begin previewing the next answer choices.

### Answer quickly and prepare for the next question.

Before each question is played preview the answer choices or picture, and try to predict as much as you can about what you are going to hear and what specifically you are going to be listening for. The better you can predict, the easier the listening will be. This applies to all listening parts except Part 2 (approaches to this part will be covered in the units).

## Reading strategies

### Keep a watch in front of you.

Time management is the key to the reading and you need to monitor exactly how much time you spend on each section to ensure you don't run out of time. You should spend roughly 60 seconds on each Part 7 question and 20–30 seconds on each Part 5 and 6 questions. This will allow you some time to check over your answers at the end.

### Do Part 7 first!

You do not have to follow the order presented in the test. In Parts 5 and 6 you can answer many questions quickly and effectively. Questions in Part 7 can take much longer to make even a basic attempt at, so start here to ensure you don't run out of time.

### Do not start by reading the whole passage

In Part 7 move immediately to the questions and focus on what you need to answer.

### Answer the easy questions first

You do not have to answer in the order presented in the test so get the easy marks first, then come back later and answer (or make your best guess). You may want to make a small mark on your test booklet to remind you which ones you haven't completed.

## Study strategies

### Build your vocabulary

This is the single most important factor for the TOEIC test. To do this you should:
- keep a vocabulary notebook and note all new words, plus the sentence they occur in
- study the word lists in this book and do the quizzes
- read, read, read!

### Study outside of class

Making big improvements on the TOEIC test requires you to significantly improve your knowledge of English. To do this in a reasonable amount of time you must be prepared to follow up on your class lessons with some additional study at home. At the end of each unit there is a "Further Study" section that gives tips to help you expand and reinforce the points you learned in the lesson.

### Learn to **use** English

The TOEIC tests your ability to understand English as it is used in everyday work and life situations. The more capable and comfortable you are in using natural English, both spoken and written, the better you will do on the TOEIC test. Make an effort to use English to communicate as much as you can and your score will go up much faster than if you do nothing but study test items, grammar and vocabulary.

## A    Strategy: Use the photo to predict what you will hear

As soon as this section starts pick out the main focus of the first photograph and start to predict the type of statements you may hear.

### 1    Language building: Brainstorm vocabulary for the focus

Match the nouns and verbs with pictures 1–3. You can use them more than once.

| Nouns | | | Verbs | | |
|---|---|---|---|---|---|
| couple | bag | meal | eat | sit | key in |
| screen | family | keyboard | hold | look | discuss |

**1**

| Nouns | Verbs |
|---|---|
| table | |

**2**

| Nouns | Verbs |
|---|---|

**3**

| Nouns | Verbs |
|---|---|
| table | |

*Follow up:* Add at least two more nouns and verbs to each picture, then compare your lists with a partner.

**Test tip**

**Don't listen to the instructions!**

You will have about 90 seconds while these are read. Use this time to skim the pictures and predict what you will hear.

## 2 Test tactic: Predict possible statements before you listen

Read the information in the box below. Then using the words from Activity 1, write two sentences about each of the pictures 1–3. Read your sentences to your partner.

> Most statements in Part 1 will take one of the following forms.
> 1. The (man/woman/people/thing) **is** / **are** *doing* (something).
>    e.g. *The man **is working** on the computer.*
> 2. The (man/woman/people/thing) **has** / **is** (something/ somewhere).
>    e.g. *The woman **has** a bag.*
>    *The family **are** at the table.*

🎧 *Follow up:* Listen to the correct answer choice for each picture. After each listening discuss with your partner how close your predictions were.

## 3 Tactic practice 🎧

For each picture 1–4, you will have two minutes to brainstorm vocabulary and predict possible statements with your partner.

Then you will hear the correct answer only for pictures 1–4. After each sentence, stop the audio and discuss with your partner how close your predictions were.

**Test tip**

**Predict the statement type**

Most statements are about
**a)** The activity, e.g. *The man is writing an email.*
**b)** The general situation, e.g. *The meal is ready.*

**Tactics checklist**

☑ Brainstorm possible nouns/verbs.
☑ Predict possible statements.

**Understanding natural English**

In natural spoken English, sounds are changed, combined and dropped. Listen to these sentences spoken naturally and write in the missing words.
The ......... discussing something.
The ......... covered in snow.

1

2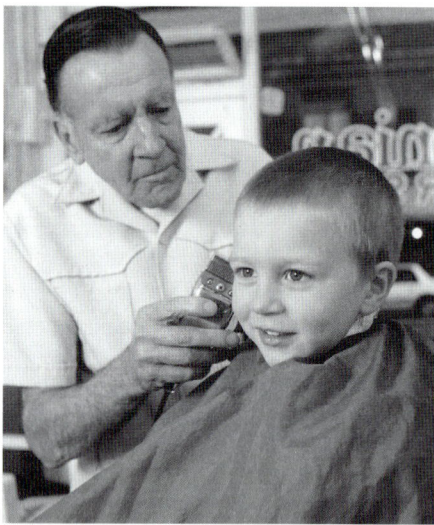

3

4

🎧 Understanding natural English

# Mini-test 🎧

Now apply the *Test tactics* at the actual test speed with questions 1–8.

> 🕐 You will have 1 minute 30 seconds to skim the pictures before the first listening starts. After that you will have exactly 5 seconds between each question to mark your answer and focus on the next picture.

**1**

**2**

**3**

**4**

**5**

**6**

**7**

**8**

| 1 | Ⓐ Ⓑ Ⓒ Ⓓ | 5 | Ⓐ Ⓑ Ⓒ Ⓓ |
|---|---|---|---|
| 2 | Ⓐ Ⓑ Ⓒ Ⓓ | 6 | Ⓐ Ⓑ Ⓒ Ⓓ |
| 3 | Ⓐ Ⓑ Ⓒ Ⓓ | 7 | Ⓐ Ⓑ Ⓒ Ⓓ |
| 4 | Ⓐ Ⓑ Ⓒ Ⓓ | 8 | Ⓐ Ⓑ Ⓒ Ⓓ |

# Learn by doing: Writing stories

**A**  Choose one of the pictures below, brainstorm vocabulary and write a three-sentence story about it. Look at the example first. Which picture does it describe?

| **Vocabulary** (nouns and verbs) | | **Sentences** |
|---|---|---|
| boy | lie | *The boy is lying on his stomach.* |
| oar | look | *There is an oar by his right side.* |
| water | watch | *He is looking in the water.* |

**1**

**2**

**3**

**4**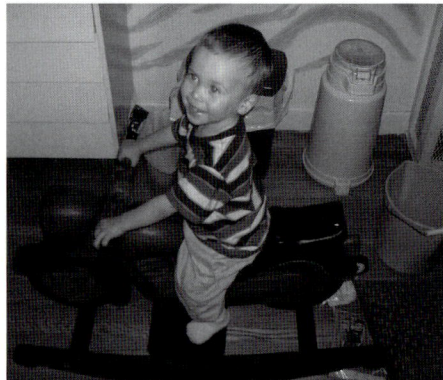

**B**  Read one of your sentences to your partner. They must guess which picture you chose.

*Follow up:* Re-write the three sentences you wrote in A above. Change one word (noun or verb) in two of the sentences so that they are wrong. Read the three sentences to a different partner and ask them to choose the correct sentence.

# Further study

Find one interesting picture and write three sentences about it. Change one word (noun or verb) in two of the sentences to test on your classmates in the next lesson.

Go to word list and quiz page 159.

# Part 2

# Question-response

**A**

## Strategy: Focus on the meaning of factual questions

Focus on what the question is actually asking for. Some answers may closely relate to the topic in the question, but not actually answer it.

**Test tip**

Answers in the TOEIC test do not always answer the question directly

Listen for answers with related details or explanations.

**Test tip**

Often the question and answer will be different tenses

Don't expect the tense to be the same, e.g. the answer to a future or present question may explain something in the past.

**Test tip**

The focus in Part 2 is on meaning

Listen for key words (nouns/verbs) to help you avoid distractors and find the correct answer choice.

**Test tip**

Watch out for common distractors

Being familiar with the ways the test tries to distract you can help you to avoid choosing the wrong answer.

## 1 Language building: Focus on meaning in *Wh-* questions

Match each question 1–3 with two answers from a–f.

1. What are you doing on Sunday?

2. Who is going to represent them at the meeting?

3. How did you get to the airport?

a  I heard Miller was chosen.

b  I always go to my brother's house.

c  Mary gave me a lift.

d  They haven't decided yet.

e  Oh, I didn't. My trip was put off until next week.

f  Actually, I don't have any plans.

*Follow up:* Write two more answers for each question. Read them to your partner and ask them which question 1–3 they are the answer to.

## 2 Test tactic: Focus on the key words and avoid common distractors

 **Focus on the key words**

Listen to sentence 1 and write number 1 next to three key words or phrases as you hear them. Compare the words with your partner, and then make a true answer for the question.

| | | | | | |
|---|---|---|---|---|---|
| Why? ...... | When? ...... | rest ...... | get ...... | company ...... | last birthday ...... |
| How? ...... | What? ...... | come ...... | improve ...... | class ...... | TOEIC score ...... |

Now do the same for the next two sentences.

**Avoid common distractors**

A  Read the information in the box carefully. It shows three common ways the test can trick you into choosing the wrong answer.

**A. Same word – unrelated meaning**

*If you hear the same word in the question and the answer choices, be careful! It is often a distractor.*

*Q. Has the <u>sale</u> improved profits?*
*A. Yes, it is for <u>sale</u>.*

**B. Related subject – doesn't answer the question**

*Often the test will use words that relate to one of the key words in the question, but don't actually answer the question.*

*Q. Where can I buy a cheap <u>air</u> <u>conditioner</u>?*
*A. I agree that it's <u>too</u> <u>hot</u>.*

**C. Similar sound – different/unrelated word**

*A word that sounds similar, but is totally different is often used to trick you.*

*Q. Have you met the new <u>staff</u>?*
*A. No, it's not the same <u>stuff</u>.*

**B** Read questions 1–3 and underline the key words. Then read the two incorrect distractors for each question and mark the type A–C from the box on page 11.

1. What did the customer cancel his contract for?

   [C] He says he can sell it quite cheap. *(cancel sounds like can sell)*

   [ ] My customers live in Boston.

2. Why did you buy a new car?

   [ ] Traffic can be terrible in this city.

   [ ] My wife usually drives the car.

3. How are they going to ship the documents?

   [ ] Have you seen the notice about the sheep?

   [ ] I just love ocean cruises.

*Follow up:* Think of a correct answer choice for each of the questions, and then compare your answers and new sentences with your partner.

**Tactics checklist**

Remember:

☑ Listen for key words and focus on meaning.

☑ Don't expect the form of the answer to be the same as the question.

☑ Listen for common distractors.

## 3 Tactic practice 🎧

You will hear six Part 2 questions. After each question stop the audio. Tell your partner the key words you heard. As soon as the answer choices start, stop speaking, and mark your answer choice.

| 1 | Ⓐ Ⓑ Ⓒ | 4 | Ⓐ Ⓑ Ⓒ |
|---|---------|---|---------|
| 2 | Ⓐ Ⓑ Ⓒ | 5 | Ⓐ Ⓑ Ⓒ |
| 3 | Ⓐ Ⓑ Ⓒ | 6 | Ⓐ Ⓑ Ⓒ |

🎧 **Understanding natural English**

In natural spoken English, sounds are changed, combined and dropped. Listen to these sentences spoken naturally and write in the missing words.

......... quit your last company?

......... get for your last birthday?

## B Mini-test 🎧

Now apply the *Test tactics* at the actual test speed with questions 1–12.

🕐 You will have 5 seconds at the end of each item to make your choice. You must then be ready to listen to the next question.

| 1 | Ⓐ Ⓑ Ⓒ | 7 | Ⓐ Ⓑ Ⓒ |
|---|---------|----|---------|
| 2 | Ⓐ Ⓑ Ⓒ | 8 | Ⓐ Ⓑ Ⓒ |
| 3 | Ⓐ Ⓑ Ⓒ | 9 | Ⓐ Ⓑ Ⓒ |
| 4 | Ⓐ Ⓑ Ⓒ | 10 | Ⓐ Ⓑ Ⓒ |
| 5 | Ⓐ Ⓑ Ⓒ | 11 | Ⓐ Ⓑ Ⓒ |
| 6 | Ⓐ Ⓑ Ⓒ | 12 | Ⓐ Ⓑ Ⓒ |

# C  Learn by doing: Factual questions

Role play:  Student A use the information below.
Student B look at Activity file 2.1 on page 151.

## Student A

You just received the following fax from the Director of your company. Unfortunately, your fax machine is broken and some of the words are unclear.

### Task

- Work with your partner and write out the questions you will ask him or her.
- Call him or her up, apologize for the problem and ask the questions to get the information you need.

---

**Fax Message**

**Important**

*Re: August 14 meeting*

Mr. Carson,

I am writing to let you know that I will be arriving on (1) ░░░░░░░░░░░. I am flying with United Airlines and my plane is scheduled to land at (2) ░░░░░░. Could you arrange my hotel for me?

The main purpose of my visit is (3) ░░░░░░░░░░ Accuron Line of watches. We have had many complaints about water damage. We must discuss (4) ░░░░░░░░░░░░░░. Please invite (5) ░░░░░░░ and ░░░░░░░ also.

Barton Donovan.

---

## Useful language

**Opening**

*I'm sorry to bother you Mr. Donovan, but I'm afraid we couldn't read your fax properly.*

**Closing**

*Thanks very much. That's all the information I need. I will take care of this right away.*

# D  Further study

Write down one of the questions you asked Mr. Donovan, and then make up your own answer and two other Part 2 type distractors to test other students in your next lesson.

Go to word list and quiz page 159.

**A** **Strategy:** Skim read to predict the context before listening

The questions and answer choices in this part of the test can help you predict what you are going to hear. Using the time available to skim read these before listening will help you focus on the key parts of the conversation.

**Test tip**

Predicting the context of the conversation can make the listening easier

Use the key information in the answer choices to make a rough guess about what you are going to hear.

**1 Language building: Paraphrasing**

Match the statements 1–4 with those with a similar meaning a–d. Underline the words which have similar meaning.

1. You can run it with an AC adapter          a   The adapter is missing
2. Look to see if they have the item          b   Buy the part
3. The part wasn't included                    c   Check the parts stock
4. Purchase an adapter                         d   You can plug it into a socket

5. ..........                                   e   Give a replacement part
6. ..........                                   f   The label is incorrect
7. ..........                                   g   It's an expensive model

 *Follow up:* Now listen to three more statements 5–7 and match them with the remaining three phrases with a similar meaning in e–g.

**2 Test tactic: Pick out key words to predict the context**

A   Skim the questions and answer choices and underline key words (10–15 seconds per item). Compare with a partner and discuss what the conversation may be about. Try to predict who and where the speakers are.

1. What does the woman want to do?
   (A) Buy batteries for her CD player
   (B) Purchase an adapter
   (C) Have a missing part replaced
   (D) Check the parts stock

2. What does the man tell her?
   (A) It doesn't run on batteries.
   (B) The label is incorrect.
   (C) The adapter isn't included.
   (D) She should buy another model.

3. What does the man offer to do?
   (A) Order the item
   (B) Check the box label
   (C) Give her a new model
   (D) Include the adapter

B   Focus on the answer choices as you listen. Mark the best answer.
    Guess if you aren't sure, and move on to the next question.

| 1 | Ⓐ Ⓑ Ⓒ Ⓓ |
| 2 | Ⓐ Ⓑ Ⓒ Ⓓ |
| 3 | Ⓐ Ⓑ Ⓒ Ⓓ |

**Tactics checklist**

☑ Use the time before and after the listening to predict the context.

☑ Think of other ways to say the answer choices.

☑ Answer quickly.

**Understanding natural English**

In natural spoken English, sounds are changed, combined and dropped. Listen to these sentences spoken naturally and write in the missing words.

......... borrow your lawnmower?

......... mail these packages?

**3** Tactic practice

Now listen to two more short conversations. Before each conversation begins, use the time to predict the context with your partner, and think of other ways to say the answer choices.

1. What are the men speaking about?
   (A) The new hardware store
   (B) Harry's job
   (C) Martha's birthday
   (D) Harry's lawnmower

2. What does the neighbor want?
   (A) To finish his model
   (B) To hire a new employee
   (C) To try Harry's birthday present
   (D) For Harry to loan him some money

3. What isn't Harry pleased with?
   (A) The price
   (B) How well it cuts grass
   (C) The new model
   (D) His old lawnmower

4. How does the man feel about their new training program?
   (A) It's not as good as the old one.
   (B) It's an improvement on their previous one.
   (C) It doesn't have any practical value.
   (D) It's full of useful ideas.

5. What did the woman ask the man about?
   (A) How many trainees attended
   (B) A package she needs
   (C) The trainees' practical skills
   (D) Comments from the participants

6. What did some trainees criticize?
   (A) There were too many ideas.
   (B) There was no opportunity for feedback.
   (C) It was too theoretical.
   (D) It was hard to say anything in the session.

| 1 | Ⓐ Ⓑ Ⓒ Ⓓ | 4 | Ⓐ Ⓑ Ⓒ Ⓓ |
| 2 | Ⓐ Ⓑ Ⓒ Ⓓ | 5 | Ⓐ Ⓑ Ⓒ Ⓓ |
| 3 | Ⓐ Ⓑ Ⓒ Ⓓ | 6 | Ⓐ Ⓑ Ⓒ Ⓓ |

Understanding natural English

**B** **Mini-test**

Now apply the *Test tactics* at the actual test speed with questions 1–12.

🕐 You will have 30 seconds to skim the questions and answer choices before the first listening starts. After that you will have exactly 8 seconds between each question to mark your answer and focus on the next question.

1. What does the man want the woman to do?
   (A) Pay the money she owes
   (B) Mail some packages
   (C) Attend a meeting
   (D) Give him the addresses

2. What does the woman ask?
   (A) For the destinations
   (B) For the time
   (C) Where the meeting is
   (D) If he wants a coffee

3. Why doesn't the man do it himself?
   (A) The woman has the list.
   (B) The woman owes him a favor.
   (C) He doesn't know the address.
   (D) He has to rush to a previous appointment.

4. What does the woman want?
   (A) To share a ride
   (B) To go shopping
   (C) To take her car
   (D) To take Eric for a drive

**GO ON TO THE NEXT PAGE**

5. What is the woman's problem?

   (A) She has missed the bus
   (B) Her car is broken
   (C) She is late to get to work
   (D) She needs to buy a new car

6. What will the man do?

   (A) Meet her at the company around 8:00
   (B) Show his appreciation
   (C) Take her to the hotel
   (D) Give her a lift to the auction

7. What does the man want the woman to do?

   (A) Go to the theater
   (B) Move to a different parking spot
   (C) Change her mind
   (D) Go to the other building

8. What is the woman concerned about?

   (A) She can't read the sign.
   (B) She is at the wrong branch.
   (C) She thinks the man is making excuses.
   (D) She may not be able to find another space.

9. Why couldn't the woman see the sign?

   (A) It was around the corner.
   (B) It had been cut down.
   (C) It was partly hidden.
   (D) It was behind the truck.

10. What's the problem with the man's watch?

    (A) It needs a new battery.
    (B) It has a crack in the face.
    (C) The buckle is damaged
    (D) It needs to be replaced.

11. What will cause the delay?

    (A) There is a problem with the battery.
    (B) They don't have the correct strap.
    (C) The new watches haven't arrived.
    (D) They must order a replacement watch.

12. When will the watch finally be ready?

    (A) This afternoon
    (B) On Tuesday
    (C) On Wednesday
    (D) On Thursday

| 1 | Ⓐ Ⓑ Ⓒ Ⓓ | 7 | Ⓐ Ⓑ Ⓒ Ⓓ |
|---|---|---|---|
| 2 | Ⓐ Ⓑ Ⓒ Ⓓ | 8 | Ⓐ Ⓑ Ⓒ Ⓓ |
| 3 | Ⓐ Ⓑ Ⓒ Ⓓ | 9 | Ⓐ Ⓑ Ⓒ Ⓓ |
| 4 | Ⓐ Ⓑ Ⓒ Ⓓ | 10 | Ⓐ Ⓑ Ⓒ Ⓓ |
| 5 | Ⓐ Ⓑ Ⓒ Ⓓ | 11 | Ⓐ Ⓑ Ⓒ Ⓓ |
| 6 | Ⓐ Ⓑ Ⓒ Ⓓ | 12 | Ⓐ Ⓑ Ⓒ Ⓓ |

## C    Learn by doing: Requests

**A** Complete the two conversations using the words in the box.

| | |
|---|---|
| I'll do it | Any time will be fine |
| Sure | Do you think I could |
| Would you mind | Sure, no problem |
| | Would that be alright |

A: ........... mailing these packages for me?

B: ........... . When do they have to arrive?

A: They need to be delivered by Tuesday at the latest.

B: OK, ........... this afternoon.

C: ........... borrow your lawnmower? Mine is broken.

D: ........... . When do you want it?

C: How about Saturday afternoon? ...........?

D: Yeah, of course. ........... .

*Follow up:* Practice the conversations.

**B** Make similar conversations with your partner using the situations 1–4 below. Before you begin, look at the useful expressions in the box and read the *Culture note*.

| More common request phrases | Response vocabulary/phrases |
|---|---|
| Would you mind (helping me with these files)? | Of course. |
| | Certainly. |
| Are you by any chance (driving down to the auction)? | |
| | Sorry, (I'm using it on the weekend). |
| I wonder if you would mind (moving your car)? | I'm afraid I can't (right now). |
| | Sorry, I'm really busy. Maybe (Bob) could |
| I need you to (replace this battery for me)? | give you a hand. |

1. Ask them to help you make some copies (you need them for a meeting in one hour).

2. Ask to borrow their calculator (yours is at home).

3. Ask for some help moving some boxes (the courier is going to pick them up in 15 minutes).

4. Ask them for a ride home (your car is in the shop).

### Culture note

If you don't know the person well, start your request with:
*Excuse me ...* or
*I'm sorry to bother you, but ...*

*Follow up:* With your partner, write down one of the conversations you had. Then write three Part 3 type questions (no answer choices) for your conversation. Join up with another pair, read out the conversation as naturally as possible and ask them the questions you wrote.

## D    Further study

Think of an actual request you made recently, or imagine one you might make, and write up the conversation in English. Write three questions (you don't need to make answer choices) to test your classmates in the next lesson.

Go to word list and quiz page 160.

**A**

## Strategy: Skim read to predict the context before listening

The questions and answer choices in this part of the test can help you predict what you are going to hear. Using the time available to skim read these before listening will help you focus on the key parts of the conversation.

### 1  Language building: Paraphrasing

Match each of the underlined words and phrases in the announcements below with the word or phrase with the closest meaning from the list a–f. The first one has been done for you.

> May I have your attention.
>
> I am sorry to announce that the ferry service to the Fairport Islands will be <u>interrupted</u> (1) ....*e*.... due to damage caused by <u>the recent typhoon</u> (2) .......... . Ticket holders may get <u>a refund</u> (3) .......... <u>immediately</u> (4) .......... . The shuttle bus back to the train station should be here in about 20 minutes and in the meantime, we will be serving <u>complimentary</u> (5) .......... <u>beverages</u> (6) .......... .

| | |
|---|---|
| a | last week's storm |
| b | without delay |
| c | money returned |
| d | drinks |
| e | ~~stopped~~ |
| f | free |

### 2  Test Tactic: Pick key words and predict the context

**A**  Skim the questions and answer choices in 1–3 and underline the key words (10–15 seconds per item). Then compare with a partner and discuss which of the situations A–C you think the talk will be about.

1. <u>Where</u> is this <u>announcement</u> being made?
   (A) At a <u>train station</u>
   (B) At an <u>airport</u>
   (C) At a <u>bus station</u>
   (D) At a <u>coffee shop</u>

2. What is the problem?
   (A) The train is delayed due to the hurricane.
   (B) Rains have damaged the Dalesville bridge.
   (C) Service has been interrupted due to the weather.
   (D) Passengers are being refused a refund.

3. What may people wishing to go to Darby do?
   (A) Wait for two hours
   (B) Take a shuttle bus to Evanston
   (C) Get replacement tickets
   (D) Go by train

| | |
|---|---|
| **A** A TV news weather report about a big storm | **C** An announcement about a change in transportation services |
| **B** A tourist information report on new travel routes | |

**Test tip**

**Answer the questions as soon as you hear the answer**

Do not wait for the voice to tell you. Answer quickly, then use the 35–40 seconds between conversations to skim the next questions.

**Tactics checklist**

☑ Use the time before and after the listening to predict the context.

☑ Think of other ways to say the answer choices.

☑ Answer quickly.

**Understanding Natural English**

In natural spoken English, sounds are changed, combined and dropped. Listen to these sentences spoken naturally and write in the missing words.

We apologize ......... inconvenience.

Check the documents ......... typos.

🎧 **B** Focus on the answer choices in A 1–3 as you listen. Mark the best answer. Guess if you aren't sure, and move on to the next question.

| 1 | Ⓐ Ⓑ Ⓒ Ⓓ |
| 2 | Ⓐ Ⓑ Ⓒ Ⓓ |
| 3 | Ⓐ Ⓑ Ⓒ Ⓓ |

## 3 Tactic practice 🎧

Listen to two more short talks. Before each talk begins, with a partner take one minute to predict the context and think of other ways to say the answer choices.

1. What is the purpose of this announcement?
   (A) To discuss the history of Antigua
   (B) To describe Antigua's beautiful landscape
   (C) To make it sound attractive to visitors
   (D) To provide an overview of its Maritime events

2. What was Antigua originally established as?
   (A) A pirate base
   (B) A center for sailing events
   (C) A resort for hiking and watersports
   (D) A military outpost

3. When was this announcement probably first broadcast?
   (A) In October
   (B) In the winter
   (C) During the summer
   (D) In April

4. Why was the meeting called?
   (A) To announce a schedule change
   (B) To move the deadline
   (C) To lend a hand
   (D) To answer any questions

5. When does the project have to be finished?
   (A) In a week
   (B) In five days
   (C) By tomorrow
   (D) By Thursday

6. What are Beth and Howard asked to do?
   (A) Finalize the image files
   (B) Check for typos
   (C) Ask questions
   (D) Write the address labels

| 1 | Ⓐ Ⓑ Ⓒ Ⓓ | 4 | Ⓐ Ⓑ Ⓒ Ⓓ |
| 2 | Ⓐ Ⓑ Ⓒ Ⓓ | 5 | Ⓐ Ⓑ Ⓒ Ⓓ |
| 3 | Ⓐ Ⓑ Ⓒ Ⓓ | 6 | Ⓐ Ⓑ Ⓒ Ⓓ |

🎧  Understanding natural English

**B** ## Mini-test 🎧

Now apply the *Test tactics* at actual test speed with questions 1–12.

🕐 You will have 30 seconds to skim the questions and answer choices before the first listening starts. After that you will have exactly 8 seconds between each question to mark your answer and focus on the next question.

1. Where is this presentation most likely taking place?
   (A) An Asian market
   (B) A board meeting
   (C) A computer conference
   (D) A college technical fair

2. What customer group saw the best sales?
   (A) Executives
   (B) Students
   (C) Small businesses
   (D) Salespeople

**GO ON TO THE NEXT PAGE** ▶

3. How were sales of their standard desktop?

   (A) Extremely good

   (B) Steady

   (C) Poor

   (D) Surprisingly good

4. Which things were noted as blowing in the breeze?

   (A) Tissues

   (B) Cat litter

   (C) Hazardous waste

   (D) Organic waste

5. What day are grass and leaves collected?

   (A) Tuesday

   (B) Wednesday

   (C) Thursday

   (D) Friday

6. What is the maximum allowed container weight?

   (A) 20 lbs

   (B) 35 lbs

   (C) 45 lbs

   (D) 50 lbs

7. Who probably produced this announcement?

   (A) An automobile dealership

   (B) The police department

   (C) The city emergency services section

   (D) An insurance company

8. Which of the following things are NOT mentioned?

   (A) Photographing the accident scene

   (B) Calling for medical assistance

   (C) Getting the other party's license number

   (D) Noting the weather conditions

9. When does the announcement suggest calling the police?

   (A) If there is injury or damage to vehicles

   (B) After checking for injury

   (C) At the first opportunity

   (D) After you have talked to witnesses

10. What is the purpose of this announcement?

    (A) To explain some important computer upgrades

    (B) To apologize for an error

    (C) To explain the cause of a system failure

    (D) To enlist aid in repairing some damage

11. What caused the problem?

    (A) A problem with the clocks

    (B) Someone must have opened an infected file.

    (C) Someone forgot to activate their firewall.

    (D) Someone shared their passwords.

12. What does the announcement say to do in the future?

    (A) Only open attachments from familiar senders

    (B) Consult the IT team before opening email files

    (C) Track the company's financial status

    (D) Assist in making repairs

| 1 | Ⓐ Ⓑ Ⓒ Ⓓ | 7 | Ⓐ Ⓑ Ⓒ Ⓓ |
| 2 | Ⓐ Ⓑ Ⓒ Ⓓ | 8 | Ⓐ Ⓑ Ⓒ Ⓓ |
| 3 | Ⓐ Ⓑ Ⓒ Ⓓ | 9 | Ⓐ Ⓑ Ⓒ Ⓓ |
| 4 | Ⓐ Ⓑ Ⓒ Ⓓ | 10 | Ⓐ Ⓑ Ⓒ Ⓓ |
| 5 | Ⓐ Ⓑ Ⓒ Ⓓ | 11 | Ⓐ Ⓑ Ⓒ Ⓓ |
| 6 | Ⓐ Ⓑ Ⓒ Ⓓ | 12 | Ⓐ Ⓑ Ⓒ Ⓓ |

# C Learn by doing: Be familiar with announcement conventions

**A** Match the beginnings of the sentences 1–4 with the appropriate endings a–d to complete the announcement.

1. Excuse me everyone, ...
2. I'm afraid that today's class is canceled ...
3. The class will be rescheduled ...
4. If you are unable to attend on that day, ...

a ... because Mr. Phillips is off with the flu today.

b ... please speak to Mr. Phillips in his office on Monday. Thank you.

c ... could I have your attention, please.

d ... for next Wednesday at 2:00.

**B** Now practice reading this announcement to your partner.

*Follow up:* With a partner, take turns to make announcements using the notes below. You may write them down first if you prefer.

**Change to meeting room**
*The room for the sales meeting has been changed.*
*The new meeting space is room 401.*
*The meeting start time is 3:15.*

**Collecting gift money**
*We are collecting money for Shelley's wedding gift.*
*Give money to Sam or Helen by Friday.*
*Also, we would like gift suggestions.*

**Farewell party**
*After work there will be a farewell party for Tom.*
*It will be held at the Nightshift Café.*
*If you need directions, please get a map from Jim.*

## Culture note

When giving news to groups of customers it is common to start with:
   *May I have your attention please.*,

   If it is unpleasant, say,
   *I am sorry to tell you ...* or *I am afraid I have to announce that ... .*

   If you are requesting something, say *please.*

   Thank them at the end.

# D Further study

Think of an announcement you have made or an event that would require a similar announcement. Prepare an announcement to give in the next lesson.

Go to word list and quiz page 161.

**A**

## Strategy: Identify the part of speech
### Use your time wisely

Parts of speech are a commonly tested feature. This unit will help you identify the type of word you need quickly and efficiently.

**1  Language building: Know what you are looking for (main parts of speech)**

**A**  Read sentences 1–6 and note the part of speech of the word that is missing (noun, verb, adjective or adverb). Compare your ideas with a partner and think of a word that would fit.

1. The children were amazed by the ...... insects in the garden.
2. Ms. Watkins was ...... pleased with her retirement present.
3. While Jane was at college, she ...... to her sister every week.
4. The project team found it very difficult to hide their ...... over the rejection.
5. The report suggested there was an immediate need to improve cost ...... .
6. The delegates seemed to find the presentation very ...... .

**B**  The complete questions are shown below. Quickly skim the answers to find the part of speech you noted above.

1. The children were amazed by the ...... insects in the garden.
   (A) color
   (B) colorful
   (C) colors
   (D) coloring

2. Ms. Watkins was ...... pleased with her retirement present.
   (A) terrified
   (B) terrible
   (C) terribly
   (D) terrific

3. While Jane was at college, she ...... to her sister every week.
   (A) writing
   (B) written
   (C) write
   (D) wrote

4. The project team found it very difficult to hide their ...... over the rejection.
   (A) disappoint
   (B) disappointing
   (C) disappointedly
   (D) disappointment

5. The report suggested there was an immediate need to improve cost ...... .
   (A) efficient
   (B) efficiency
   (C) efficacious
   (D) efficiently

6. The delegates seemed to find the presentation very ...... .
   (A) interests
   (B) interest
   (C) interesting
   (D) interestingly

## Test tip

**Manage your time wisely**

Answer the easy questions first, very quickly. After you have answered all the easy ones come back and spend a maximum of 20 seconds each on the rest.

## Test tip

**Try to predict answers**

On the first pass, try to think of possible answers before you look at the answer choices.

## Test tip

**Don't waste time on questions you don't know**

Spending more than 30 seconds on a Part 5 question probably won't help you find the answer. If you don't know the answer, guess and move on.

## Tactics checklist

☑ Determine the part of speech that fits the blank.

☑ Look for answer choices of the correct type.

☑ Think of words that might fit before you look at the answer choices.

☑ Use the 2-Pass method to answer quickly. If you aren't sure, guess and move on.

## 2 Test tactic: The 2-Pass method

You will have one minute only to read six sentences, think of a word that would fit, then choose the best answer. If you don't know the answer within 10 seconds, move on to the next question.

### Pass 1: Easy questions – 1:00 minute (10 seconds per question)

1. Ms. Jennings suggests ...... increase our sales margin by streamlining our distribution system.
   - (A) us to
   - (B) plans
   - (C) we
   - (D) that

2. To ...... an outside call, please dial "9", then the number you wish to reach.
   - (A) ring
   - (B) telephone
   - (C) reach
   - (D) place

3. What time does the courier come ...... in the evenings?
   - (A) with
   - (B) to
   - (C) by
   - (D) for

4. If shipping costs are not fully covered, ...... for delivery will be the responsibility of the recipient.
   - (A) pay
   - (B) payment
   - (C) paying
   - (D) to pay

5. ...... an emergency, press the red alarm button.
   - (A) In case of
   - (B) When
   - (C) If encounter
   - (D) Due to

6. The director was very ...... in the quality of his accommodations.
   - (A) disappointed
   - (B) disappointment
   - (C) disappointing
   - (D) disappoints

### Pass 2: Remaining questions – maximum 20 seconds per question

Go back and answer the questions you didn't answer on the first pass. If you don't know the answer within 20 seconds, guess and move on. Answer all questions within the time limit.

## 3 Tactic practice

A Read sentences 1–4, decide the part of speech of the missing word, and think of a word that would fit. Compare your ideas with your partner.

1. It has long been ............ that small downturns in the US economy can have a global impact.

2. The assistant was outraged at the ............ charges of misuse of company property.

3. Due to his father's bankruptcy, the funds ............ for entry into the expensive university were unavailable.

4. The city welfare fund collects donations to aid local ............ and underprivileged citizens.

**B** Choose the correct answer for sentences 1–4 on page 23.

**1.** (A) say
(B) known
(C) define
(D) identify

**2.** (A) unproven
(B) disapproval
(C) misappropriated
(D) disproportionately

**3.** (A) money
(B) receivable
(C) payment
(D) required

**4.** (A) needing
(B) needful
(C) need
(D) needy

## **B** Mini-test

Now apply the *Test tactics* at the actual test speed with questions 1–12.

> You have 6 minutes to complete 12 items. To use your time wisely, use the 2-pass method. Spend no more than 30 seconds on each item. If you don't know the answer, guess and move on.

**1.** Young adults who are ...... with their use of credit, may find themselves in trouble sooner than they expect.
(A) careless
(B) uncaring
(C) carelessly
(D) uncared for

**2.** The attorney was warned against trying to ...... the young witness.
(A) influential
(B) influence
(C) influent
(D) influencing

**3.** Inexperienced investors are ...... to enter the junk bond market with care.
(A) advice
(B) suggest
(C) advised
(D) decision

**4.** The journalist refused ...... the federal investigator the names of his sources.
(A) talk
(B) talkative
(C) telling
(D) to tell

**5.** All the components for Hanson scooters are ...... right here in the state.
(A) make
(B) production
(C) building
(D) manufactured

**6.** The ...... is likely to have serious repercussions in future negotiations.
(A) incident
(B) happened
(C) accidental
(D) opportune

**7.** I don't want to tell her how I actually ...... about the gift.
(A) liked
(B) feel
(C) bought
(D) opinion

**8.** I am afraid that the date of ...... we were quoted is too optimistic.
(A) completion
(B) finish
(C) ending
(D) done

9. The complexity of modern economic systems makes them far from ...... .

(A) believed
(B) predictable
(C) safety
(D) knowing

10. I am not ...... that the consultant's recommendation will help the situation.

(A) convince
(B) convinced
(C) conviction
(D) convincing

11. Adam Smith is generally considered to be one of the most ...... philosophers of the eighteenth century.

(A) brilliantly
(B) impressed
(C) importance
(D) significant

12. The woman was staring at me ...... as I left the conference hall.

(A) intently
(B) angered
(C) looks
(D) to go

## C  Vocabulary practice

A  Read sentences 1–12 and note the part of speech of the word that is missing. Use the abbreviations: noun (n), verb (v), adjective (adj), adverb (adv).

1. The owner of the largest factory in town was a very ........... ( adj ) member of the town council.

2. The company president faced criminal charges because he ........... (    ) money from his workers' retirement fund.

3. John's skill in quickly and ........... (    ) solving the problem saved his company thousands of dollars and avoided weeks of lost production.

4. The rich businessman made thousands of dollars worth of ........... (    ) to help cancer research each year.

5. The salesman made many promises and offers to try to ........... (    ) the manager to purchase his company's product.

6. The golf pro stared ........... (    ) at the hole as he carefully lined up his shot.

7. An ........... (    ) person always sees the good side of any situation.

8. The fact that Mary graduated from a famous university was a ........... (    ) advantage when she started job hunting.

9. With 15 million dollars in debt and the bank's refusal of a new loan, the company was forced into ........... (    ).

10. Regular exercise and a good diet can ........... (    ) your health and fitness.

11. We hired a motorcycle ........... (    ) to deliver the package by hand.

12. I don't know what to order. Can you ........... (    ) something that isn't too spicy?

B  Note the part of speech for each of the following words. If you aren't sure, confirm the meaning with a classmate or look in the word list on page 162.

| efficiently | adv | intently | | improve | | suggest | |
| courier | | influential | | bankruptcy | | optimistic | |
| misappropriated | | donations | | convince | | significant | |

C  Now put the words into the sentence that they best fit.

Go to word list and quiz page 162.

## A

## Strategy: Choose the correct verb form: present, past

Verb forms are a commonly tested feature. This unit will help you to find clues in the questions and choose the correct answer choice.

### Test tip

**Choose the correct verb form**

Many questions focus on choosing the correct verb form. Look at the sentence and decide what verb form it requires, then choose an answer of the same type.

### Test tip

**Look at the sentence first**

You usually do not need to read the text to answer the questions. Go straight to the first question and look for time clues.

### Test tip

**Sometimes the sentence may not give clues to the required tense**

In this case look at the rest of the text to find when the action happens.

## 1 Language building: Present/Past tense verb forms

**Present tense verb forms**

Read the information about verb forms. Then complete sentences 1–4 by putting the verb in the correct tense.

| **Present simple** | **Present continuous** |
|---|---|
| base form (*he/she/it* statements + s) (Happening regularly or always true) | *am/is/are* + verb + *ing* (Happening right now and not finished yet) |
| e.g. *Cheetahs <u>run</u> very fast.* *She <u>runs</u> 5 km twice a week.* | e.g. *I <u>am waiting</u> to see the doctor.* *He <u>is waiting</u> till Christmas to buy the present.* |

1. They often ............ (play) golf with their customers on Saturday.
2. The parts ............ (still/sit) on the truck waiting to be unloaded.
3. The customer  ............ (sign) his name on the insurance form as we speak.
4. Mary ............ (work) as a cashier in the bank on Wilkins Street.

*Follow up:* Now write one true present simple and one true present continuous sentence about yourself and compare with your partner.

**Past tense verb forms**

Read the information about verb forms. Then complete sentences 1–6 by putting the verb in the correct tense.

| **Past simple (+)** | **Past simple (– / ?)** | **Past continuous** |
|---|---|---|
| base form + *ed* or irregular past (single or completed action, finished in the past) | *did/didn't* + base form (single or competed action, finished in the past) | *was/were* + base form + *-ing* (past action that continued for a period of time when another interrupted it.) |
| e.g. *I <u>dropped</u> a ball on my foot!* *She <u>lived</u> in Spain when she was young.* *He <u>ate</u> the cake.* (irregular verb) | e.g. *<u>Did</u> you <u>see</u> the movie?* *I <u>didn't meet</u> him!* | e.g. *He <u>was driving</u> slowly when he saw the accident.* *As they <u>were sleeping</u>, the man entered the house.* |

1. The workers ............ (stand) around waiting for the foreman to arrive for over an hour.
2. ............ he ............ (take) the package with him?
3. While we ............ (sleep) the thieves broke into our house and stole our TV.
4. How long ago ............ the package ............ (arrive)?
5. I ............ (drop) Sally off at the bus stop more than an hour ago.
6. They ............ ............ (not/go) to the conference.

*Follow up:* Write one true past simple statement, one true past simple negative statement and one true past continuous sentence about yourself and compare with your partner.

## 2  Test tactic: Use clues to choose the correct present/past forms

A   Read the text and decide if the missing verb should be in the present or past form. Circle the part of the text that tells you this.
Then with a partner guess the words that could go in each blank.

| | |
|---|---|
| All first-year engineering students (1) ............ the story of Herbert Mansfield when they enter university. | 1 ✔ Present ☐ Past |
| Before his invention of the steam converter in 1903, Herbert (2) ............ as a design engineer for a manufacturing company. | 2 ☐ Present ☐ Past |
| He (3) ............ in a small, tidy, very average house outside Billington. | 3 ☐ Present ☐ Past |
| He (4) ............ at the National Institute before receiving his degree in engineering. | 4 ☐ Present ☐ Past |
| It wasn't until several years later that he (5) ............ the invention that would change the world. | 5 ☐ Present ☐ Past |
| Many of the most influential scientists still (6) ............ it to be the greatest breakthrough of the century. | 6 ☐ Present ☐ Past |
| Currently the city (7) ............ a monument to this very important individual. | 7 ☐ Present ☐ Past |

B   Complete the text using the verbs in the box. Did you guess correctly?

| made | believe | lived | studied | is building | worked | learn |
|---|---|---|---|---|---|---|

## 3 Tactic practice

Read the sentences for questions 1–4, decide which tense is needed and think of a word that would fit. Compare your ideas with a partner. Then quickly choose the correct answer.

**Questions 1–4** refer to the following letter.

Re: Diesel generator – Order No. B90008

Dear Mr. Johnson

I am writing to complain about the above noted large diesel generator that we ............... from

1. (A) get
   (B) received
   (C) taken
   (D) are accepting

you yesterday.

Upon unpacking the equipment, we found the width of the mounting brackets to be almost 8 inches longer than we ............... in our design specifications. These will have to be replaced

2. (A) noted
   (B) writing
   (C) picture
   (D) say

immediately as the generator must be installed by the end of the week.

Furthermore, the unit was sent without the wiring harness for the main control unit. Please ............... this out in the same shipment as the correct mounting bracket.

3. (A) to send
   (B) sending
   (C) sent
   (D) send

It is vital that we receive these parts by Tuesday. Late delivery ............... our own installation schedule.

4. (A) affects
   (B) affected
   (C) will affect
   (D) has affected

Yours Sincerely

*Thomas Hardings*

Thomas Hardings
Director

## B  Mini-test

Now apply the *Test tactics* at the actual test speed with questions 1–12.

> 🕐 You have 6 minutes to complete 12 items. To use your time wisely, use the 2-pass method you learnt in Unit 5.1. Spend no more than 30 seconds on each item. If you don't know the answer, guess and move on.

**Questions 1–4** refer to the following letter.

---

Mr. Robert Cheung
Sea Dragon Shipping
372 Clementi Ave 2#03–149A
SINGAPORE
120356

March 23

Dear Mr. Cheung,

I am writing on behalf of one of our clients, Mikra Electronics, Jakarta, who ................ us that the

**1.** (A) have sent
  (B) telling
  (C) have informed
  (D) written

SS Liberty Star, due to arrive in Auckland on March 22 ................ failed to arrive as scheduled.

  **2.** (A) will
    (B) is
    (C) having
    (D) has

This vessel was carrying a consignment (B/L 8974) for our client and they would like to know why the vessel has been ................ and when it is expected to arrive.

  **3.** (A) delayed
    (B) stop
    (C) going
    (D) done

Since this delivery was being made through your Priority Express system, we must also inform you that you will be held responsible for any late delivery penalties our client may ................ due to the delay.

  **4.** (A) owing
    (B) have paid
    (C) be
    (D) face

A prompt reply would be appreciated in this matter.

Yours sincerely,

*Emerson Filho*

Emerson Filho

---

GO ON TO THE NEXT PAGE ▶

---

## Memorandum

**To:** Alvin Kurosawa, Vancouver Branch Manager

**From:** Melville Bromwich, Accounting Section

---

Alvin,

I am just ............... to confirm that my colleague Tom Brooks and I will be

     **5.** (A) write
        (B) writing
        (C) written
        (D) been writing

in Vancouver from the end of next week for the annual expenses audit. Could you please ask one of your staff to arrange our accommodation? We plan to arrive on the 14th and ............... on the 19th.

      **6.** (A) left
         (B) leaving
         (C) is leaving
         (D) will be leaving

Also, I don't know if you have heard yet, but the board has ............... us to evaluate

            **7.** (A) asking
               (B) tell
               (C) instructed
               (D) ordering

the travel andentertainment expenses starting from the last quarter. Since we are likely to be extremely busy, I ............... we will be unable to find time to take in a

      **8.** (A) think
         (B) will say
         (C) have thought
         (D) am saying

hockey game as you had previously suggested.

Thanks in advance for any assistance with the hotels, and looking forward to seeing you next week.

Yours truly,

Mel

Mr. Niels Kirstein
Olaf and Bohr Furnishings
Kristianiagade 19
2100 Copenhagen
Denmark

Dear Mr. Kirstein,

We ................ your delivery of 150 hardwood table and chair sets (order# DH4589)

**9.** (A) receive
  (B) received
  (C) will receive
  (D) receives

this morning, but unfortunately, when we opened them we discovered that there is one leg missing from ................ table.

**10.** (A) each
   (B) all
   (C) some
   (D) any

Obviously we will need this problem corrected as soon as possible. We would appreciate if you could ................ the missing 150 legs to our warehouse by this

**11.** (A) be sent
   (B) sending
   (C) send
   (D) sent

Friday (August 16) at the latest. The tables are ................ to go on display in our

**12.** (A) wanting
   (B) hoped
   (C) planning
   (D) scheduled

showroom the following Monday.

I look forward to hearing from you in the next day or so.

Yours sincerely,

*Alfred Axely*

Alfred Axely
Purchasing Director

Read three short texts and put the verbs in the correct tense.

1. **Business letter**

> Dear Mr. Jones,
>
> I (1) ……….. (write) in connection with the article in this month's American
> Engineer. Our company (2) ……….. (make) parts for the aerospace industry and we
> think that your invention meets our specifications. Would you be willing
> (3) ……….. (meet) with one of our design engineers to discuss licensing your
> design?

2. **Complaint letter**

> Last month your company (1) ……….. (put) in new automatic doors on our
> warehouse. Since then we have twice had problems with the motors. In the first
> case, they didn't (2) ……….. (open) when the operator (3) ……….. (press) the
> button and we had to call in a mechanic to fix them. In the second case, the
> doors suddenly closed when a truck (4) ……….. (come) into the garage. This
> (5) ……….. (delay) the delivery of an important consignment of goods. I am
> afraid we must hold you responsible for any penalties.

3. **Email**

> Sally,
> Have you been told that Jack Benson (1) ……….. now ……….. (work) on the
> Dorfin Project? As you know he (2) ……….. previously ……….. (manage) our
> Texas outfit, but he (3) ……….. just ……….. (arrive) this morning from Dallas
> and (4) ……….. (need) accommodation near the office.

Go to word list and quiz page 163.

## A  Strategy: Scan the questions to decide which to answer first

Looking at the questions first will allow you to find exactly what you are looking for in the reading text so you can answer the questions most efficiently.

### 1  Test tactic: Answer easier/faster questions first

Look at the list of question types below. This is the order in which you should do them to make best use of your time.

1. **Specific information (positive)**
   These are the easiest and quickest to find the answer for. Do these first.
   - *According to the author, what will x be used for?*
   - *Where did x come from?*
   - *Which x will benefit from this?*

2. **Vocabulary questions**
   (See Unit 7.2)
   These should be answered quickly. If you don't know the word or words, guess and move on.
   - *The word "x" in paragraph 1 line 3 is closest in meaning to ...*

3. **Main idea/inference questions**
   (See Unit 7.2)
   Doing the previous question types first will help prepare you for these.
   - *What is the **purpose** of this memo?*
   - *Why is Mr. Jones writing this letter?*
   - *What **can be said/inferred** about...?*
   - *Who might read this advertisement?*

4. **Specific information (negative)**
   (See Unit 7.3)
   These can be the most time consuming. Leave them till last, when you may have already got information to help you with the answers.
   - *Which of the following is NOT true?*
   - *Which of the following positions is NOT available?*

For each question below mark in the box the order it should be done. The first one has been done for you.

1. What is this notice mainly about?  `3`
2. Where might you see this notice?  ☐
3. By when must you give notice in order to get the maximum refund?  ☐
4. What will happen if you withdraw prior to the second lesson?  ☐
5. Which of the following is NOT true?  ☐
6. The word "constitute" in paragraph 3, line 5, is closest in meaning to  ☐

### 2  Test tactic: Answer specific information questions (positive) first

A  Circle the specific information questions from the list below.

| | |
|---|---|
| 1  At what time does the club open? | 5  Where did the man buy his bicycle? |
| 2  The word "robust" in paragraph 1, line 2, is closest in meaning to | 6  How long should the man wait for a reply? |
| 3  What is the price of the guitar? | 7  What can be inferred about the woman's job? |
| 4  Who might reply to this advertisement? | |

**B** Look at the specific information questions from activity 1.

Underline the key words in the question and answer choices, and then scan the passage below to find the sentence that answers the question.

**3.** By when must you give notice in order to get the maximum refund?

    (A) Just after the first class

    (B) Before the second class is held

    (C) Five business days before the first lesson

    (D) Within four to six weeks

**4.** What will happen if you withdraw prior to the second lesson?

    (A) All costs will be refunded by check.

    (B) You will receive the full amount minus $25.

    (C) No refunds or credits will be issued.

    (D) You will pay for the first lesson plus admin fee.

*Follow up:* Compare your answers with your partner.

**Questions 1–6** refer to the following notice.

---

**Summer program refund policy**

The effective date of the withdrawal/cancellation is the date the withdrawal notice is received by the center, regardless of the date the participant stopped attending the class.

Withdrawal requests from all registered courses must be made before the second class is held. If the request is received 5 business days prior to the first class, the amount refunded will be the full amount, less the refund administration fee ($25.00). If the request is received after the first class, but before the second class, the amount refunded will be the full amount, less the cost of the first class and less the administration fee ($25.00). From the second lesson onwards, no refunds/credits will be issued.

If there is a medical reason for the request, it must be received prior to the mid-point of the program. Refunds for sports and fitness programs will NOT be processed until ALL gym and pool passes have been returned.
Please note that advising an instructor or not attending a program will not constitute a notice of withdrawal.

Cash/check remittances will be refunded by check. Please allow our office 4 to 6 weeks to process your refund. Credit card refunds will go back on the original card.

---

**Tactics checklist**

☑ Don't read the text first.

☑ Skim the questions and do the specific questions first.

☑ Skim the text to find the answer to the question. (Be careful! It may use different words.)

☑ Answer the question yourself, then choose the best answer choice.

## 3 Tactic practice: Specific information

Use the tactics you have practiced to answer the following questions.

1. Who is the intended recipient of this letter?
   (A) Alberto Romero
   (B) Benjamin Weintraub
   (C) John Teirney
   (D) Alex Andreas

2. What kind of job did the person apply for?
   (A) Human resources
   (B) Administrative work
   (C) Marketing
   (D) Sales

3. Where was Mr Romero applying for a job?
   (A) In Britain
   (B) In America
   (C) In Europe
   (D) In Asia

**Questions 1–3** refer to the following letter.

---

Alberto Romero
3254 Turney Road
Garfield Heights
OH 44125
USA

Dear Mr Romero,

This letter is to thank your for your application to join our International sales team. Unfortunately, we must inform you that due to the large number of highly-qualified applicants that applied for the position of Eastern European sales representative, we have already filled all the positions that were advertised in the May issue of the Human Resources Bulletin.

As you know, administrative and marketing positions in our European and Asia-Pacific offices regularly become available during the year and we would welcome your application for future international postings.

Yours truly,

Alex Andreas

p.p. Benjamin Weintraub
Human Resources Manager
London Office
John Teirney & Sons Ltd.

---

Now apply the *Test tactics* at the actual test speed with questions 1–9.

 You have 12 minutes to complete 12 items.

**Questions 1–3** refer to the following advertisement.

---

*Printing for your personal & small business needs*

# Gaines Bros Printing

*A commitment to quality and service since 1959*

New opening hours:
Monday to Saturday from 9 a.m. – 7 p.m.

- Business Forms
- Business Cards
- Envelopes
- Folders
- Letterhead
- Full Color Printing

- Graphic Design
- Digital Copying
- Invitations
- Graduation and Wedding Announcements

**Special offers, only for June:**

- Order 10 sets of letterhead and get matching envelopes at a 50% discount
- 2 for 1 business cards or invitations for any order over $100
- Purchase over $250 and you will receive a voucher worth 10% off the your next order during the coming year

---

Order by phone, fax or in person.

## 555–3467 • FAX 555–3478

458 Notting Drive Unit 119 • Alansburg

---

**1.** Who would NOT be a potential customer for this company?
- (A) A couple whose daughter is getting married
- (B) A major corporation
- (C) A local real estate agent
- (D) A restaurant in need of new menus

**2.** What could customers who spend 150 dollars get?
- (A) A 10% discount
- (B) Double the number of invitations
- (C) A discount on envelopes
- (D) Two free sets of business cards

**3.** What will happen from July 1?
- (A) The time the shop opens will change
- (B) You will not be allowed to make fax orders
- (C) Discount vouchers will become invalid
- (D) No bonus will be given for large letterhead orders

Questions 4–6 refer to the following notice.

# Welcome to the Groveland library service

We would like to invite all Groveland residents to become members of the public library.

Interested applicants should follow the procedure below to receive their library card promptly and make use of the full range of facilities.

Please complete the accompanying personal information form and submit it to the applications desk in any of the Groveland branch libraries or to your local ward office community service desk.

Within two working days (Monday–Friday) of the application being submitted:

- You will receive a library barcode number via email (enabling you to place reservations and access online databases before collecting your card).
  Note: You will require a PIN to place reservations and to access your record online. Please note that the default PIN number is the last four digits of your telephone number. If you would prefer to specify a different number please do so on the application form.

- Your card will be available for collection at the branch library you have nominated.

If you are under the age of 18, we require a parent or guardian's signature on a permission letter (Form 103) which will need to be brought into the library when you are collecting your card.

4. The word "promptly" in paragraph 2, line 2 is closest in meaning to
   (A) correctly
   (B) quickly
   (C) appropriately
   (D) suitably

5. What will NOT be possible two working days after submitting the application?
   (A) You will receive a number that will let you reserve books.
   (B) You will be able to collect your card at your nominated branch library.
   (C) You get a barcode that will let you check book availability online.
   (D) You will be able to change your PIN number.

6. What special conditions apply to children?
   (A) They need a parent or guardian to collect their card.
   (B) They must wait until they are 18.
   (C) They need a signed permission letter.
   (D) They must sign a form.

**GO ON TO THE NEXT PAGE**

---

## Online water/sewer payment

Welcome to the Worthwood Water/sewer Account Payment System. You can now pay your bill online via credit card using the most secure online payment system available.

Please enter your Worthwood Water/sewer account number below, then click "Submit". Your account number can be found in the upper left-hand corner of your bill. If you do not know your account number, please call 555-8375.

If your door has been tagged for non-payment, you must call 555-0874 to stop termination of water service.

Please do not use this website if your payment is intended for overdue sewer charges related to sewer certification. If you recently received a notice about unpaid sewer charges, please follow the payment instructions on the notice.

Sewer payments can be mailed to Division of Water, P.O. Box 139012, Worthwood, NP 8926-2412. Payments must be received by Feb 16.

A two dollar ($2.00) or two percent (2%) processing fee (whichever is GREATER) will be added to your payment.

All general inquiries should be addressed to the Information Section, Worthwood Public Works Section, P.O. Box 138976, Worthwood, NP 8926-2469, or call 555-2378 (ext. 124).

---

**7.** Who would be most interested in this notice?
(A) People who need sewer certification
(B) People who don't wish to pay additional processing charges
(C) People who want to pay by computer
(D) People who wish to receive a Water/sewer account number

**8.** What number should you call if you don't want your water disconnected?
(A) 555-0874
(B) 555-8375
(C) 555-2378
(D) 8926-2412

**9.** What must people who have been notified of an overdue sewer bill do?
(A) Call the Division of Water
(B) Pay an additional processing fee
(C) Address their inquiries to the Information Section
(D) Follow the instructions given

A   You are Sam Hong, the branch manager for Sea Star Shipping in Singapore. Read the notice your company has recently sent you and answer questions 1–4.

---

## Notice

The recent typhoon has caused delays in some of our shipping contracts of up to three days. Because of this we anticipate complaints from our customers due to late delivery.

Our official policy is that we are not responsible for any costs resulting from failure to meet delivery schedules due to natural disasters. This is clearly stated in all our shipping contracts.

To assist customers with especially time-sensitive deliveries, we can offer a special 50% discount on Express air freight costs. Especially valued customers may be offered a 15% discount on their next order.

---

1. What problem does this company have?
2. Will Sea Star pay for any extra costs customers may have due to the delay?
3. What can the company do for customers who need quick delivery?
4. What bonus can the company offer important customers?

B   One hour ago you received the following letter from the agent for MegaCo, one of your largest customers. Read the letter, then discuss the situation with your partner. Say what you think Mr. Hong should do. Then complete the reply to the letter of 16 February 2006.

---

16 February 2006

Mr. Hong,

We were recently informed that the recent typhoon and suspension of shipping out of Singapore has delayed the delivery of product shipment SD1278 to San Francisco by an estimated five days.

This is an extremely time-sensitive shipment for our customer, and because of this we will have to pay late penalties of approximately $7,500 per day.

I am writing to inform you that we hold you responsible for these and any additional fees resulting from your failure to deliver as per our shipping contract.

I look forward to hearing from you soon.

*Martha Rogers*

---

### Culture note

When talking about amounts of money, we often use the letter K, to mean thousand
*The job offers a starting salary of **$40K**.*
(meaning $40,000)

Dear Ms Rogers,

We received your letter of 16 February concerning the delay to your shipment, consignment number (1) ................. .

We are very sorry for the unfortunate delays to your shipment, but I am afraid however that we are not responsible for any
(2) ................................................................................. due to
(3) ............................................................ . This is clearly stated in your
(4) ........................................ .

As you are a valued customer, however, we would like to assist you as much as possible in making the delivery to (5) ............................... on time. We are prepared to offer you a special (6) ................................. . In addition to this we will give you a (7) ................................. off the costs of your next order.

Please let us know as soon as possible about your intentions.

Yours sincerely,

Sam Hong

## D Further study

Write a short report on how you handled the delayed shipping problem. Be prepared to describe what you did in your next lesson.

Go to word list and quiz page 164.

**A**   **Strategy:** Listen for the correct verb

Many of the incorrect answer choices in this section feature an inappropriate verb for the situation. This section will focus on identifying the sentence with the verb that best describes what is seen in the picture.

## 1   Language building: Present continuous/present simple

**A**   Look at the list of verbs and make possible sentences about each of the pictures using the present continuous or present simple tense. The first one is done for you.

**1**      **2**

| | |
|---|---|
| study → They are studying in the library. | run → The highway runs under the overpass. |
| read → They're all … | run → The overpass … |
| sit → The students … | be (a sign) → There is … |
| stand → Nobody … | be (cars) → There … |
| revise → They … | divide (a guardrail) → A guardrail … |

 **B**   Listen to four correct sentences about these pictures. Listen carefully, and after each one stop the audio and try to echo as much of the sentence as possible. Decide with a partner which picture you think the sentence matches.

*Follow up:* Make up one new sentence for each picture. You may use different verbs. Test your partner to echo your sentence and choose the correct picture.

## 2   Test tactic: Select an answer quickly

 **A**   Listen to three sentences describing the pictures.  Hold your pencil over the answer choices and try to echo each statement as you listen. If you think the sentence is correct, hold your pencil over that answer. When you have listened to all the sentences, choose an answer quickly.

**1.** (A) ☐
  (B) ☐
  (C) ☐

**2.** (A) ☐
  (B) ☐
  (C) ☐

**B** Now write two sentences to describe the following pictures.

Example: *The woman is holding a coffee cup.*

**1**

**2**

**C** You will hear four sentences describing each picture. After each sentence, stop the audio and tell your partner the verbs you heard, then mark below whether you think it is correct or wrong.

**1**

(A) ☐ Correct ☐ Wrong

(B) ☐ Correct ☐ Wrong

(C) ☐ Correct ☐ Wrong

(D) ☐ Correct ☐ Wrong

**2**

(A) ☐ Correct ☐ Wrong

(B) ☐ Correct ☐ Wrong

(C) ☐ Correct ☐ Wrong

(D) ☐ Correct ☐ Wrong

*Follow up:* With your partner compare the sentences you first made and the correct sentence.

## 3 Tactic practice 🎧

Use the tactics you have practiced for the next three photographs. You will have one minute to a) brainstorm vocabulary and b) predict possible sentences with your partner. Then listen to and echo (silently) the answer choices, and as you listen, tick whether you think it is correct, maybe correct, or wrong.

**1**

(A) ☐ Correct ☐ Maybe correct ☐ Wrong

(B) ☐ Correct ☐ Maybe correct ☐ Wrong

(C) ☐ Correct ☐ Maybe correct ☐ Wrong

(D) ☐ Correct ☐ Maybe correct ☐ Wrong

**2**

(A) ☐ Correct ☐ Maybe correct ☐ Wrong

(B) ☐ Correct ☐ Maybe correct ☐ Wrong

(C) ☐ Correct ☐ Maybe correct ☐ Wrong

(D) ☐ Correct ☐ Maybe correct ☐ Wrong

3

(A) ☐ Correct  ☐ Maybe correct  ☐ Wrong

(B) ☐ Correct  ☐ Maybe correct  ☐ Wrong

(C) ☐ Correct  ☐ Maybe correct  ☐ Wrong

(D) ☐ Correct  ☐ Maybe correct  ☐ Wrong

*Follow up:* Compare your answers with your partner, explain your reasons, and say what you remember hearing.

🎧 Understanding natural English

## B  Mini-test 🎧

Now apply the *Test tactics* at the actual test speed with questions 1–8.

> 🕐 You will have 1 minute 30 seconds to skim the pictures before the first listening starts. After that you will have exactly 5 seconds between each question to mark your answer and focus on the next picture.

1

2

3

4

5

6

| 1 | Ⓐ Ⓑ Ⓒ Ⓓ |
| 2 | Ⓐ Ⓑ Ⓒ Ⓓ |
| 3 | Ⓐ Ⓑ Ⓒ Ⓓ |
| 4 | Ⓐ Ⓑ Ⓒ Ⓓ |
| 5 | Ⓐ Ⓑ Ⓒ Ⓓ |
| 6 | Ⓐ Ⓑ Ⓒ Ⓓ |
| 7 | Ⓐ Ⓑ Ⓒ Ⓓ |
| 8 | Ⓐ Ⓑ Ⓒ Ⓓ |

7

8

# Learn by doing: Picture bingo

Choose one of the words on your bingo card, then pick a picture you think relates to that word. Tell your partner the picture number and ask them to make a sentence about the picture. There are some words to help you below. Listen to your partner's sentence and, if you hear the word, you can mark it off on your bingo card. Take turns until one person has marked off all their words. Bingo! They are the winner.

**Student A:** Look at Activity file 1.2a on page 151.

**Student B:** Look at Activity file 1.2b on page 152.

1

2

3

4

5

6

| **1.** family | road | **2.** passenger | get into | **3.** car | woman |
|---|---|---|---|---|---|
| mother | walk | taxi | take | boats | door |
| father | lift | suit | travel | dock | sit |
| children | hold | street | | men | open |

| **4.** customers | outdoors | **5.** boy | ground | **6.** old man | push |
|---|---|---|---|---|---|
| wine | drink | gate | wear | bicycle | walk |
| glasses | sit | hat | open | lake | going fishing |
| table | sip | sweater | walk | sun | wear |
| café | enjoy | snow | stand | cap | shine |

## D    Further study

Find three pictures from newspapers or magazines. Write Part 1 type statements (one correct answer, three that are close but wrong) to test on your classmates in the next lesson. The incorrect answers should include correct subject or object words, but incorrect verbs.

Go to word list and quiz page 165.

**A** **Strategy:** Be familiar with different ways of answering direct questions

Be aware of similar sounding words

In this part of the test, you will often hear direct questions. The correct answer will not usually be an answer with *yes*, *no* or *don't know*, and will often be in a different tense.

**Test tip**

Often direct questions will not be answered with *yes*, *no* or *don't know*

Look for options that use different words to express these meanings.

**Test tip**

Often the question and answer choice will be different verb tenses

Do not expect the grammar of the question to match the answer.

Example
*Are you going tonight? → I've made plans.*

**Test tip**

Distractors using the same (or similar-sounding) words are common in Part 2

Be careful of choosing responses that use the same or similar-sounding words.

## 1 Language building: Choosing the correct answer

Choose two correct answers for each question.

a. Is Mr. Clemens coming to the presentation?

b. Did she say when she would be available?

c. Could you help Laura to prepare the documents?

d. Do you think they would mind if I came along?

1. She thinks she'll be free later today.
2. No. Everyone has been invited.
3. Unfortunately, he's on holiday then.
4. Sure. Where is she?
5. You should probably call them first.
6. No, I forgot to ask her.
7. Sorry, I have to help Michael.
8. Yes, but he'll be a few minutes late.

 *Follow up:* Now listen to four more responses and match each one to questions a–d above.

1. a. b. c. d.
2. a. b. c. d.
3. a. b. c. d.
4. a. b. c. d.

## 2 Test tactic: Look out for same or similar-sounding words

A Look at the following questions and responses. Tick the correct response and circle any SAME or SIMILAR-SOUNDING words used in the distractors.

1. Are you going to the party tonight?
   (A) Yes, it's tonight.
   (B) No, he's departing tomorrow.
   ✓ (C) I haven't decided yet.

2. Have you handed in the report yet?
   (A) I've already reported it.
   (B) I put it on her desk yesterday.
   (C) I thought it was very handy.

3. Could you rearrange the venue for me?
   (A) Yes, it's new.
   (B) Sure. Is the meeting room better?
   (C) No, I didn't arrange it.

4. You called Simon back, didn't you?
   (A) No, I don't have his number.
   (B) Yes, he'll be back tomorrow.
   (C) No, he's called David.

B Now compare your answers with your partner.

**Test tip**

**Short-term memory is important**

Repeat each response in your head and check if it answers the question or has same word/similar sound distractors.

*Follow up:* Now listen to five more questions. Repeat each response as you hear it, and tick whether it is correct, or wrong with a same word or similar word distractor. Then compare your answer with your partner's.

1. Is this the last stop?

(A) ☐ Correct  ☐ X – Same word  ☐ X – Similar sound
(B) ☐ Correct  ☐ X – Same word  ☐ X – Similar sound
(C) ☐ Correct  ☐ X – Same word  ☐ X – Similar sound

2. Did you call the customer back?

(A) ☐ Correct  ☐ X – Same word  ☐ X – Similar sound
(B) ☐ Correct  ☐ X – Same word  ☐ X – Similar sound
(C) ☐ Correct  ☐ X – Same word  ☐ X – Similar sound

3. You're working tomorrow, aren't you?

(A) ☐ Correct  ☐ X – Same word  ☐ X – Similar sound
(B) ☐ Correct  ☐ X – Same word  ☐ X – Similar sound
(C) ☐ Correct  ☐ X – Same word  ☐ X – Similar sound

4. Can you remember the details?

(A) ☐ Correct  ☐ X – Same word  ☐ X – Similar sound
(B) ☐ Correct  ☐ X – Same word  ☐ X – Similar sound
(C) ☐ Correct  ☐ X – Same word  ☐ X – Similar sound

5. You read through the notes, didn't you?

(A) ☐ Correct  ☐ X – Same word  ☐ X – Similar sound
(B) ☐ Correct  ☐ X – Same word  ☐ X – Similar sound
(C) ☐ Correct  ☐ X – Same word  ☐ X – Similar sound

**Tactics checklist**

☑ Don't always expect *Yes/No* responses.

☑ Be careful of same/similar-sounding words.

☑ Verb tenses may be different.

## 3 Tactic practice 🎧

You will hear six question-response questions. After each question, stop the audio and repeat the response to your partner. Then mark your answer choice. Then compare your answers with your partner.

| 1 | Ⓐ Ⓑ Ⓒ | 4 | Ⓐ Ⓑ Ⓒ |
| 2 | Ⓐ Ⓑ Ⓒ | 5 | Ⓐ Ⓑ Ⓒ |
| 3 | Ⓐ Ⓑ Ⓒ | 6 | Ⓐ Ⓑ Ⓒ |

🎧 **Understanding natural English**

In natural spoken English, sounds are changed, combined and dropped.
Listen to these sentences spoken naturally and write in the missing words.

I'm ......... go after work.

Are you ......... wait for Mark?

## B Mini-test 🎧

Now apply the *Test tactics* at the actual test speed with questions 1–12.

🕐 You will have 5 seconds at the end of each item to make your choice.
You must then be ready to listen to the next question.

| 1 | Ⓐ Ⓑ Ⓒ | 7 | Ⓐ Ⓑ Ⓒ |
| 2 | Ⓐ Ⓑ Ⓒ | 8 | Ⓐ Ⓑ Ⓒ |
| 3 | Ⓐ Ⓑ Ⓒ | 9 | Ⓐ Ⓑ Ⓒ |
| 4 | Ⓐ Ⓑ Ⓒ | 10 | Ⓐ Ⓑ Ⓒ |
| 5 | Ⓐ Ⓑ Ⓒ | 11 | Ⓐ Ⓑ Ⓒ |
| 6 | Ⓐ Ⓑ Ⓒ | 12 | Ⓐ Ⓑ Ⓒ |

# C — Learn by doing: Checking information

**A** Complete the questions and responses by choosing the correct items from the boxes.

1. A: ..................... the **printer paper** kept in the **storeroom**?
   B: ..................... next to the photocopier.

   | Is | Does | That's | No, it's |

2. A: This is your **bag**, ..................... ?
   B: Thanks. I ..................... looking for that.

   | was | isn't it | wasn't | am |

3. A: The new **boss** seems really **nice**, ..................... ?
   B: ..................... , but I heard he can be very **strict** too.

   | doesn't he | isn't he | He does | He will |

4. A: ..................... show me how to use the **photocopier**?
   B: ....................., it's really easy.

   | Could you | Do you | Of course | Sorry |

5. A: The **meeting** begins at **2:30**, ..................... ?
   B: ....................., it's starting **now**.

   | doesn't it | didn't it | Probably | Actually |

6. A: ..................... that the last **report**?
   B: ..................... .

   | Were | I'll think about it | Was | I think so |

**B** Now make similar conversations by replacing the words in bold with the following words.

1. key/boss's office?
2. calculator
3. accountant/friendly/rude
4. fax machine
5. presentation/11:30/after lunch
6. box

*Follow up:* Ask your partner some more questions using auxiliary verbs and tag questions. Try to give some answers without *Yes* or *No*.

# D — Further study

Choose two sets of question words from the list below and make two Part 2 type questions. Then, add three responses (one correct, two incorrect) to test your partner on, in the next lesson.

| Are you ... ? | Could you ... ? | Is she ...? | ..., aren't you? |
| Did he ...? | Does this ...? | Do you ...? | ..., isn't she? |

Go to word list and quiz page 165.

**A** **Strategy:** Be aware of same word distractors

In this part of the test, the recording can often use words that are the same or have the same meaning as words in the answer choices. Usually this is to distract you to choose an incorrect answer. Be careful not to choose an answer simply because you heard something similar in the listening.

**Test tip**

Part 3 commonly uses the same words in the recording and answer choices, but with the wrong meaning

If you hear the same words in a conversation answer choice, be careful. It will often be the wrong answer.

**1** **Test tactic: Be aware of same word distractors**

**A** Quickly skim Question 1 below and underline the key words. The question and 1A have been done for you.

1. Why <u>didn't</u> George <u>attend</u> the <u>meeting</u>?
   (A) He was in the <u>Human Resources</u> section.
   (B) He doesn't get along with Mr. Stubbs.
   (C) He had to go to Anaheim.
   (D) He was in New York.

**B** Now quickly skim the tapescript below to find sentences with the key words. For each one decide if it answers the question or not. Cross out the wrong answer choices. When you think you have found the answer, circle the correct answer choice. Compare your answer with a partner.

> **Tapescript**
>
> Man A:   *Hey, Taylor. How did the Human Resources meeting go? I couldn't make it because I was on a visit to the Anaheim office.*
>
> Man B:   *Oh, hi George. You're lucky you missed it. It turned into a major argument between Mr. Stubbs and the New York team over employee numbers.*
>
> Man A:   *Really? What was the problem?*
>
> Man B:   *Mr. Stubbs wants to drastically cut back on the sales staff on the East Coast. Jameson and the New York team were strongly in favor of increasing staff to increase sales.*

**C** Continue as above, with the remaining two questions.

2. What was the meeting about?
   (A) To discuss a recent argument with employees
   (B) The purchase of a Major league team in New York
   (C) It was a seminar on natural resources
   (D) Changes in the number of workers

3. What happened during the meeting?
   (A) They discussed an increase in the number of bargain sales.
   (B) There was a disagreement between staff members.
   (C) They talked about the increase in the sales figures.
   (D) Taylor was lucky to draw the winning number.

**Test tip**

**Answers to Part 3 questions often use different words from the recording**

The correct answer choice often uses different words to say the same thing as the recording.

🎧 **D**  Underline the key words in the following questions and answer choices. Then listen to one short conversation for each question and cross out the answer choices with similar word distractors.

1.  What is the man looking for?
    (A) The stove
    (B) The coffee maker
    (C) The CD player
    (D) The kitchen

2.  What happened to Dave?
    (A) He was injured.
    (B) He was given a lot of money.
    (C) He had a traffic accident.
    (D) He won the lottery.

3.  What is the man complaining about?
    (A) He hates filing documents.
    (B) He was given directions to the wrong place.
    (C) His work is always the same.
    (D) A worker's carelessness

🎧 *Follow up:* Listen again and choose the correct answer. Compare your answers with your partner.

| 1 | Ⓐ Ⓑ Ⓒ Ⓓ |
|---|---|
| 2 | Ⓐ Ⓑ Ⓒ Ⓓ |
| 3 | Ⓐ Ⓑ Ⓒ Ⓓ |

## 2  Test tactic: Listen for who says what

**A**  Quickly skim Question 1 below and underline the key words.

1.  What is the man planning to do?

| | | | |
|---|---|---|---|
| (A) To work in Chicago | ☐ Woman | ☐ Man |
| (B) To get a new job | ☐ Woman | ☐ Man |
| (C) To move away from his family | ☐ Woman | ☐ Man |
| (D) To move closer to his dad | ☐ Woman | ☐ Man |

**Test tip**

**Listen to who says what**

Often the answer choice will have key words used by one of the speakers, but it may not be the speaker specified in the question. Noticing this can help you spot distractors.

🎧 **B**  Listen to the sample conversation and tick who says each of the key words (the man or the woman). Because the question is asking about the man's plans, the words the woman says can be ignored. Choose the best answer from the things the man says. Check your answer with your partner.

🎧 **C**  Continue as above, with the question below. This time it's important what the woman says.

2.  What does the woman want?

| | | | |
|---|---|---|---|
| (A) A red sweater | ☐ Woman | ☐ Man |
| (B) A discount | ☐ Woman | ☐ Man |
| (C) Free shipping | ☐ Woman | ☐ Man |
| (D) A green sweater | ☐ Woman | ☐ Man |

## Tactics checklist

☑ Be careful if you hear the same words in the conversation as in the answer choices.

☑ Listen to who says what.

## Understanding natural English

In natural spoken English, sounds are changed, combined and dropped. Listen to these sentences spoken naturally and write in the missing words.

......... be some time before he can run again.

......... get us there in five minutes.

## 3 Tactic practice

Use the tactics you have practiced for the next six questions. Before each passage begins use the time to a) predict the context and b) think of other ways to say the answer choices with your partner.

1. What is the woman unhappy about?
   (A) She made a mistake at work.
   (B) The people she works with are inexperienced.
   (C) She doesn't like her new boss.
   (D) She dislikes working in the advertising field.

2. What does the man suggest?
   (A) Talking to her boss
   (B) Changing to a job in advertising
   (C) Looking for another job
   (D) Talking with her co-workers

3. Why does she suspect she got the job?
   (A) The supervisor liked her.
   (B) She has a lot of experience.
   (C) Her company has high employee turnover.
   (D) She had worked there a year previously.

4. What does the woman request?
   (A) Her money back
   (B) To get a receipt
   (C) A new coffee machine
   (D) A discount

5. What does she say is the problem?
   (A) The machine is broken.
   (B) The cups are too small.
   (C) She comes from a very large family.
   (D) The unit doesn't make enough coffee.

6. What does the man say?
   (A) The woman can have a refund.
   (B) She can change to a different one.
   (C) He needs to see the receipt.
   (D) Replacing the unit will take a week.

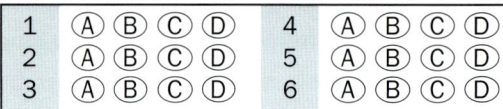

| 1 | Ⓐ Ⓑ Ⓒ Ⓓ | 4 | Ⓐ Ⓑ Ⓒ Ⓓ |
|---|---|---|---|
| 2 | Ⓐ Ⓑ Ⓒ Ⓓ | 5 | Ⓐ Ⓑ Ⓒ Ⓓ |
| 3 | Ⓐ Ⓑ Ⓒ Ⓓ | 6 | Ⓐ Ⓑ Ⓒ Ⓓ |

 Understanding natural English

## B    Mini-test

Now apply the *Test tactics* at the actual test speed with questions 1–12.

🕐 You will have 30 seconds to skim the questions and answer choices before the first listening starts. After that you will have exactly 8 seconds between each question to mark your answer and focus on the next question.

1. How long has the man been working?
   (A) One year
   (B) Two years
   (C) Since he graduated
   (D) Since the summer

2. What does the man plan for the future?
   (A) To continue his education
   (B) To open his own business
   (C) To move to a new city
   (D) To change careers

3. How does the man feel about the company?
   (A) Unsatisfied
   (B) Content
   (C) Unappreciated
   (D) Over-worked

4. Where are the speakers?
   (A) A bus stop
   (B) A garage
   (C) A power plant
   (D) A used car lot

5. What is the woman unhappy about?
   (A) She can hear a strange noise.
   (B) She can't get a ride home.
   (C) Her electricity has been cut off.
   (D) She doesn't want to wait.

6. What does the man suggest?
   (A) Having it looked at
   (B) Going home
   (C) Waiting a few hours
   (D) Making a cup of coffee

7. What is the man's job?
   (A) Baseball player
   (B) Insurance agent
   (C) Farmer
   (D) Cab driver

8. Why is the woman upset?
   (A) She doesn't want to be late.
   (B) The game was terrible.
   (C) She doesn't have insurance.
   (D) The market closed five minutes before.

9. What will the man do?
   (A) Get to the game on time
   (B) Drive to the market
   (C) Exceed the speed limit
   (D) Take a special route

10. What is the woman doing?
    (A) Discussing a sports event
    (B) Talking about her accident
    (C) Inquiring about the man's relative
    (D) Trying to borrow a motorcycle

11. What does the woman think is unfortunate?
    (A) The insurance company won't pay.
    (B) The man will miss the race.
    (C) She needs to have an operation.
    (D) She will miss a lot of work.

12. Who will pay the expenses?
    (A) Brandon
    (B) The man's parents
    (C) The insurance company
    (D) The other driver

| 1 | Ⓐ Ⓑ Ⓒ Ⓓ | 7 | Ⓐ Ⓑ Ⓒ Ⓓ |
| 2 | Ⓐ Ⓑ Ⓒ Ⓓ | 8 | Ⓐ Ⓑ Ⓒ Ⓓ |
| 3 | Ⓐ Ⓑ Ⓒ Ⓓ | 9 | Ⓐ Ⓑ Ⓒ Ⓓ |
| 4 | Ⓐ Ⓑ Ⓒ Ⓓ | 10 | Ⓐ Ⓑ Ⓒ Ⓓ |
| 5 | Ⓐ Ⓑ Ⓒ Ⓓ | 11 | Ⓐ Ⓑ Ⓒ Ⓓ |
| 6 | Ⓐ Ⓑ Ⓒ Ⓓ | 12 | Ⓐ Ⓑ Ⓒ Ⓓ |

## C  Learn by doing: Complaining

**A**  Conversations complaining about goods and services or about other things are common in Part 3. Practice the following complaints with your partner. Then change the underlined words in the conversations using the phrases from the box.

**Complaints about goods and services**

Staff: Good Afternoon. <u>May I help you?</u>

Customer: Yes, I bought this <u>wallet</u>, but <u>the zipper is broken</u>. <u>Could you replace it?</u>

Staff: Yes, that should be fine. <u>May I see</u> your receipt?

Customer: <u>Here you are.</u>

Staff: Thank you, just let me see if we have the same make and color.

**Complaints about other things**

A: How <u>is</u> your <u>work these days</u>?

B: <u>I'm afraid I'm not very happy.</u>

A: Why, what's the matter?

B: Well, my <u>boss</u> is very <u>demanding</u>. <u>He is never satisfied.</u>

A: What are you going to do?

B: I think I may <u>try to find a new job.</u>

| | | | |
|---|---|---|---|
| Can I help you?<br>How can I help? | Can I see …<br>Could I have … | … is/new car?<br>… is/new<br>  apartment?<br>… are/classes<br>  going? | … the gas mileage/<br>low.<br>It is quite<br>expensive. |
| jacket<br>CD player | Here you go.<br>Here it is. | | … the rent/high. I<br>can't afford it. |
| it's the wrong size.<br>it doesn't work<br>  properly. | | Well, there are a<br>few problems.<br>Not great, I'm<br>afraid. | … my teacher/tough.<br>He gives so much<br>homework. |
| I'd like my money<br>back.<br>Could you fix it? | | Not very well. | … sell it and get a<br>smaller one.<br>… look for a new<br>place.<br>… have to work<br>harder! |

**B**  Now make another conversation using your own ideas.

*Follow up:* Write three Part 3 type questions (no answer choices) for your conversation to test other students.

> ### Culture note
> When making a complaint, it is important to state what the problem is and how you would like it resolved, in a polite way.

## D  Further study

Think of something you were unhappy with recently, and write a conversation complaining about it. Write three questions (no answer choices) to test your classmates in the next lesson.

Go to word list and quiz page 166.

**A** **Strategy:** Be familiar with different kinds of "what" questions

"What" questions are very common in the TOEIC test. Sometimes they ask for an overview or the main idea of the talk. Other times they ask for specific information. This unit will help you to deal with both types.

## 1 Language building: Vocabulary for overview questions

**A** Use the words on the right to complete the overview questions.

1. What is the ...... of the presentation?                          being described
2. What is this report .......... ?                                 addressing
3. What is the speaker's reason for .......... the group?           about
4. What product is .......... ?                                      topic

**B** Look at the key words listed for four short talk questions. Circle the likely topic from the list on the right.

1. sales figures, increase, report, final quarter

   (A) A financial report     (B) A sales demonstration     (C) A school report

2. closure, bankrupt, debt, failure

   (A) It is very successful.     (B) It is doing badly.     (C) It hasn't changed.

3. tremor, relief workers, aid, landslide

   (A) A war     (B) A charity campaign     (C) An earthquake

4. ink, paper, documents, high quality, photographs

   (A) A camera     (B) A printer     (C) An office chair

*Follow up:* Discuss your answers with your partner and explain why you selected them.

## 2 Test tactic: Listen for answers in order

**A** Underline the key words in the following questions and answer choices. Then skim the tapescript and underline the words that tell you the answers.

1. What kind of people might be interested in this advertisement?

   (A) Teenagers
   (B) Elderly people
   (C) Businessmen

2. What can early bookers receive?

   (A) A better room
   (B) A 10% discount
   (C) Special tour offers

3. What kind of holidays does Alto-Pacific offer?

   (A) Relaxing resort holidays
   (B) Enjoyable golfing holidays
   (C) A range of different holidays

**Tapescript**

*Retired travelers get a break with Alto-Pacific holidays. With a special discount rate for senior citizens, summer never has to end for travelers aged over 60. We offer discounts starting at 10% off regular rates, as well as room upgrade deals for early bookers. Not only do we offer cheaper than standard prices, but also special tour offers, complimentary breakfasts and a guaranteed quiet room. Whether you are looking to relax in a world-class resort surrounded by the blue waters of Micronesia, or enjoy a round of golf at one of our Hawaiian resorts, or perhaps explore the historical castles of Japan, we have something to cater for every taste.*

**Mark answers as you listen**

If you hear an answer that is definitely correct, mark it as you listen. If you hear answers that are possibly correct, leave a small pencil mark by these. Answer all questions as quickly as possible.

**B** Listen to the three parts of a short talk in turn. You have 30 seconds to skim the questions and answer choices. Then, listen and mark the answers as correct, maybe correct, or wrong. Note how the answers appear in order.

1.  What kind of people might listen to this announcement?

    (A) Politicians            (A) ☐ Correct ☐ Maybe Correct ☐ Wrong
    (B) Venture capitalists     (B) ☐ Correct ☐ Maybe Correct ☐ Wrong
    (C) Shareholders           (C) ☐ Correct ☐ Maybe Correct ☐ Wrong

2.  What has changed in the European market in the last year?

    (A) It has become twice as big.        (A) ☐ Correct ☐ Maybe Correct ☐ Wrong
    (B) It has increased by one quarter.    (B) ☐ Correct ☐ Maybe Correct ☐ Wrong
    (C) It has decreased by 50%.            (C) ☐ Correct ☐ Maybe Correct ☐ Wrong

3.  What does the speaker say about the company's finances this year?

    (A) The North American market was strong.     (A) ☐ Correct ☐ Maybe Correct ☐ Wrong
    (B) There were good and bad results.          (B) ☐ Correct ☐ Maybe Correct ☐ Wrong
    (C) The European market was disappointing.    (C) ☐ Correct ☐ Maybe Correct ☐ Wrong

**Tactics checklist**

☑ Identify any overview questions.

☑ Skim the questions and answer choices before listening to identify key words.

☑ Listen for answers in order.

☑ Answer any specific information questions as you listen.

# 3 Tactic Practice

Use the tactics you have practiced for the next two short talks. You will have one minute before you listen to a) skim the questions and identify key words, and b) identify any overview questions.

1.  What does the speaker say about the house?

    (A) It is old but well maintained.
    (B) It was built 40 years ago.
    (C) It hasn't been renovated.
    (D) There are two bedrooms.

2.  What is mentioned about the living room?

    (A) It is a little dark.
    (B) There is a bright lamp.
    (C) It was renovated six months ago.
    (D) It has a lot of space.

3.  What will the speaker do next?

    (A) Show the visitors the kitchen
    (B) Take the visitors to the second floor
    (C) Leave the house
    (D) Talk about the price

4.  What is the aim of this announcement?

    (A) To describe Daniel Kanemoto
    (B) To advertise a club
    (C) To boast about achievements
    (D) To improve people's fitness

5.  What is the minimum age for members?

    (A) 6
    (B) 66
    (C) 2
    (D) 10

6.  What is special about the dojo master?

    (A) He is 66 years old.
    (B) He is a junior regional champion.
    (C) He won a title twice.
    (D) He knows some basic self-defence.

| 1 | Ⓐ Ⓑ Ⓒ Ⓓ |
|---|---|
| 2 | Ⓐ Ⓑ Ⓒ Ⓓ |
| 3 | Ⓐ Ⓑ Ⓒ Ⓓ |
| 4 | Ⓐ Ⓑ Ⓒ Ⓓ |
| 5 | Ⓐ Ⓑ Ⓒ Ⓓ |
| 6 | Ⓐ Ⓑ Ⓒ Ⓓ |

**Understanding natural English**

In natural spoken English, sounds are changed, combined and dropped. Listen to these sentences spoken naturally and write in the missing words.

As you ........ see, it is in remarkable condition.

You ........ keep your entire photo collection safe.

# Mini-test 🎧

Now apply the *Test tactics* at the actual test speed with questions 1–12.

> 🕐 You will have 30 seconds to skim the questions and answer choices before the first listening starts. After that you will have exactly 8 seconds between each question to mark your answer and focus on the next question.

1. What is this report about?
   (A) The effect of a natural disaster
   (B) A piece of good news
   (C) Problems with trucks
   (D) The dangers of winter

2. Why are relief workers unable to deliver aid?
   (A) The roads are blocked.
   (B) The weather is too bad.
   (C) There isn't enough aid.
   (D) The trucks are damaged.

3. What is the good news that is mentioned?
   (A) Governments are sending helicopters.
   (B) Some people were rescued.
   (C) The aftershocks have stopped.
   (D) Nobody was killed.

4. Who is most likely listening to this talk?
   (A) The customer service department
   (B) Customers
   (C) New employees
   (D) The head of the department

5. Why is the speaker addressing the group?
   (A) To resolve customers' problems
   (B) To introduce himself and the training goals
   (C) To respond to customer needs
   (D) To introduce new employees

6. When should the listeners ask questions?
   (A) When the speaker has finished
   (B) When they have got to know him
   (C) If they are confused about something
   (D) After the next three days

7. What product is being described?
   (A) A cordless telephone
   (B) An all-in-one printer
   (C) A laptop computer
   (D) A digital camera

8. Which of the following best describes the product?
   (A) It creates a lot of desktop clutter.
   (B) It is an older model with many features.
   (C) It is quite large.
   (D) It is an innovative design.

9. What is described as the unique feature?
   (A) The color printer
   (B) The fax machine
   (C) The hard disk drive
   (D) The scanner

10. What is the purpose of this announcement?
    (A) To ask for donations for a gift
    (B) To introduce a new staff member
    (C) To ask people to keep the office clean
    (D) To start a new club

11. When is Chuck leaving?
    (A) At the end of the year
    (B) At the end of this month
    (C) In a couple of months
    (D) Next week

12. Why shouldn't people tell Chuck about this?
    (A) He doesn't know he is leaving.
    (B) He doesn't need the money.
    (C) It is meant to be a surprise.
    (D) It hasn't been decided yet.

| 1 | Ⓐ Ⓑ Ⓒ Ⓓ |
|---|---|
| 2 | Ⓐ Ⓑ Ⓒ Ⓓ |
| 3 | Ⓐ Ⓑ Ⓒ Ⓓ |
| 4 | Ⓐ Ⓑ Ⓒ Ⓓ |
| 5 | Ⓐ Ⓑ Ⓒ Ⓓ |
| 6 | Ⓐ Ⓑ Ⓒ Ⓓ |
| 7 | Ⓐ Ⓑ Ⓒ Ⓓ |
| 8 | Ⓐ Ⓑ Ⓒ Ⓓ |
| 9 | Ⓐ Ⓑ Ⓒ Ⓓ |
| 10 | Ⓐ Ⓑ Ⓒ Ⓓ |
| 11 | Ⓐ Ⓑ Ⓒ Ⓓ |
| 12 | Ⓐ Ⓑ Ⓒ Ⓓ |

**C** ## Learn by doing: Tonight's news

With a partner read over the questions about the business and world news reports below and make sure you understand all the words. Try to guess what the reports are about.

**Business news report**

1. What did FHL Electronics announce?
2. What caused the closure of the factories?
3. What did the president say about labor costs in Asia?
4. What did the president promise?
5. What is the best newspaper headline for this report?
   - Drop in Asian Labor Costs
   - FHL Announces Record Losses
   - President Introduces New Product

**World news report**

1. What time did the event happen?
2. What were people doing when it happened?
3. What was totally destroyed?
4. How are supplies reaching the area?
5. What is the best newspaper headline for this report?
   - 1975 Quake Remembered
   - Disaster Hits Togassa
   - Helicopter Hits Bridge

**Student A:** Look at Activity file 4.2a on page 152. Read your report to your partner.
**Student B:** Listen to your partner's news report and answer the questions. When you are finished, switch roles. Look at Activity file 4.2b on page 154.

 **D** ## Further study

Write four or five sentences about your company, school or family, and write three "what" questions. Test your classmates in the next lesson.

Go to word list and quiz page 167.

## Strategy: Choose gerunds and infinitives correctly
## Improve your knowledge of phrasal verbs

Being familiar with the correct use of gerunds and infinitives and understanding phrasal verbs is helpful for many parts of the TOEIC test. This unit will make you more aware of how they are used, especially in Part 5.

## 1 Language building: Gerunds and infinitives

Gerunds are verbs in their base + -ing form, e.g. *doing*. Infinitives are verbs in their base form.

### Verbs that take a gerund

All the verbs below can be followed by gerunds, but some do not fit into the sentences. Choose the verbs from each list that do NOT fit the sentence. The first one is done for you.

1. I have a very bad memory. I can't .......... meeting you before. ☐ recall ☒ admit ☐ remember

2. He .......... smoking after his doctor warned him of the dangers. ☐ contemplated ☐ gave up ☐ quit

3. I .......... traveling on the subway when it's really busy. ☐ can't stand ☐ dislike ☐ forgive

4. It starts at 5 a.m. but I .......... getting up early. ☐ can't help ☐ don't mind ☐ am used to

5. The professor was .......... improving his spoken English. ☐ interested in ☐ keen on ☐ afraid of

*Follow up:* Now write one sentence about yourself using a verb followed by a gerund and compare with a partner.

### Verbs that take infinitives

All the verbs below can be followed by infinitives, but some do not fit into the sentences. Choose the verbs from each list that do NOT fit the sentence. The first one is done for you.

6. Although it was a reasonable offer, we .......... them to increase it by 10%. ☒ pretended ☐ persuaded ☐ forced

7. Did you .......... to meet Mr. Yamamoto when you were in Tokyo? ☐ intend ☐ expect ☐ hesitate

8. It was a very successful meeting as they .......... to purchase fifty units. ☐ decided ☐ threatened ☐ agreed

9. Because he had a lot of experience, he .......... to be promoted. ☐ expected ☐ prepared ☐ deserved

10. Although he wasn't fully fit, he still .......... to complete a full marathon. ☐ managed ☐ decided ☐ reserved

*Follow up:* Now write one sentence about yourself using a verb followed by an infinitive and compare with your partner.

## 2 Test tactic: Familiarize yourself with phrasal verbs

**A** Choose the correct phrasal verb on the right to match the meaning given.

| | | | |
|---|---|---|---|
| 1. | to arrange (e.g. a meeting) | ☐ set up | ☐ call up |
| 2. | to complete a blank in a form | ☐ fill out | ☐ take in |
| 3. | to support (e.g. a colleague) | ☐ fall through | ☐ back up |
| 4. | to become interested in (e.g. jazz music) | ☐ get into | ☐ take over |
| 5. | to stop using something gradually | ☐ back out of | ☐ phase out |
| 6. | to become behind schedule | ☐ fall behind | ☐ buy out |
| 7. | to investigate | ☐ look into | ☐ look for |
| 8. | to continue (doing something) | ☐ keep on | ☐ go through |
| 9. | to succeed in something (e.g. a great deal) | ☐ pull off | ☐ ask around |

**B** Choose the correct phrasal verb to complete the following sentences.

1. Despite working overtime every day for two weeks, he still .......... with his work.
   - (A) kept up
   - (B) set up
   - (C) fell behind

2. The lawyer called three times this morning to .......... a meeting.
   - (A) set up
   - (B) set to
   - (C) set on

3. Nobody expected him to play well, but he managed to .......... a shock win over the favorite.
   - (A) get into
   - (B) stem from
   - (C) pull off

4. The police promised to .......... any new evidence that came to light.
   - (A) look out of
   - (B) look into
   - (C) look after

5. Passengers traveling to the United States are required to .......... an immigration questionnaire, prior to arrival.
   - (A) fill up
   - (B) fill in for
   - (C) fill out

6. When color televisions became standard in most homes, black and white sets were gradually .......... .
   - (A) phased out
   - (B) backed up
   - (C) set up

**Tactics checklist**

☑ Predict gerund/infinitive questions, and eliminate any obviously wrong answers.

☑ Say phrases to yourself and try to hear if they sound "wrong".

☑ Familiarize yourself with as many phrasal verbs as possible.

## 3 Tactic practice

Use the tactics you have practiced to answer the following questions.

1. Although I advised her to invest in steel, she decided .......... silver instead.
   (A) buy
   (B) to buy
   (C) buying
   (D) bought

2. He was out when I called, but the receptionist kindly offered .......... a message for me.
   (A) to take
   (B) taken
   (C) took
   (D) taking

3. It appears that our principal rivals are considering .......... our takeover proposal.
   (A) to accept
   (B) accept
   (C) accepting
   (D) the acceptance

4. When buying a new car, it is advisable to .......... to find the best deal.
   (A) look around
   (B) look for
   (C) look into
   (D) look after

5. We're all .......... you to make a good impression at the conference next month.
   (A) expected
   (B) counting on
   (C) sure
   (D) considering

6. After waiting for more than thirty minutes for my entrée to arrive, I demanded .......... the manager.
   (A) that he spoke
   (B) speaking
   (C) spoken
   (D) to speak

## B Mini-test

Now apply the *Test tactics* at the actual test speed with questions 1–12.

 You have six minutes to complete 12 items. To use your time wisely, use the 2-pass method you learnt in Unit 5.1. Spend no more than 30 seconds on each item. If you don't know the answer, guess and move on.

1. The president's limousine should be here soon, as we are expecting him .......... by 7p.m.
   (A) arrival
   (B) to arrive
   (C) arrive
   (D) arriving

2. During the winter months many people enjoy .......... a variety of winter sports.
   (A) play
   (B) to play
   (C) to be playing
   (D) playing

**GO ON TO THE NEXT PAGE**

3. The CEO was due to retire. ..........
   we started looking for a
   replacement.
   (A) Furthermore
   (B) Consequently
   (C) Moreover
   (D) However

4. Although I was pleased when I
   bought the camera, I later
   regretted .......... for a more
   advanced model.
   (A) not waiting
   (B) waiting
   (C) not to wait
   (D) to wait

5. She was .......... by her grandparents
   from the age of seven.
   (A) brought up
   (B) grown up
   (C) taken up
   (D) held up

6. The product was not a commercial
   success, .......... a lot of money was
   spent on advertising.
   (A) despite
   (B) in spite of
   (C) even though
   (D) because of

7. The first applicant seemed to
   resent .......... about his previous
   experience in the field.
   (A) to be ask
   (B) asking
   (C) being asked
   (D) to ask

8. He .......... to see the presentation
   before he made the decision.
   (A) likes
   (B) would like
   (C) would have liked
   (D) had liked

9. Their low prices were matched by
   their .......... to quality.
   (A) committed
   (B) commitment
   (C) committal
   (D) commensurate

10. Most workplace accidents ..........
    careless practices amongst
    employees.
    (A) stem from
    (B) start out
    (C) leave from
    (D) get out of

11. .......... visitors to the region omit to
    visit the unique Al Hasqua
    mosque.
    (A) Almost
    (B) More
    (C) The most
    (D) Most

12. Union leaders agreed to meet
    with management in order to
    .......... an alternative proposal.
    (A) talk with
    (B) talk at
    (C) talk to
    (D) talk over

# C Vocabulary practice

A Most phrasal verbs are made from very simple and common words. The articles below can be completed using phrasal verbs that start with *take* or *look*. Choose the correct particle to complete the phrasal verbs below.

### Advertisement

If you are looking (1).................... a relaxing vacation, then perhaps you should consider the Hotel du Rhône. Here, you'll be taken (2).................... by our professional staff, and wined and dined to your heart's content. You'll have memories you'll look (3).................... for years to come.

### Company statement

As you know, we were in a three-way battle for ownership of Mediacom. We tried our best to take (4).................... two much larger competitors, but unfortunately our attempt to take (5).................... Mediacom was unsuccessful. However, it may not be all bad news, as the police are currently looking (6).................... some reports of illegal trading in the deal.

### Phrasal verbs with *take* and *look*

| Verb | Meaning | Verb | Meaning |
|------|---------|------|---------|
| take over | assume control of (*The smaller firm was taken over by its larger competitor.*) | look after | care for, nurture (*My mother looked after me when I was sick.*) |
| take in | learn (*There is so much to take in when starting a new job.*) | look for | search (*I've been looking for my car keys everywhere, but I can't seem to find them.*) |
| take up | start a new activity (*I decided to take up karate after watching a few action movies.*) | look up to | admire, respect (*I really look up to my father. He's achieved so much in his life.*) |
| take care of | be in charge of (*I'll take care of the arrangements for tomorrow's meeting.*) | look into | investigate (*I'll look into the best way of getting to the airport.*) |
| take off | remove (*He took off his jacket when he came home from work.*) | look on | watch passively (*It seems that several people were just looking on when the robbers ran out of the jeweller's.*) |
| take on | challenge (*Sydney take on Melbourne in tonight's rugby match.*) | |  |
| take out | dispose of (*Take out the garbage when you leave, would you?*) | look back on | consider the past (*When he looked back on his life, he was glad he had done so many different things.*) |
| take back | retract (*I'm sorry I called you a fool. I take it back.*) | look forward to | Anticipate eagerly (*I am really looking forward to the Christmas holidays this year.*) |
| | | look out for | be careful (*When you are in the city, look out for pickpockets.*) |

B Now write four sentences about your life using phrasal verbs with *take* and *look*. Tell them to your partner in the next lesson. Check a dictionary for other examples of phrasal verbs and note how they are used.

Go to word list and quiz page 169.

 **A**

## Strategy: Choose the correct part of the speech: adjectives and adverbs

Choosing the correct part of speech is a commonly tested feature of the TOEIC test, and being able to identify appropriate use of adjectives and adverbs will help improve your score. This unit focuses on raising your awareness of how these words are used.

### 1 Language building: Adjective and adverb endings

The sentences below use some of the most common adjective and adverb endings found in the TOEIC test. Choose the correct adjective or adverb to complete each sentence.

1. Your new chair looks very ........... . (comfort**able**/ comfortab**ly**)

2. We have ........... problems in our Tokyo office. (seri**ous**/serious**ly**)

3. John's marks were poor because he never listened ........... in class. (attent**ive**/attentive**ly**)

4. Our sales have been ........... good in the last three months. (consist**ent**/consistent**ly**)

5. Mary looked ........... in her new dress. (beauti**ful**/beautifu**lly**)

6. I ........... asked you yesterday not to forget to bring the file. (specif**ic**/specifical**ly**)

*Follow up:* With a partner think of two or three other words for each of the adjective and adverb endings below.

| -able (-ible) | |
|---|---|
| -ous | |
| -ive | |
| -ent (-ant) | |
| -ful | |
| -ic | |
| -ly | |

Now choose two of the words from the chart above and make sentences (either true or false) about someone or something in the room. Read your sentence to your partner and see if they agree or not.

Example
**A:** *Min Joon always studies English very carefully.*
**B:** *I don't really.*

## 2 Test tactic: Be aware of correct comparative and superlative forms

A Look at the examples of comparative and superlative forms common in the TOEIC test.

... *as* hard *as* steel.

... *more* difficult *than* skiing.

... fast*er than* a bullet.

... *the* fast*est* ship.

... *his/their/my* great*est* problem.

... *the most* important thing.

Use the examples above to help you choose the best word to complete the sentences.

1. The ........... (good/better/best) thing about this car is the price.

2. This system has the ........... (advanced/more advanced/most advanced) technology on the market.

3. He may not be as ........... (big/bigger/biggest) as the other man, but he is much ........... (strong/stronger/the strongest).

4. They are our ........... (important/more important/most important) customers by far.

5. A cheetah is much ........... (fast/faster/fastest) than a buffalo.

6. I really thought the steak was ........... (delicious/most delicious/more delicious) than the chicken.

*Follow up:* Compare your answers with a partner. If you have any different answers, tell your partner why you chose your answer.

B With your partner, make comparative and superlative sentences about the animals below.

Example
*An elephant isn't as big as a whale.*
*A bear is much stronger than a mouse.*

elephant     bear     mouse     whale     gorilla

## 3 Tactic practice

Use the tactics you have practiced to answer the following questions.

**Questions 1–4** refer to the following article.

High among the many triumphs of man's courage and spirit is Sir Edmund Hillary and Sherpa Tenzing's ............... climb to the summit of Mount Everest in 1953.

1. (A) amazement
   (B) amazing
   (C) amazingly
   (D) say

Their struggle against the harshness of Mother Nature and the limits of human endurance is one of the ............... events of the twentieth century.

2. (A) excitement
   (B) interest
   (C) more thrillingly
   (D) most inspiring

Although several attempts to climb Everest had been made in the previous 30 years, none had been successful, and many climbers had died. At dawn on the morning of 29 May, Hillary and Tenzing emerged from their tents to begin ............... moving up the south

3. (A) cautiously
   (B) careful
   (C) slow
   (D) difficulty

ridge towards the summit, which they reached after a grueling climb at 11:30. They lingered ............... on the summit and then, about fifteen minutes later, began the tiring

4. (A) momentary
   (B) short
   (C) briefly
   (D) soon

climb down the mountain, and into the history books.

## B  Mini-test

Now apply the *Test tactics* at the actual test speed with questions 1–12.

> 🕐 You have six minutes to complete 12 items. To use your time wisely, use the 2-pass method you learnt in Unit 5.1. Spend no more than 30 seconds on each item. If you don't know the answer, guess and move on.

**Questions 1–4** refer to the following article.

---

### Attention film fans

National Pictures is proud to announce the release of some of the most famous films of the 30's, 40's and 50's. Now, for the first time in decades, you can see such ............... gems as, Corsini's

    **1.** (A) famously
       (B) attracted
       (C) of
       (D) classic

*Roma Viva Roma*, the original 1937 *The Odd Angry Man*, and long-thought destroyed, *Drums Along The Khyber*. These and the other films in our collection are ............... of the most respected and

    **2.** (A) some
       (B) many
       (C) any
       (D) something

talked about films of the early days of talking pictures. The original prints have been re-mastered, ............... restored to modern digital standards by our

    **3.** (A) careful
       (B) repaired
       (C) lovingly
       (D) complete

experienced film technicians, and burned onto DVD for a lifetime of enjoyment. To see the full ............... of restored films, and order your own set, log on to

    **4.** (A) costs
       (B) sample
       (C) movie
       (D) catalog

www.nationalclassics.com today.

---

**GO ON TO THE NEXT PAGE** ▶

**From:** Kurt Redmond, Site Supervisor
**To:** Peter Burnaby, Personnel Manager
**Subject:** Report on new employee, Jackson Silvers

Peter, you asked me for a progress report on Jackson Silvers, No. 3490. I am afraid that he isn't ................. out well. He seems eager, but in the two weeks he has been assigned

     **5.** (A) doing
         (B) working
         (C) going
         (D) trying

to this job he has been late twice.
Even more worrying, and something I have spoken to him about on several ................. are

**6.** (A) problems
   (B) things
   (C) times
   (D) occasions

his safety habits. I have had to caution him a number of times about our ................. enforced

**7.** (A) strictly
   (B) careful
   (C) always
   (D) complete

policy on safety glasses and hard hats, but even today had to warn him again about working without his glasses on. As you know, there is just no place on a ................. site like this

**8.** (A) dangerous
   (B) this
   (C) constructing
   (D) such

for someone who can't follow safety rules. As I said, he has a good attitude, but I am afraid I will have to recommend him for retraining or assignment to a different section.

Questions 9–12 refer to the following letter.

Dear Joe,

Thanks very much for the present you sent out for Dad's birthday.
We ................ the party at

9. (A) have had
   (B) have
   (C) are having
   (D) had

the community center and it was much bigger than the one we gave him last year.
He was really pleased with the watch. I bet it was really ................! It was too bad
that you couldn't make it.

10. (A) expensive
    (B) amazed
    (C) timely
    (D) present

Janet and I spent weeks ................ planning every detail and it came off very well,

11. (A) preparation
    (B) meticulously
    (C) precise
    (D) extensive

if I do say so myself.
Do you think you will be able to make it home some time ................ the summer?

12. (A) at
    (B) for
    (C) during
    (D) middle

Tom and I have just put in a pool and we plan to have a lot of garden parties.
Take care and write back soon.

Lots of love

Grace

**Adjectives and adverbs**

A Look at the gapped sentences and decide whether they require an adjective or adverb. Then select the best word of the correct type from the list on the right.

1. John ................ got the highest scores on his English assignments because he always put so much effort into them.

   | a | specifically |
   |---|---|

2. Marathon runners need ................ endurance to do well in competitions.

   | b | precise |
   |---|---|

3. The ................ and graceful movements of the dancer impressed the judges.

   | c | consistently |
   |---|---|

4. Mary ................ displayed the trophy she had won for the speech contest.

   | d | proudly |
   |---|---|

5. Mr. Ellis quit his job as a traveling salesman because the long hours and ................ travel were affecting his health.

   | e | grueling |
   |---|---|

6. All new sales staff are ................ told not to wear flashy jewelry or heavy perfume.

   | f | amazing |
   |---|---|

B Choose four adjectives or adverbs from the list in activity A and write new sentences using them. Then test your classmates to see if they can choose the right words.

**Comparative and Superlative**

A Change the words to the correct form (if necessary) in order to complete the sentences.

1. Diamonds are much ................ than rubies. (expensive)

2. When they were filming the original *King Kong*, the Empire State Building was the ................ building in the world. (tall)

3. The pro wrestler looked as ................ as a house. (big)

4. The summit of Mt Everest is the ................ place on earth. (high)

5. Antarctica is ................ for the harshness of its climate than the beauty of its landscapes. (famous)

6. Many people believe that a pound of lead is ................ than a pound of feathers. (heavy)

B Write four more sentences about yourself, your family, or your country. Compare your sentences with your classmates.

Go to word list and quiz page 170.

**A** **Strategy:** Scan the questions to decide which to answer next

This unit follows on from Unit 7.1 and focuses on vocabulary, main idea and inference questions. Doing the questions in order of the easiest to the most difficult lets you make the most efficient use of your time.

**Test tip**

**The context of the passage can give clues to vocabulary meaning**

Read the sentences around the target word to try to guess the meaning.

**Test tip**

**These questions intentionally use challenging vocabulary**

If you don't know all of the words, ignore the ones you do know that don't answer the question. This will increase your chances of a successful guess.

## 1 Test tactic: Use context to answer vocabulary questions

**A** Look at vocabulary question 1 below. Find the word in the passage and cross it out. Brainstorm other words that might fit in the sentence and discuss your ideas with a partner.

1. The word "constitute" in (paragraph 2,) line 2, is closest in meaning to …

> If there is a medical reason for the request, it must be received prior to the mid-point of the program. Refunds for sports and fitness programs will NOT be processed until ALL gym and pool passes have been returned.
> Please note that advising an instructor or not attending a program will not constitute a notice of withdrawal.
> Cash/check remittances will be refunded by check. Please allow our office 4 to 6 weeks to process your refund. Credit card refunds will go back on the original card.

**B** Look at the answer choices and choose the one that seems closest to your idea.

(A) begin
(B) indicate
(C) remove
(D) understand

If you aren't familiar with some of the words and can't see an obvious answer, ignore any words you do know and make a guess with the remaining choices. Read the sentence (silently) with each remaining choice and choose the one that "sounds" the best.

**C** Do the same for the following question.

The word "remittances" in (paragraph 3,) line 1, is closest in meaning to
(A) requirements
(B) costs
(C) payments
(D) bills

**Test tip**

Use what you've learned to answer main idea questions

Doing the other questions should help you to answer these ones. If not, skim the passage to confirm the most likely answer choice.

## 2 Test tactic: Answering main idea and inference questions

**A** Underline the key words in the answer choices. Choice (A) is done for you.

   **2.** What is this notice mainly about?
   (A) The <u>costs</u> of <u>summer</u> <u>college</u> <u>programs</u>
   (B) The way to obtain refunds for unattended courses
   (C) Details of payment for summer programs
   (D) Common reasons for withdrawal from college courses

*Follow up:* Compare your choices with a partner.

**B** Now answer the question. You should already have enough understanding of the passage to make a choice (it is the same one you used with specific information questions in Unit 7.1). If you still aren't sure, skim the passage and choose the one that seems closest to the overall meaning.

---

**Summer program refund policy**

The effective date of the withdrawal/cancelation is the date the withdrawal notice is received by the center, regardless of the date the participant stopped attending the class.

Withdrawal requests from all registered courses must be made before the second class is held. If the request is received 5 business days prior to the first class, the amount refunded will be the full amount, less the refund administration fee ($25.00). If the request is received after the first class, but before the second class, the amount refunded will be the full amount, less the cost of the first class and less the administration fee ($25.00). From the second lesson onwards, no refunds/credits will be issued.

If there is a medical reason for the request, it must be received prior to the mid-point of the program. Refunds for sports and fitness programs will NOT be processed until ALL gym and pool passes have been returned.
Please note that advising an instructor or not attending a program will not constitute a notice of withdrawal.

Cash/check remittances will be refunded by check. Please allow our office 4 to 6 weeks to process your refund. Credit card refunds will go back on the original card.

---

**Test tip**

Inference questions use words related to the correct answer choice

Use your knowledge of related vocabulary to choose the correct option.

**C** Both main idea and inference questions require you to look for vocabulary and ideas related to the choices. Write the letter of the answer choice above the related words it best matches in the chart on page 71. Choice (A) is done for you.

   **3.** Where might you see this notice?
   (A) A student alumni magazine
   (B) An insurance policy
   (C) A medical journal
   (D) A community services bulletin

| | | | **A** |
|---|---|---|---|
| Things that are insured and things that aren't covered<br><br>Monthly payments<br><br>The insurance company name<br><br>Policy number/date | Profile of a famous doctor<br><br>Research on diseases<br><br>Descriptions of new medical techniques<br><br>Ads for health services | Upcoming courses, services, or events<br><br>Details of costs and schedules for community services<br><br>Available facilities | Profiles of famous ex-students<br><br>Fund-raising information<br><br>Information on student admission<br><br>Upcoming special events at the university |

## 3 Tactic practice

Use the tactics you have practiced to answer the following questions. First, number the questions in the order they should be done, then answer them as quickly as you can.

1. What is the purpose of this letter?
   - (A) To set up a meeting
   - (B) To confirm the launch dates for the New Health product line
   - (C) To outline the marketing strategy for the product
   - (D) All of the above

2. What can be inferred about the New Health product line?
   - (A) It is aimed at women.
   - (B) It is going to be expensive to buy.
   - (C) It will sell well.
   - (D) It is a cosmetic.

3. The word "anticipated" in paragraph 1, line 2 is closest in meaning to
   - (A) expected
   - (B) promised
   - (C) required
   - (D) confirmed

**Tactics checklist**

☑ Use context to answer vocabulary questions.

☑ Use what you've learned to answer main idea questions.

☑ For inference questions, look for words or ideas in the passage related to the things noted in each answer choice.

**Questions 1–3** refer to the following letter.

---

Roger,

It was a great pleasure to speak with you last week regarding our new product line that we will be introducing next year in Europe. Unfortunately, at that time, I was unable to confirm the anticipated launch date for the New Health line and the expected level of marketing support this product will receive.

I am now able to confirm that the launch date for our new range in our non-U.S. markets will be April 1. Prior to this date we will be launching a major marketing campaign for our new products which will include the placing of two-page spreads in leading health care and fashion magazines, and TV advertisements. We are expecting to confirm a well-known model as the face for the campaign shortly.

I will be coming to London early next month and I was wondering if we could meet to discuss our products and pricing strategies in more detail? I will be able to supply you with more information about not only the New Health line, but also the other skincare products that we offer.

I look forward to meeting you and discussing this sales opportunity with you further.

Regards,
Lewis

---

**B** **Mini-test**

Now apply the *Test tactics* at the actual test speed with questions 1–9.

🕐 You have 9 minutes to complete 9 items.

**Questions 1–2** refer to the following memo.

---

Memorandum

To: Sales Department Staff
From: P.B. Anderson, Office Administrator
Subject: Garbage disposal

We received a complaint last Wednesday about improper garbage disposal by your department. Despite the recent guidelines, several bags of garbage were found in black plastic bags. We would therefore like to remind you of the following:
• Ensure that the new transparent garbage bags are used for all garbage.
Also note for future reference that:
• Burnable and non-burnable items should be separated as previously advised.
• All garbage must be taken out before 6 p.m. on Tuesday and Friday evenings. If garbage is not out by this time, the collection will be missed.
• All glass and metal waste should be placed in the separate receptacle near the rear gate for pickup on Monday morning before noon.

---

1. When must burnable garbage be taken out?
   (A) Every Monday
   (B) Before noon
   (C) On Tuesdays and Fridays
   (D) After 6 p.m.

2. Which of the following has the sales staff failed to do?
   (A) Always use the new garbage bags
   (B) Separate the garbage
   (C) Place metal waste in the correct receptacle
   (D) Take out the garbage at the correct time

**Questions 3–5** refer to the following advertisement.

---

Muscles Gym

Add power to your dreams
Opening campaign
Muscles Gym is the place for serious fitness, with over 50 multi-purpose gyms nationwide. We are pleased to announce that a new Muscles Gym is set to open in January in your area next to Main Street Station. This new Muscles Gym features a fully stocked workout gym including free weights, machines and a range of cardiovascular equipment. There is also an exercise studio, which will offer a comprehensive program of dance, aerobic and martial arts classes. Membership in the Main Street branch also allows full use of the pool and aquatics programs in either the Central or Lansdowne branches.

We are now open for membership applications, so please visit us, take a tour of our wonderful facilities and see how we can truly add power to your dreams!

- Monthly membership rates from as little as $60
- Family packages available from $100
- 20% discount for group membership (min. of 4 members)
- Many other membership rates and packages
- Bonus discount for all new members signing by December 31

Membership inquiries:
Reception open 12–6 p.m. weekdays, 9 a.m.–6 p.m. Sat/Sun

---

3. What is the main purpose of this advertisement?
   (A) To announce the opening of a new gym
   (B) To give details of membership rates
   (C) To describe the benefits of exercise
   (D) To describe the facilities programs that will be available

4. What do people who apply for group membership before the end of the year get?
   (A) A $60 membership rate
   (B) A 20% discount
   (C) A bonus discount
   (D) A 20% discount and a bonus discount

5. Which of the following is true of this new branch?
   (A) People may sign up from 9–6 all week.
   (B) Joining will be more expensive after the new year.
   (C) Children are not able to use this gym.
   (D) It is convenient for swimmers.

GO ON TO THE NEXT PAGE

People think that hurricanes just do not occur in northern Europe, but in October 1987 there was a 'storm' during the night in the south of England that caused unprecedented damage to this usually hurricane free part of the globe.
By the time most people went to bed, exceptionally strong winds had not even been mentioned in national radio and TV weather broadcasts.

Rescue workers faced an unprecedented number of emergency calls as winds hit 94 mph in the capital and over 110 mph in the Channel Islands. Along the south coast, damage to yachts and boat yards was extensive and a famous pier was even reduced to driftwood. Many houses were also damaged by the hurricane.

The hurricane resulted in an estimated 1.7 billion dollars in repairs and clear-up costs. The insurance industry faced huge payouts. Most household policies cover storm damage, and thousands of homeowners made claims.

Weather forecasters soon faced criticism for failing to predict the severity of the weather. The stormy weather was first predicted at the beginning of the week but forecasters incorrectly assumed that the weather system would track along the English Channel, but instead it cut a swathe right across the south of the country.

6. What is this article mainly about?
   (A) The difficulties rescue workers face during hurricanes
   (B) The limited chance of hurricanes occurring in northern Europe
   (C) The impact of a hurricane on southern England
   (D) The inaccuracy of some weather forecasts

7. The word "swathe" which appears in paragraph 4, line 4 is closest in meaning to
   (A) current
   (B) path
   (C) command
   (D) collision

8. According to the article, why were people NOT warned about the hurricane?
   (A) It wasn't expected to hit land.
   (B) Severe damage wasn't anticipated.
   (C) The news didn't mention the impending storm.
   (D) Hurricanes don't occur in Europe.

9. What do most household insurance policies cover?
   (A) Damage caused by freak natural occurrences
   (B) Damage caused by strong winds
   (C) Damage to cars
   (D) Damage to yachts

## C  Reading in action

**Role play**

You bought a watch (a Seimex Accuron) a month ago. Last night you were relaxing in your Jacuzzi when you realized your watch wasn't working. You noticed there was some water inside the face. The watch is clearly labeled as "water-resistant" and is almost brand new!

Read the warranty below and note:

1. How long is the warranty good for?

2. What two things may the company do if it is broken?

3. What situations does the warranty not cover?

4. What should you do if you want to make a warranty claim?

---

SEIMEX INTERNATIONAL WARRANTY

Your SEIMEX watch is warranted against manufacturing defects by Seimex Corporation for a period of ONE YEAR from the original purchase date. Please note that Seimex may, at its option, repair your watch or replace it with an identical or similar model.

IMPORTANT — PLEASE NOTE THAT THIS WARRANTY DOES NOT COVER DEFECTS OR DAMAGES TO YOUR WATCH:

1) if the watch was not originally purchased from an authorized Seimex retailer.
2) from repair services not performed by Seimex.
3) from accidents, or use for purposes outside of those specified in the users manual.

Report all warranty claims to your local authorized SEIMEX dealer for prompt service.

---

**Task**

With your partner write a complaint letter to the local Seimex dealer where you bought the watch and:

- Tell them when you bought the watch (note the model).
- Explain what happened.
- Point out that the watch hasn't been bumped or dropped and because it is supposed to be water-resistant there must be a problem with the watch.
- Since it is still under warranty, find out how soon they can repair or replace the watch.

> ### Culture note
> When making complaints, try not to sound rude or personal, e.g. *You must fix the problem you caused ...*
>
> It is better to say, *The problem must be fixed ...*

To whom it may concern,


I am writing to complain about a Seimex _____ watch I purchased

_____ in your shop. I was quite happy with it until last night,

after coming out of the Jacuzzi, _____ and

_____ inside the face.

During the time I have owned it, it hasn't been _____ and since it is

clearly labeled as water-resistant there is obviously a _____

_____.

Since it is still under warranty I would like to _____

_____.


I look forward to hearing from you soon.

Yours sincerely,

**D** **Further study**

Using your completed letter, write two Part 7 type questions to test a partner in the next lesson.

Go to word list and quiz page 170.

**A**   **Strategy:** Listen carefully to every detail

Most incorrect choices in this part will use some correct subject, verb and object words and some wrong ones. This unit will help you to pick out and eliminate incorrect answer choices.

## 1   Language building: Listen for subject/verb/object words

A   Look at the list of possible subjects/objects and verbs and make up sentences about each of the pictures with a partner.

1 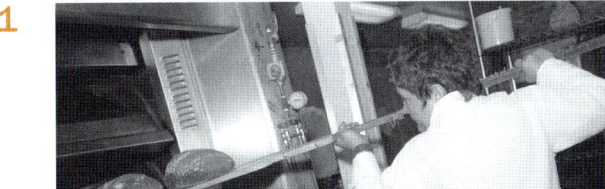    2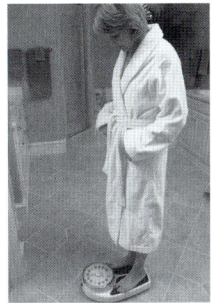

| Possible subjects/objects used | | | Possible verbs used | | |
|---|---|---|---|---|---|
| woman | weight | bathrobe | standing | checking | looking at |
| baker | scales | oven | weighing | making | baking |
| bread | | | wearing | putting | |

B   Listen to four correct sentences about these pictures. Listen carefully to the subjects/objects and verbs, and after each one stop the audio and tell your partner the words you heard. Decide together which picture you think the sentence matches.

*Follow up:* Write one new sentence for each picture. You may use different words. Test your partners to pick out the SVO words and choose the correct picture.

## 2   Test tactic: Be careful of subject/verb/object problems

A   For the following sentences underline the incorrect words and say how you could correct them.

   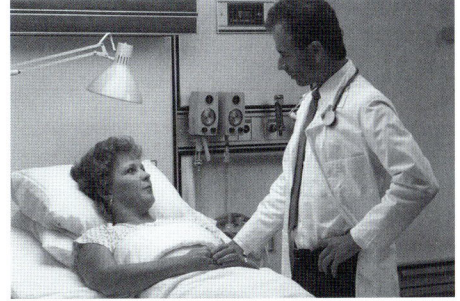

1. The woman is hitting the baby.
2. The shopping cart is empty.

3. The woman is crying on the bed.
4. The doctor is sitting on the bed.

**B**   Now write two correct sentences about each of the following pictures. Underline the subjects, verbs and objects.

Example: *The hiker is sitting on the ground.*

**1**

**2**

**C**   You will hear four sentences about each picture. After each sentence, stop the audio and tell a partner the SVO words you heard, then mark below whether you think the sentence is Correct or Wrong.

**1**
(A) ☐ Correct    ☐ Wrong
(B) ☐ Correct    ☐ Wrong
(C) ☐ Correct    ☐ Wrong
(D) ☐ Correct    ☐ Wrong

**2**
(A) ☐ Correct    ☐ Wrong
(B) ☐ Correct    ☐ Wrong
(C) ☐ Correct    ☐ Wrong
(D) ☐ Correct    ☐ Wrong

*Follow up:* Compare with your partner the sentences you first made and the correct sentence.

## 3   Tactic practice 🎧

Use the tactics you have practiced for the next three photographs. You will have one minute to a) brainstorm vocabulary and b) predict possible statements with a partner. Then listen to and echo (silently) the answer choices, and after you hear each, tick whether you think it is correct, maybe correct, or wrong.

**Tactics checklist**

☑ Listen for SVO words.

☑ Listen for wrong subjects, verbs (and objects).

**1**

(A) ☐ Correct    ☐ Maybe correct    ☐ Wrong
(B) ☐ Correct    ☐ Maybe correct    ☐ Wrong
(C) ☐ Correct    ☐ Maybe correct    ☐ Wrong
(D) ☐ Correct    ☐ Maybe correct    ☐ Wrong

**2**

(A) ☐ Correct    ☐ Maybe correct    ☐ Wrong
(B) ☐ Correct    ☐ Maybe correct    ☐ Wrong
(C) ☐ Correct    ☐ Maybe correct    ☐ Wrong
(D) ☐ Correct    ☐ Maybe correct    ☐ Wrong

**3**

(A) ☐ Correct   ☐ Maybe correct   ☐ Wrong
(B) ☐ Correct   ☐ Maybe correct   ☐ Wrong
(C) ☐ Correct   ☐ Maybe correct   ☐ Wrong
(D) ☐ Correct   ☐ Maybe correct   ☐ Wrong

*Follow up:* Now compare your answers with your partner, explaining your reasons, and what you remember hearing.

🎧 Understanding natural English

**Understanding natural English**

In natural spoken English, sounds are changed, combined and dropped. Listen to these sentences spoken naturally and write in the missing words.

A forest grows in ......... valley.

The man is drawing ......... diagram.

---

## B   Mini-test 🎧

Now apply the *Test tactics* at the actual test speed with questions 1–6.

🕐 You will have 1 minute 30 seconds to skim the pictures before the first listening starts. After that you will have exactly 5 seconds between each question to mark your answer and focus on the next picture.

**1**

**2**

**3**

**4**

**5**

**6**

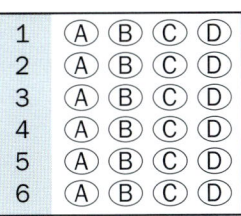

```
1  Ⓐ Ⓑ Ⓒ Ⓓ
2  Ⓐ Ⓑ Ⓒ Ⓓ
3  Ⓐ Ⓑ Ⓒ Ⓓ
4  Ⓐ Ⓑ Ⓒ Ⓓ
5  Ⓐ Ⓑ Ⓒ Ⓓ
6  Ⓐ Ⓑ Ⓒ Ⓓ
```

## C     Learn by doing: Three in a row game

To win this game you must make a line of three pictures in a row.

Choose a picture and say the number. Your partner will read a sentence and you must say if it is correct or wrong (and explain why). If you are right, you get the square. Take turns until you have a winner.

**Student A:** Look at Activity file 1.3a on page 153.

**Student B:** Look at Activity file 1.3b on page 156.

## D     Further study

Choose two pictures from C above, and write Part 1 type statements (one correct answer, three that are close but wrong) to test on your classmates in the next lesson. The incorrect answers should include some correct SVO words and at least one wrong one.

Go to word list and quiz page 172.

# Part 2    Question-response    Unit 2.3

## A    Strategy: Be familiar with time and location structures

Questions about time and location are common in the TOEIC test. This will familiarize you with the types of questions and answer choices you will see in this section.

### 1 Language building: Be familiar with time and location marker words

A   The table below contains sentences that answer different time and location questions. Common marker words are shown in **bold**.

Match each answer to the correct question type. The first one is done for you.

|   |   |   |
|---|---|---|
| | a | We will be finished **in February**. |
| | b | It's **at** Eastern State University, **on** the 3rd floor. |
| **1 Where/Directions?** b | c | She's been working here **for** several months. |
| | d | **Down** the hall, **turn left** and it's just **across** from the cafeteria. |
| **2 How long?** | e | The package was delivered about **an hour ago**. |
| | f | They've been in the meeting **since** 6:00. |
| | g | **To** Florida, as usual. |
| **3 When?** | h | I've had it **about** a month. |
| | i | **On Tuesday July 7th, at** 1:00. |
| | j | It's **in** the refrigerator, **behind** the vegetables. |

B   Some questions do not have obvious time or location marker words. Write in the space whether the answer is for "Where/Directions", "How long", or "When" questions. The first one is done for you.

| 1 Where / Directions? | Berlin. |
|---|---|
| 2 | It could take all night. |
| 3 | Sorry, I'm not from around here. |
| 4 | Bermuda again. I can't wait! |
| 5 | It hasn't arrived yet. |

C   Now listen to four answer choices, and for each tick whether it is a "Where/Directions", "When" or "How long" question. After the recording compare your answers with a partner.

1. ☐ Where/Directions?   ☐ When?   ☐ How long?
2. ☐ Where/Directions?   ☐ When?   ☐ How long?
3. ☐ Where/Directions?   ☐ When?   ☐ How long?
4. ☐ Where/Directions?   ☐ When?   ☐ How long?

**Test tip**

Learn to identify "When" questions

Usually "When" questions involve the phrases
*How long ...?,* or
*When .../*
*What time ...?*

## 2 Test tactic: Identify and answer time and location questions

**A** For each question below, tick whether it is a "Where", "Directions", "When" or "How long" question. The first one is done for you.

1. Excuse me. Where are the stairs?
   - ☑ Where?
   - ☑ Directions?
   - ☐ When?
   - ☐ How long?

   (A) Go out this door and walk around the corner.
   (B) They are away on business.
   (C) It's not polite to stare.

2. When did they cancel the order?
   - ☐ Where?
   - ☐ Directions?
   - ☐ When?
   - ☐ How long?

   (A) Back in March, I think.
   (B) Yes, they were ordered to do it.
   (C) I really think we have to cancel it.

3. How long did you have to wait?
   - ☐ Where?
   - ☐ Directions?
   - ☐ When?
   - ☐ How long?

   (A) Yes, it is very long.
   (B) I was waiting for it on Tuesday.
   (C) Not as long as I thought I would.

4. Do you know where my keys are?
   - ☐ Where?
   - ☐ Directions?
   - ☐ When?
   - ☐ How long?

   (A) Yes, it's the wrong key.
   (B) In the drawer, as usual.
   (C) I locked the front door.

5. Do you know of a good cleaners near here?
   - ☐ Where?
   - ☐ Directions?
   - ☐ When?
   - ☐ How long?

   (A) I think it's not so clean.
   (B) I prefer a different cleaner.
   (C) There's one on Bank Street.

🎧 **B** Now listen and choose the best answers for each question. Be careful of the distractors noted in activity 1.

*Follow up:* Compare your answers with a partner.

**Understanding natural English**

In natural spoken English, sounds are changed, combined and dropped. Listen to these sentences spoken naturally and write in the missing words.

......... A4 paper kept?

......... taxi coming?

## 3 Tactic practice 🎧

Use the tactics you have practiced for the next five questions.

| 1 | Ⓐ Ⓑ Ⓒ |
|---|--------|
| 2 | Ⓐ Ⓑ Ⓒ |
| 3 | Ⓐ Ⓑ Ⓒ |
| 4 | Ⓐ Ⓑ Ⓒ |
| 5 | Ⓐ Ⓑ Ⓒ |

*Follow up:* Discuss with a partner which answers you chose and why.

🎧 Understanding natural English

**Tactics checklist**

☑ Listen for location questions, decide the type and listen for the appropriate answer.

☑ Listen for marker words in time questions.

## B Mini-test

Now apply the *Test tactics* at the actual test speed with questions 1–10.

> 🕐 You will have 5 seconds at the end of each item to make your choice. You must then be ready to listen to the next question.

| 1 | Ⓐ Ⓑ Ⓒ | 6 | Ⓐ Ⓑ Ⓒ |
| 2 | Ⓐ Ⓑ Ⓒ | 7 | Ⓐ Ⓑ Ⓒ |
| 3 | Ⓐ Ⓑ Ⓒ | 8 | Ⓐ Ⓑ Ⓒ |
| 4 | Ⓐ Ⓑ Ⓒ | 9 | Ⓐ Ⓑ Ⓒ |
| 5 | Ⓐ Ⓑ Ⓒ | 10 | Ⓐ Ⓑ Ⓒ |

## C Learn by doing: Time and location questions

**A** Look at the model conversation below. Use the words on the right to complete the conversation.

A: Where do you live, Ken?
B: Right now ........... .
A: Oh yeah? How long have you lived there?
B: Oh, ........... . I moved there ........... .
A: Really? Where did you live before?
B: ........... .

I lived in Georgetown with my family
just after University
I'm living in Hamilton
for about 5 years

**B** Now make a similar conversation with a partner, using the questionnaire below. Add some more questions of your own.

---
**Interview your partner**

Where do you live?
How long have you lived there?
Where did you live before?
How long does it take you to come to class?

Where do you think is the best place to eat around here?
If you could take a holiday anywhere in this country, where would you go?
How long would you like to stay there?
What time of year do you think would be best to go?
What other country would you most like to visit?

How long have you been studying for the TOEIC test?
When do you think you will be able to get the score you want?

---

## D Further study

Think of a famous person and write two "Where", two "When", and two "How long" questions you could ask them. Then write the answers you think they would give. In the next class read the answers you wrote to see if your partner can guess the questions you asked and the famous person you chose.

Go to word list and quiz page 173.

**A**

## Strategy: Use vocabulary clues to infer meaning

The answers for many of the questions in this part of the test are not stated directly. You will have to listen carefully and use your knowledge of related vocabulary and context to choose many of the answers.

**Test tip**

Sometimes the answers are not stated directly in the passage

Before the listening, think of other words related to the answer choices and listen to infer the general meaning.

**1** **Language building: Brainstorm vocabulary for locations, activities and occupations**

**A** For each of the following, choose the words that best relate to each answer choice, then add two more words for each answer choice. The first word is done for you.

**1.** Where is the woman?

| | | |
|---|---|---|
| (A) A hotel | | ~~rail~~ |
| | | room |
| | | track |
| (B) A car rental agency | | bed |
| | | stadium |
| (C) A train station | *rail* | fans |
| | | car |
| (D) A sports event | | license |

*Follow up:* Compare your list with a partner. Then think of another common place and brainstorm three related words. Say your words to your partner and see if they can guess the location.

**2.** What is the man doing?

| | | |
|---|---|---|
| (A) Making a hotel reservation | | table |
| | | bride |
| (B) Getting married | | room |
| (C) Borrowing a book | | dinner |
| from the library | | library card |
| | | vacancies |
| (D) Making a restaurant | | novel |
| reservation | | dress |

*Follow up:* Compare your list with your partner. Then think of another common activity and brainstorm three related words. Say your words to your partner and see if they can guess the activity.

**3.** What is the man's job?

| | | |
|---|---|---|
| (A) A delivery man | | deposit |
| | | truck |
| | | discount |
| (B) A musician | | concert |
| | | withdrawal |
| (C) A banker | | order |
| | | recording |
| (D) A salesman | | package |

*Follow up:* Compare your list with your partner. Then think of another common job and brainstorm three related words. Say your words to your partner and see if they can guess the job.

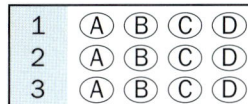 **B** Now listen to the three conversations and choose the correct answer. After each one, circle the word(s) on the lists in A that helped you find the answer.

1  Ⓐ Ⓑ Ⓒ Ⓓ
2  Ⓐ Ⓑ Ⓒ Ⓓ
3  Ⓐ Ⓑ Ⓒ Ⓓ

## 2 Test tactic: Identify inference markers

Look at the three common inference questions in **bold**. Read the conversation below, choose the correct answer and underline the words in the tapescript that tell you it is correct.

1.  **What can be said** about the weather?
    (A) It is often wet.
    (B) It is warmer than Arizona.
    (C) It has no effect on transportation.
    (D) It is moderate.

2.  **What can be inferred** about the speakers' location?
    (A) They are in a restaurant.
    (B) They are waiting at a bus stop.
    (C) They are at work.
    (D) They are in a taxi.

3.  **What is implied** about the woman?
    (A) She often walks to work.
    (B) She used to live in another city.
    (C) She dislikes her job.
    (D) She is often late.

### Tapescript

M: *Look, I'm soaked to the skin. And I'm late, too! The buses are always slower on days like this.*

W: *Oh no. I don't have an umbrella, and I have to walk across town to get Mr. Johnson's signature on these documents before lunch.*

M: *Well, you had better take a taxi. It's supposed to stay like this all day.*

W: *I bet it's not going to be easy to catch one. I am really starting to miss living in Arizona!*

*Follow up:* Compare the words that you have underlined with a partner and discuss your answers.

## Understanding natural English

In natural spoken English, sounds are changed, combined and dropped. Listen to these sentences spoken naturally and write in the missing words.

That's what we were ......... expect.

You've always ......... work overseas.

## 3 Tactic practice

Use the tactics you have practiced for the next six questions. Before each passage begins, use the time to a) predict the context and b) think of other ways to say the answer choices with a partner.

1. Where are the speakers?
   (A) In a library
   (B) In a book store
   (C) In a music store
   (D) In a gift shop

2. What is the woman doing?
   (A) Recording a CD
   (B) Looking for a present
   (C) Taking an order
   (D) Paying for something

3. What does the man imply?
   (A) The item is in stock.
   (B) The item will arrive very soon.
   (C) The item is extremely rare.
   (D) The item is popular.

4. What are the speakers doing?
   (A) Watching the news
   (B) Going overseas
   (C) Looking at a job ad
   (D) Planning a holiday

5. What can be inferred about the speakers' relationship?
   (A) They've known each other for a time.
   (B) They've just met.
   (C) They work together.
   (D) They live together.

6. What does the man imply?
   (A) He's desperate to work overseas.
   (B) He wants to go on holiday.
   (C) He has enough money to live for a while.
   (D) He'd like to get a new place.

| 1 | Ⓐ Ⓑ Ⓒ Ⓓ | 4 | Ⓐ Ⓑ Ⓒ Ⓓ |
|---|---|---|---|
| 2 | Ⓐ Ⓑ Ⓒ Ⓓ | 5 | Ⓐ Ⓑ Ⓒ Ⓓ |
| 3 | Ⓐ Ⓑ Ⓒ Ⓓ | 6 | Ⓐ Ⓑ Ⓒ Ⓓ |

Understanding natural English

## B    Mini-test

Now apply the *Test tactics* at the actual test speed with questions 1–12.

🕐 You will have 30 seconds to skim the questions and answer choices before the first listening starts. After that you will have exactly 8 seconds between each question to mark your answer and focus on the next question.

1. What does the man assume about the woman's trip?
   (A) It was remarkable.
   (B) It was unpleasant.
   (C) It was amusing.
   (D) There were lots of presents.

2. What can be inferred about the woman's feelings about her trip?
   (A) She would like to have stayed longer.
   (B) She had a relaxing time.
   (C) She didn't enjoy it at all.
   (D) She found it tiring.

3. Where was the woman's hotel located?
   (A) On the right of the first aid center
   (B) In the center of the carnival area
   (C) Out of town
   (D) Near a dance hall

4. Where does the conversation probably take place?
   (A) In a bank
   (B) In an office
   (C) In a restaurant
   (D) At the doctor's

5. How much should the man pay?
   (A) 10 dollars
   (B) 15 dollars
   (C) 5 dollars
   (D) 2 dollars

6. What can we infer about the situation?
   (A) The man didn't fully read the sign.
   (B) The woman has made a mistake.
   (C) The price was incorrectly marked.
   (D) The man will pay the cheaper price.

7. What can be inferred about the man's manager?
   (A) He is away on business.
   (B) He checks all reports carefully.
   (C) He sometimes sets unreasonable deadlines.
   (D) He thinks there is a problem.

8. What does the woman initially think?
   (A) The work needs to be checked.
   (B) Her team can do the calculations.
   (C) The problem will go away.
   (D) The work can be done on time.

9. What is the man waiting for?
   (A) Some calculations
   (B) Some results
   (C) The typists
   (D) His manager

10. How long does the man say it will take?
    (A) It depends
    (B) Less than two hours
    (C) It can be finished right away
    (D) It was finished last night

11. Who is the man?
    (A) A truck driver
    (B) A gardener
    (C) A repairman
    (D) A guest

12. Where are the speakers?
    (A) In a hotel
    (B) At a garage
    (C) At a home and garden center
    (D) At the woman's house

| 1 | Ⓐ Ⓑ Ⓒ Ⓓ |
| 2 | Ⓐ Ⓑ Ⓒ Ⓓ |
| 3 | Ⓐ Ⓑ Ⓒ Ⓓ |
| 4 | Ⓐ Ⓑ Ⓒ Ⓓ |
| 5 | Ⓐ Ⓑ Ⓒ Ⓓ |
| 6 | Ⓐ Ⓑ Ⓒ Ⓓ |
| 7 | Ⓐ Ⓑ Ⓒ Ⓓ |
| 8 | Ⓐ Ⓑ Ⓒ Ⓓ |
| 9 | Ⓐ Ⓑ Ⓒ Ⓓ |
| 10 | Ⓐ Ⓑ Ⓒ Ⓓ |
| 11 | Ⓐ Ⓑ Ⓒ Ⓓ |
| 12 | Ⓐ Ⓑ Ⓒ Ⓓ |

# C  Learn by doing

**Student A:** Look at Activity file 3.3a on page 152.

**Student B:** Look at Activity file 3.3b on page 154.

Take turns to read one of the sentences from your file to your partner. They must say the job, location OR activity from the lists that best matches the sentence.

| Jobs | Locations | Activities |
| --- | --- | --- |
| office worker | restaurant | buying clothes |
| shoe salesman | art museum | talking about a movie |
| teacher | supermarket | changing an appointment |
| train conductor | sports club | asking for directions |

*Follow up:* Now choose a job, location or activity and make up your own sentences to test your partner.

# D  Further study

Think of a common job, location and an activity and write a short conversation. In the next class read your conversation and see if the other students can guess the job, location and activity you chose.

Go to word list and quiz page 174.

**A**

## Strategy: Be familiar with re-statements
Be aware of questions involving numbers and quantities

Numbers and quantities are a commonly tested feature in the TOEIC test. The tactics in this section will help you to pick out the correct answers when dealing with Part 4 and other listening parts of the test.

**Test tip**

The correct answer choice often uses different words from what you will hear

Be aware of this and listen for meaning, not just the key words.

**Test tip**

Specific information questions appear in the same order they appear in the listening

Focus on the questions in order. When you hear the answer, mark it and move on immediately.

**1 Language building: Re-statements of key vocabulary**

A Look at the three questions with just the correct answer choice. Circle the words in the tapescript which have the same meaning as each answer choice.

1. Where is the announcement made?

   (A) **At an annual convention**

2. Which of the following is NOT true about Dr. Abrahams?

   (B) **He has less than three qualifications.**

3. What will Dr. Abrahams do tomorrow?

   (C) **Take part in a seminar**

**Tapescript**

*Our final speaker today was also our guest presenter at last year's conference. Dr. Harel Abrahams is perhaps best known for his best-selling work "Meeting business challenges", but his area of expertise extends far beyond the topics dealt with in that book.*

*A graduate of Yale University, with no fewer than three PhD degrees to his name, he is the current chair of Economics at McGuire University, and we are delighted that he has agreed to speak to us once more. As well as today's lecture, Dr. Abrahams has kindly agreed to join tomorrow's round table discussion, which I am sure you will all be keen to attend.*

*So, without further ado, to speak on "Small companies and macro economics", let me present Dr. Harel Abrahams.*

**Test tip**

Be careful of questions involving number and quantity

Read the question and carefully note what it is asking, then quickly read the answer choices. When you hear one of the numbers in the listening decide whether it answers the question or not.

 B Now listen to three sets of sentences and mark the answer choice that is closest in meaning.

1. Part of the shipment was damaged.    ☐ A ☐ B ☐ C
2. They started the job a month ago.    ☐ A ☐ B ☐ C
3. Mr. Holmes has always been a huge help to the team. ☐ A ☐ B ☐ C

*Follow up:* Compare your answers with a partner.

**2 Test tactic: Choosing the correct number/quantity answer**

A Underline the key words in the question below, then quickly read the answer choices.

1. How many boats will join the event?

   (A) 14    (B) 17    (C) 35    (D) 70

**B** Scan the following tapescript for the numbers in 1 A–D. When you find one, decide if it answers the question or not. Remember, the words in the question and the tapescript may be different even if the meaning is the same.

> **Tapescript**
>
> *The Jamestown regatta kicks of Saturday afternoon at 14 hundred hours, that's 2 p.m. to you landlubbers. With 70 racing yachts competing this year for 3500 dollars in prizes, this is sure to be one of the sailing events of the season. Spectators should try ...*

**C** Underline the key words in the question below. Now listen to the rest of the passage and choose the best answer.

2. How many salvaged civil-war items are on display?
   (A) 19
   (B) 90
   (C) 150
   (D) 200

## 3 Tactic practice

Use the tactics you have practiced for the next three questions. Before the start of each question a) predict the content and b) think of other ways to say the key words or phrases.

1. How many people are required to attend the conference?
   (A) One
   (B) Two
   (C) Three
   (D) Four

2. How long does the conference last?
   (A) One afternoon
   (B) All day Saturday
   (C) A couple of hours
   (D) Two days

3. How much time off can volunteers expect?
   (A) About an hour
   (B) Two days
   (C) About four hours
   (D) A day

| 1 | Ⓐ Ⓑ Ⓒ Ⓓ |
|---|---------|
| 2 | Ⓐ Ⓑ Ⓒ Ⓓ |
| 3 | Ⓐ Ⓑ Ⓒ Ⓓ |

**Understanding natural English**

In natural spoken English, sounds are changed, combined and dropped. Listen to these sentences spoken naturally and write in the missing words.

... both ......... conference.

She's ......... top designers.

Now apply the *Test tactics* at the actual test speed with questions 1–12.

🕐 You will have 30 seconds to skim the questions and answer choices before the first listening starts. After that you will have exactly 8 seconds between each question to mark your answer and focus on the next question.

1. Who can attend the last show of *Indigo Heart*?
   (A) Everyone
   (B) People over the age of 13
   (C) People over the age of 18
   (D) People under the age of 18

2. Which movie features Deborah Legg?
   (A) *Monterrey*
   (B) *Long Vacation*
   (C) *Phantom Knight*
   (D) *Indigo Heart*

3. How many movies are showing?
   (A) 3
   (B) 2
   (C) 4
   (D) 9

4. What does Elvira Kaur do?
   (A) She is a video game designer.
   (B) She works in the fashion industry.
   (C) She is a student.
   (D) She is an actress.

5. How long has Elvira been working for the company?
   (A) 2 months
   (B) 19 years
   (C) Since she graduated
   (D) From September

6. What is Elvira planning to speak about today?
   (A) Her designs
   (B) Next year's sales target
   (C) How to understand fabrics
   (D) Her project group

7. How many crimes is the man wanted for?
   (A) 6
   (B) 7
   (C) 8
   (D) 10

8. How many of the man's family are said to live in the area?
   (A) 1
   (B) 2
   (C) 3
   (D) 5

9. Who is this announcement intended for?
   (A) Social workers
   (B) Police
   (C) Lawyers
   (D) Local citizens

10. What kind of product is being advertised?
    (A) Exercise equipment
    (B) A training video
    (C) A fitness club
    (D) A suitcase

11. Why might people use the single-hand technique?
    (A) To strengthen their arms
    (B) To build flexibility
    (C) To work on their abs
    (D) To carry it with them

12. How much is the product?
    (A) $9.99 plus post and packaging
    (B) $555 plus delivery
    (C) More than $30 including delivery
    (D) The advertisement doesn't say

| 1 | Ⓐ Ⓑ Ⓒ Ⓓ |
| 2 | Ⓐ Ⓑ Ⓒ Ⓓ |
| 3 | Ⓐ Ⓑ Ⓒ Ⓓ |
| 4 | Ⓐ Ⓑ Ⓒ Ⓓ |
| 5 | Ⓐ Ⓑ Ⓒ Ⓓ |
| 6 | Ⓐ Ⓑ Ⓒ Ⓓ |
| 7 | Ⓐ Ⓑ Ⓒ Ⓓ |
| 8 | Ⓐ Ⓑ Ⓒ Ⓓ |
| 9 | Ⓐ Ⓑ Ⓒ Ⓓ |
| 10 | Ⓐ Ⓑ Ⓒ Ⓓ |
| 11 | Ⓐ Ⓑ Ⓒ Ⓓ |
| 12 | Ⓐ Ⓑ Ⓒ Ⓓ |

 **C** ## Learn by doing: Introducing people

**A** Look at the biography speech below describing Bill Gates. With a partner write down the questions you would need to ask to get the information that is underlined in the text.

Examples

Bill Gates – *May I have your name please?*
being the head of the computer company Microsoft – *What are you famous for?*

> *Today I would like to give you some background on* Bill Gates*. Although he is quite famous for* being the head of the computer company Microsoft*, that is not what I am going to talk about today.*
>
> *Born on* Oct. 28, 1955*, Bill grew up in* Seattle, Washington *with* his two sisters. *His father,* William H. Gates II*, was a Seattle* attorney *while his late mother,* Mary Gates*, was a* schoolteacher*.*
>
> *In* 1973*, Gates entered* Harvard University*, where he* developed a computer operating system*. This interest in* computers *continues to this day.*
>
> *Apart from* computers *Bill enjoys* reading*, and* playing golf *and* bridge*.*

**B** Interview your partner using the questions you wrote. Note their answers and make a similar speech, then write two or three questions about it.

*Follow up:* Test another group of students with your speech and questions.

**D** ## Further study

Write a similar short biography about someone in your family or a famous person. Write two questions and answer choices to test your classmates in the next lesson.

Go to word list and quiz page 175.

## A     Strategy: Improve your knowledge of suffixes and prefixes

Knowledge of suffixes and prefixes can help you guess the meaning of unfamiliar words. This unit will familiarize you with some of the most common forms.

**Test tip**

**Learn suffixes to identify nouns and verbs**

Questions that require nouns or verbs are common in the TOEIC test. Learning to recognize noun and verb suffixes will help you to choose the right one.

**1**  **Test tactic: Noun and verb suffixes**

**A**  The words below feature some of the most common suffixes used with nouns and verbs. For each word decide whether it is a noun or a verb.

| cooperation | ☐ N ☐ V | simplify | ☐ N ☐ V | security | ☐ N ☐ V |
|---|---|---|---|---|---|
| criticize | ☐ N ☐ V | quickness | ☐ N ☐ V | widen | ☐ N ☐ V |
| partnership | ☐ N ☐ V | activate | ☐ N ☐ V | assistance | ☐ N ☐ V |
| department | ☐ N ☐ V | celebration | ☐ N ☐ V | realize | ☐ N ☐ V |

**B**  Now look at the list of suffixes and mark whether each is a noun or verb suffix.

| -tion/-sion | ☐ noun ☐ verb | -ise/-ize | ☐ noun ☐ verb |
|---|---|---|---|
| -ity | ☐ noun ☐ verb | -en | ☐ noun ☐ verb |
| -ness | ☐ noun ☐ verb | -ate | ☐ noun ☐ verb |
| -ment | ☐ noun ☐ verb | -(i)fy | ☐ noun ☑ verb |
| -ance/-ence | ☐ noun ☐ verb | -ship | ☑ noun ☐ verb |

**C**  For each sentence below, first decide if it requires a noun or verb, then choose the best word of the correct type to fit the gap.

| investigation | identify | devastate | repetitiveness | criticize |
|---|---|---|---|---|
| document | internship | renovate | dependence | soften |

1. The stockholders have called for a(n) ...... to find out where the money went.

2. Jon's boss would often loudly ...... him for even the smallest mistakes that he made.

3. Doing a(n) ...... is a good way for students to get work experience.

4. Miller Manufacturing's ...... on one supplier caused serious problems when that company went bankrupt.

5. A consultant was hired to ...... the company's main weaknesses, and suggest solutions.

6. Bill panicked when he realized he had left a key ...... on his desk at home.

7. The company spent millions to ...... its main office in order to impress its customers.

8. Officials worry that the hurricane will ...... the coastal areas if it changes its course.

9. Many people dislike the ...... of working on a factory assembly line.

10. Cyclists often use special pads to ...... the seat for long-distance rides.

**Test tip**

Being able to guess the meaning of unknown words is important for all parts of the test

Learning common prefixes can help you guess the meaning of words you don't know.

## 2 Test tactic: Use prefixes to help decide the best answer

A Look at the list of some of the most common prefixes below. Match the prefix to the meaning on the right. The first one is done for you.

| 1 dis- | discomfort (n), discontinue (v) |
| un- | unable (adj), unfasten (v) |
| non- | non-fiction (adj), non-political (adj) |
| im-/in-/ir-/il- | inconvenient (adj), illegal (adj) |

| 2 co- | co-founder (n), cooperate (v) |
| 3 sub- | submarine (n), subsection (n) |
| 4 inter- | interaction (n), international (adj) |
| 5 re- | re-organization (n), review (v/n) |
| 6 over- | overwork (v), overpriced (adj) |
| 7 mis- | mislead (v), misunderstanding (n) |

☐ a badly or wrongly

☑ b reverses the meaning

☐ c between

☐ d joint or together

☐ e again or back

☐ f below, under

☐ g too much

B Now use your understanding of prefixes to help you choose the best word to complete each sentence.

1. The company's bid was rejected because the quality of their work was ............... .

2. Jake Thomson and Phil Greene ............... the project, each looking after one team.

3. There is a(n) ............... in each room to allow all the staff to communicate easily, even between different floors.

4. After the plane crash they needed to completely ............... the damaged runway.

5. Many people believe that lawyers are ............... and charge too much for their services.

6. Sorry, I think I ............... you. I thought you said you were going to book the meeting room.

7. He didn't pay his phone bill so they came to ............... his line.

8. The children couldn't wait to ............... their presents on Christmas Day.

9. I often get very ............... if there is heavy traffic when I am in a hurry.

10. Since the gift was in the sale it was ............... .

a   misheard

b   disconnect

c   unwrap

d   impatient

e   co-supervise

f   overpaid

g   resurface

h   non-refundable

i   intercom

j   sub-standard

**Tactics checklist**

☑ Learning common prefixes can help you guess the meaning of words you don't know.

☑ Learn suffixes to identify nouns and verbs.

## 3 Tactic practice

Use the tactics you have practiced to answer the following questions.

1. The two presidents maintained a close .......... despite their rival businesses.
   (A) friendly
   (B) friend
   (C) friendship
   (D) friends

2. Efforts were made to .......... the sizes of track gauge across Europe in the late twentieth century.
   (A) standard
   (B) standards
   (C) standardization
   (D) standardize

3. The program seems easy to use, but the interface needs to be .......... .
   (A) simplified
   (B) simply
   (C) simplest
   (D) simplification

4. My tennis racket will need to be .......... to return it to its original condition.
   (A) circumscribed
   (B) restrung
   (C) detached
   (D) mishandled

5. He transferred from the parent company to one of its smaller .......... .
   (A) partnerships
   (B) subsidiaries
   (C) conglomerates
   (D) multinationals

6. To resolve their differences, an .......... was employed to deal with the two sides.
   (A) investigation
   (B) intermediary
   (C) assistance
   (D) impatient

## B Mini-test

Now apply the *Test tactics* at the actual test speed with questions 1–12.

🕒 You have 6 minutes to complete 12 items. To use your time wisely, use the 2-pass method you learnt in Unit 5.1. Spend no more than 30 seconds on each item. If you don't know the answer, guess and move on.

1. Disagreements over the .......... of the design eventually led to a court case.
   (A) owner
   (B) ownership
   (C) owning
   (D) owned

2. The addition of steel girders was designed to .......... the roof support beams.
   (A) strong
   (B) strongly
   (C) strength
   (D) strengthen

3. It is essential to fully .......... on the operation of the machinery in order to avoid accidents.
   (A) concentration
   (B) concentrating
   (C) concentrate
   (D) concentrates

4. He was known in the business for his .......... attitude and astute business sense.
   (A) uncompromising
   (B) international
   (C) preventative
   (D) secretarial

5. The levels of adult .......... in the developing world have fallen by five percent in the last ten years.

   (A) educational

   (B) immortality

   (C) illiteracy

   (D) supervision

6. The trip to Boston will be postponed until next week, .......... there is an improvement in the weather.

   (A) because

   (B) since

   (C) for

   (D) unless

7. Plans to .......... the highway from four to six lanes were blocked by the local government.

   (A) wide

   (B) width

   (C) narrow

   (D) widen

8. The meeting will have to be .......... to a later date.

   (A) arranged

   (B) rescheduled

   (C) planned

   (D) prepared

9. This is the kind of decision that only a .......... businessman can make.

   (A) hard-nosed

   (B) wide-eyed

   (C) straight-lipped

   (D) flat-headed

10. The contract .......... if the parties hadn't come to a last-minute agreement.

    (A) was canceled

    (B) could be canceled

    (C) would have been canceled

    (D) might not have canceled

11. Gift giving is considered standard amongst hosts, and guests should feel no .......... to return the favor.

    (A) oblige

    (B) obliged

    (C) obliges

    (D) obligation

12. Tax .......... is available for those with dependents earning less than the statutory minimum.

    (A) refund

    (B) relief

    (C) compensation

    (D) awareness

Use the following words to complete the crossword puzzle below. Two have been done for you. Refer to the word list on page 176 if you need help.

| devastate | interaction | overstocked | illiteracy |
|---|---|---|---|
| impatient | ~~mislead~~ | ~~uncompromising~~ | discontinue |
| criticize | obligation | renovate | intermediary |

### Across

1. Showing no willingness to reduce their demands or back down

3. To have too much of a product or item

6. An inability to read and write

7. Somebody who carries messages to try to bring about agreement

8. Seriously damage or destroy

9. Upset or annoyed at having to wait

10. To complain about something you think is wrong

11. To make something like new again

### Down

2. To cause somebody to have a false opinion or belief

4. To stop doing something

5. Something that must be done because of legal or moral duty

6. Activity between two or more people or things

Go to word list and quiz page 176.

**A**     **Strategy:** Choose the correct verb form: future, perfect

This unit will familiarize you with the way that future and perfect forms are used and how they can appear in the TOEIC test.

**1** **Language building: Using the future form**

A   Look at the common future forms shown in the examples below.

> ***will/be going to*** – plus base verb form
> Examples
> *Are you <u>going to</u> play tennis on Saturday?*
> *They're <u>going to</u> buy the parts in Australia.*
> *Do you think they <u>will accept</u> the offer?*
> *I <u>won't go</u> to the show tomorrow.*

> **Present continuous** – *am/is/are* plus verb + *-ing*
> Examples
> *I'm <u>meeting</u> the chairman at 3.00.*
> *He <u>isn't coming</u> to Paris next week.*
> *<u>Are</u> they <u>bringing</u> the documents?*

B   Complete the sentences with the correct form of the verb.

1.  Will they ……… (send) us the agenda?

2.  I'm ……… (discuss) the contract with them at the upcoming meeting.

3.  I'm going to ……… (see) him at next May's sales meeting.

4.  I promise that I will ……… (send) the invoices to you by the end of the week.

5.  He isn't ……… (take) the samples to the customer.

6.  Why aren't they going to ……… (meet) the schedule?

*Follow up:* Now write one true *will/going to*, and one true present continuous (future) sentence about yourself. You could write about a job, studies, holidays, travel, or other plans. Compare with a partner.

## 2 Test tactic: Choose the correct perfect form

**A** Look at the form shown in the examples below.

| **Perfect simple (past/present/future)** |
| --- |
| – *has/have/had* + past participle |
| Examples |
| *Have you ever played at St. Andrews?* |
| *He hasn't seen the new outlines yet.* |
| *He had already eaten by the time I arrived.* |

| **Perfect continuous (past/present)** |
| --- |
| – *has/have/had been* + verb + *-ing* |
| Examples |
| *They have been discussing the plans for more than three hours.* |
| *He hadn't been paying the sales staff for several months, prior to the closure.* |

**B** Choose the correct form of the verb to complete the sentences.

1. How long have you ......... (employ) by your present company?
   (a) been employed
   (b) being employed
   (c) employed
   (d) be employed

2. Bill has been ......... (work) in Belgium since 1994.
   (a) worked
   (b) works
   (c) working
   (d) worker

3. The interviewer had already been ......... (wait) for an hour when she arrived.
   (a) waiter
   (b) waits
   (c) waited
   (d) waiting

4. I hadn't ......... (have) a chance to meet the new director before the conference.
   (a) having
   (b) have
   (c) had
   (d) been having

*Follow up:* Now write one true perfect simple, and one true perfect continuous sentence about yourself. You could write about past experiences or jobs and hobbies you have been doing for some time. Compare with a partner.

**Tactics checklist**

☑ Watch for word clues for future forms.

☑ Watch for word clues for perfect forms.

☑ Sometimes you may have to read the other sentences to find out when the action happens.

## 3 Tactic practice

Use the tactics you have practiced to complete the following. For each answer underline the words that helped you and compare your answer with a partner.

**Questions 1–4** refer to the following letter.

Dear Mr. Blackburn,

I'm writing about the position in the accounting department that we spoke about last month. As you know I ................ to work for a year to save money before

1. (A) was planned
   (B) had been planning
   (C) will plan
   (D) was going to plan

returning to school to finish my masters course.

I'm afraid since we spoke, my situation has changed. Recently I have come into a bit of money and I ................ be able to afford to return to school earlier than I had originally

2. (A) to
   (B) can
   (C) going to
   (D) will

thought possible. I ................ start my course this coming September which means that I will

3. (A) am going to
   (B) did
   (C) want
   (D) am hoping

have to refuse your offer of a job for the coming year.

I really hope this won't cause you any inconvenience. You have been extremely kind to my family and me. Without your help we wouldn't ................ able to secure the loan on the new

4. (A) be
   (B) be going to
   (C) have been
   (D) have

equipment for the farm last year.

Thank you again for your offer, and all your help.

Sincerely

Brad Jenkins

# Mini-test

Now apply the *Test tactics* at the actual test speed with questions 1–12.

> 🕐 You have 6 minutes to complete 12 items. To use your time wisely, use the
> 2-pass method you learnt in Unit 5.1. Spend no more than 30 seconds on each
> item. If you don't know the answer, guess and move on.

**Questions 1–4** refer to the following newspaper story.

---

### Problems at Beeton Steel

Beeton Steel Company ................ this afternoon that they will be closing their Milltown plant

       **1.** (A) renounced
          (B) denounced
          (C) pronounced
          (D) announced

at the end of this year. John Leighton, a spokesman for Beeton reported that costs at the facility had been rising for some time and at recent talks the company ................ to resolve a six-month-long labor

      **2.** (A) had failed
         (B) will fail
         (C) fails
         (D) could have failed

dispute. Union officials are claiming that this ................ result in a loss of over 2000 jobs for the Milltown area

              **3.** (A) unfortunate
                 (B) will
                 (C) did
                 (D) unfair

and have accused Beeton of closing the plant as a move to break the union. They have promised strikes and protests in all Beeton factories ................ the closure is canceled.

**4.** (A) after
   (B) when
   (C) unless
   (D) if

---

Questions 5–8 refer to the following advertisement.

---

## The classical music event of the season!

Fans of classical music are in for a rare treat in December. The famed Dusseldorf Chamber Orchestra ................ a one-night performance of Handel's *Xerxes* at the Rondel Theatre.

5. (A) has given
(B) gave
(C) will be giving
(D) gives

The DCO is touring North America from October until the new year and we are very lucky that they ................ to make a stop in our fair city. Based upon the glowing reviews their performances

6. (A) decide
(B) will have decided
(C) have been decided
(D) have decided

have ................ this year already, this is going to be a night true music lovers will never forget.

7. (A) received
(B) given
(C) done
(D) seen

This is likely to be the last tour for famed conductor Vasily Krampfstein, as he has announced his retirement, so be sure not to miss this ................ in a lifetime opportunity.

8. (A) sometimes
(B) always
(C) never
(D) once

---

---

## Annual PAWS Fundraiser

The Pollville Animal Welfare Society would like to announce its annual fundraising dinner. For over 25 years PAWS ................, protected and provided a home for thousands of abused

**9.** (A) had been rescuing
(B) rescues
(C) will rescue
(D) has rescued

and abandoned animals in Pollville and surrounding Duxham county.

This year they are hoping to ............... $4500 to provide a new roof for the shelter and repair the

**10.** (A) take
(B) raise
(C) prepare
(D) donate

damage caused to the fence in the large livestock run by the recent tornado.

As usual the dinner ............... to be held in the Pollville community hall and will be followed by

**11.** (A) is going
(B) will
(C) plans
(D) is planning

a series of amusing skits put on by our PAWS-patrol volunteers from Duxham High School and then square-dancing with music ............... by our very own Paw McGruder.

**12.** (A) instruments
(B) provided
(C) playing
(D) performance

The tickets are $25 and may be purchased in all local shops.

Come on down and have a great time supporting a worthy local cause.

---

# C  Grammar practice

Match the sentence beginnings on the left to the best ending on the right.
The first one is done for you.

| | | |
|---|---|---|
| 1. | The annual conference has been ... | ☐ ... ask for increased taxes on foreign livestock imports. |
| 2. | The famed musician announced that he is ... | ☐ ... meeting Joe to study for the upcoming math test. |
| 3. | The agricultural board announced that they will ... | ☐ ... denounced the court decision to take the child away from her parents. |
| 4. | Although Kenji had read the word before, he had ... | ☐ ... won't start negotiations until the rebels have renounced violence and surrendered their weapons. |
| 5. | I'm afraid I can't come to the party tonight. I am ... | ☐ ... will change the cargo invoices and send them to us next week. |
| 6. | Several protesting religious and social groups have ... | ☐ ... going to refuse the multi-million dollar recording contract. |
| 7. | The man lost his job several years ago and since then has been ... | ☐ ... going to leave all her money to worthy charities. |
| 8. | The minister of the war-torn country stated on TV that they ... | ☐ ... I'll quickly get tired of the inconvenience and long travel times. |
| 9. | I spoke to the shipping agent and he said he ... | ☐ ... been rescued, he was placed in a secure and loving home. |
| 10. | I may enjoy the quiet of living in the country but I'm sure ... | ☑ ... canceled this year due to lack of money. |
| 11. | The rich woman decided that she was ... | ☐ ... living in an abandoned car. |
| 12. | A month after the abused dog had ... | ☐ ... never heard it pronounced. |

# D  Further study

**Truth or lies**

A  Make three sentences about the most interesting things you have done.
Two should be true, one should be a lie.

Examples

*I have scuba dived.*

*I have ridden an elephant.*

*I have slept in the Sahara desert.*

Tell a partner and see if they can guess which one is the lie!

B  Now make three sentences (two true, one lie) about things you plan to do in the future and play the same game.

Go to word list and quiz page 176.

**A**

**Strategy:** Learn how to answer "NOT" questions, and questions with names, numbers, dates or times

Both "NOT" questions and questions that focus on names, numbers, dates, and times require you to first pick out the key words in the question, then skim the passage to find the correct answer.

**1** **Test tactic: Dealing with "NOT" questions**

**A** Underline the key words in the question and each answer choice. The question is done for you.

**1.** Which of the following is <u>NOT true</u> about the <u>refund policy</u>?

(A) You must return your pool pass if you want a refund.

(B) Cancelations will be accepted for medical reasons.

(C) Credit card customers will not receive refund checks.

(D) You must inform your instructor when leaving the course.

**B** If you know the answer, mark it and move on. If not, cross out the letter of any of the answer choices above you feel are wrong.

**C** For each of the answer choices remaining, skim the text below to find words with the same meaning as the answer choice, and decide if the meaning is different (the answer) or the same (wrong choice).

---

**Summer program refund policy**

The effective date of the withdrawal/cancelation is the date the withdrawal notice is received by the center, regardless of the date the participant stopped attending the class.

Withdrawal requests from all registered courses must be made before the second class is held. If the request is received 5 business days prior to the first class, the amount refunded will be the full amount, less the refund administration fee ($25.00). If the request is received after the first class, but before the second class, the amount refunded will be the full amount, less the cost of the first class and less the administration fee ($25.00). From the second lesson onwards, no refunds/credits will be issued.

If there is a medical reason for the request, it must be received prior to the mid-point of the program. Refunds for sports and fitness programs will NOT be processed until ALL gym and pool passes have been returned.
Please note that advising an instructor or not attending a program will not constitute a notice of withdrawal.

Cash/check remittances will be refunded by check. Please allow our office 4 to 6 weeks to process your refund. Credit card refunds will go back on the original card.

---

**Test tip**

For "NOT" questions, use what you've learned doing the easier questions

Doing the other questions should help you to answer these ones. If not, skim the passage to confirm the most likely answer choice.

**D** For each of the following choose the sentence which is NOT the same as the answer choice.

1. Pets are not allowed in this establishment
   a Animals prohibited from entry
   b No dogs or cats allowed
   c Owners are responsible for their pets' behavior

2. No refunds for opened goods
   a Goods must be returned in a sealed condition
   b All products come with an unconditional money-back guarantee
   c Exchange only, on unopened products

3. Discounts for seniors
   a Flat price all ages
   b Senior citizens get special rates
   c Reduced price for the elderly

## 2 Test tactic: Name, number, date, and time questions

**A** Underline the key words in the question.

1. What time will Dr. Lee catch a plane?

   (A) 08:30          (C) 11:30
   (B) 09:00          (D) 21:00

**B** Scan the passage to find the first answer choice. Read the sentence it is in and decide if it has the same meaning or a different one. If it has the same meaning, mark your answer. If it is different, scan for the next choice. Continue until you have found the correct answer.

---

**Memo**

John, here is the outline for Dr. Lee's visit.

You will meet Dr. Lee at the airport on Monday night at 8:30 and drive him to the hotel. The next day Tuesday, just after breakfast, we will bring him to the senior staff meeting which is set for 11:30. We aim to have the conference call with the Zurich laboratories from 3:00 but we may have to reschedule it if the Swiss team are delayed.

Wednesday will be taken up with touring the plant and the research building. So that should leave him enough time to interview the team leaders on Thursday before his flight back to Singapore at 9:00 on Friday evening.

Time is very tight on this visit and it is important that things go smoothly. Please ensure that all arrangements are made at your end.

Malcolm McPeg

Director

---

**C** Use the same tactics for the question below.

2. When is it planned for Dr. Lee to have the conference call with Zurich?
   (A) Monday night
   (B) Tuesday afternoon
   (C) Tuesday just after breakfast
   (D) Friday afternoon

*Follow up:* Confirm your answers with a partner.

## 3 Tactic practice: Name, number, date, and time questions

Use the tactics you have practiced to answer the following questions.

1. Which of the following is NOT true?
   (A) The party will be held in a bar.
   (B) Alison is writing to Susan.
   (C) They are planning a birthday party.
   (D) They won't be able to have food at the party.

2. What time will the party start?
   (A) 12:15 p.m.
   (B) 3:31 p.m.
   (C) 5 p.m.
   (D) 6:30 p.m.

3. When are they planning to have the party?
   (A) 29th May
   (B) 10th June
   (C) 11th June
   (D) 15th December

**Questions 1–3** refer to the following email.

---

**From:** Alison Lockwood <ali_cat@inmail.com>
**To:** susan77@yourmail.com
**Date:** 29 May 20—, 15:31:06
**Subject:** Julia's Party

---

Hi Susan,

Just a quick note to remind you we really need to organize Julia's party as soon as possible. Her birthday is on 10th June, but she's not working that day so I thought we could have it on her first day back, June 11th. This might be a good day to have it as everyone in the section is working an early shift that day. That means they will finish at 5 p.m. so there should be plenty of time to get to the bar for a 6:30 start ... what do you think?

I've already spoken to the landlord about it all. He says it's fine, but just needs to get the numbers by Friday so he can organize the food. I think we should book for around 12–15 people ... is that OK?

Let me know what you think,

Ali

---

## B  Mini-test

Now apply the *Test tactics* at the actual test speed with questions 1–10.

 You have 10 minutes to complete 10 items.

**Questions 1–3** refer to the following memo.

---

### Memorandum

**To:** All staff
**From:** Dave Perrett.
**Re:** Trip to Breakout Adventure Center

As promised, here's the revised itinerary for next week's activities. I've spoken to the staff at the center and they've agreed that the changes can be made at no extra cost to the fees we've already paid. Anyway, looks like a great week, so see you all bright and early on Monday morning in the staff parking lot. (Please be there by 8 a.m. as the bus will depart promptly at 8:15.)

| Date | Time | Activity | Place |
|------|------|----------|-------|
| Mon 16th | PM | Arrival<br>Barbeque | Center<br>Beach |
| Tue 17th | All Day | Orienteering | Holden Forest |
| Wed 18th | AM<br>PM | Canoeing<br>Surfing/Wind surfing | Lydford Gorge<br>Beach |
| Thu 19th | All Day<br>9 p.m. | Mountain Biking<br>'Music Night' | Center/Axe Valley<br>Center |
| Fri 20th | All Day<br><br>7 p.m. | Mountain Climbing<br>OR<br>Paragliding*<br>Barbeque | Center/Axe Valley<br><br>Stratton Hill<br>Beach |

\* Sorry, up to a maximum of 12 people for this activity so sign up early.

---

1. Which of the following is NOT true?
   (A) Canoeing will take place after orienteering.
   (B) Everyone can do the mountain climbing activity.
   (C) Both barbeques are at the beach.
   (D) Participants can go paragliding and mountain climbing.

2. What time is the bus scheduled to leave on Monday?
   (A) 8 a.m.
   (B) 8:15 a.m.
   (C) 7 p.m.
   (D) 9 p.m.

3. Where will the staff be on Monday morning?
   (A) At work
   (B) At the centre
   (C) On their way to the center
   (D) At the beach

**GO ON TO THE NEXT PAGE** ▶

Questions 4–6 refer to the following table.

## Breakdown of Company Staff
## (1st April 2006)

Total Number of Employees: 267

| Positions | |
|---|---|
| Senior Management | 7 |
| Section Heads | 14 |
| All Other Positions | 246 |

| Type | |
|---|---|
| Full-time Employees | 181 |
| Part-time Employees | 86 |

| Number of Years of Service | |
|---|---|
| 5 or under | 95 |
| 6–10 | 90 |
| 11 or more | 82 |

| Gender | |
|---|---|
| Male | 162 |
| Female | 105 |

| Age | |
|---|---|
| 20 or under | 24 |
| 21–30 | 91 |
| 31–40 | 72 |
| 41–50 | 43 |
| 51–60 | 25 |
| 61 or over | 12 |

| Education | |
|---|---|
| School | 61 |
| College | 48 |
| University | 158 |

4. How many employees are aged 30 or under?
   (A) 24
   (B) 67
   (C) 91
   (D) Over 100

5. Which group of employees is the largest?
   (A) Male employees
   (B) Full-time employees
   (C) Employees with more than eleven years' experience
   (D) Employees who are university educated

6. How many people work for the firm?
   (A) 267
   (B) 246
   (C) 181
   (D) 534

## Countdown to Christmas!

Only 2 Days to Go
to place your order and get

# FREE DELIVERY*
for delivery by December 24th

It's almost your last chance to place your Christmas gift orders and ensure free delivery* by December 24th. Don't miss out on this great deal and avoid leaving loved ones disappointed by submitting your order before 5pm on Friday 16th December.

Orders placed after this time and before 3pm on Thursday 22nd December will still be guaranteed to arrive by December 24th using our standard delivery option. This remains at our year-round low price of $7 per item (to mainland US addresses).

**Don't forget to wrap it:** If you are short of time, go to our Gift Wrapping corner on this floor for a number of great options (at just $3.95 per item) and put a personalized message on your complimentary card.

\* Free delivery applies to gifts delivered to mainland US addresses only and for orders of $42 or more. For all other delivery rates (including international), please ask the staff at our Delivery Service on the ground floor of this store.

7. What is the last day orders can be placed to get free delivery before Christmas?
   (A) December 16th
   (B) December 22nd
   (C) December 24th
   (D) December 25th

8. How much does it cost to have an item gift wrapped?
   (A) $3.05
   (B) $3.95
   (C) $7
   (D) $42

9. Where is this information most likely to appear?
   (A) On a website
   (B) In a newspaper
   (C) In the store
   (D) In a manual

10. What is said about orders under $42?
    (A) They are delivered free.
    (B) They cannot be delivered free.
    (C) They cannot be sent overseas.
    (D) They cannot be delivered before Christmas.

## C    Reading in action: Names, numbers, dates and times

The text below is a brochure for upcoming events in Bakerstown.

**Student A** look at the top three events (1 Jan–1 April)
**Student B** look at the bottom three events (3 April–10 June)

**Choose:**
Two names      Two numbers      Two times/dates

Make questions for each to test a partner.
Examples
**A:** *Who should I call to get information on the Winter Carnival?*
**B:** *Sally Jameson.*

**B:** *What time is the Fiesta Days re-enactment?*
**A:** *It's from 2:30.*

**A:** *How much does the JazzFest cost?*
**B:** *It's free.*

---

### Upcoming events in Bakerstown

• **Polar Bear Dip, 1 January:** The Bakerstown Polar Bear Club hosts this popular, annual splash-around in the icy York river from 9:00. Afterwards, everyone joins in the local New Year's Day tradition of warming up with home made bean and bacon soup, good music and beverages. Tickets $15 on the day. Call Burton Henderson at 555-8611.

• **Winter Carnival, 6–21 February:** One of the county's original festivals and parades, this year with 75 floats, as well as various contests and culinary festivals. Call Sally Jameson at 555-1234.

• **Festival on the Green, 31 March–1 April:** Festivities at this year's event will include a fine arts show and craft fair, dog show, musical performances, sporting events, over 25 local food vendors, a children's fair and more. FREE and open to the public. Open from 8:30–10:00. Call Billy Madison at 555-3000.

• **Bakerstown JazzFest, 3–9 April:** Bakerstown historic Seville Square hosts this event filled with great jazz music performed by local and national talents. Over 16 hours of great music! Free admission. Call Monica Bell at 555-8382.

• **23rd Annual Bakerstown Salmon Toss, 28–30 April:** This is the twenty-third year in a row for the wacky annual tournament where participants compete in an actual salmon toss. Open from 10 a.m. but fish tossing starts from 1:00. Live music, food, and drinks accompany this weekend. Admission (plus 1 fish) $35. Call 555-6838 and talk to Billy-Bob.

• **Fiesta Days Celebration and Boat Parade, 1–10 June:** The 56th annual Fiesta Days Celebration starts with a light-hearted re-enactment of the founding of the city by English explorer Francis Baker, who first landed in Bakerstown in 1779. Immediately following is an evening of outdoor musical entertainment. Re-enactment from 2:30, but the park is open all day. Free admission. Call Herman Frost at 555-6512.

---

## D    Further study

Write three more questions about things in the text, and for each write three answer choices. One should be correct and two should be in the passage but incorrect. Test your classmates in the next lesson.

Go to word list and quiz page 179.

**A** **Strategy:** Listen for the correct prepositions
Be aware of similar sounding words

Some questions in this section test your understanding of position and direction. Being familiar with the words used to describe where things are and where they are going will help you score well on this part of the test.

**1** **Language building: Listen for prepositions of position and motion**

**A** Look at Pictures 1 and 2, then read the sentences below. Work with your partner and decide which picture is being described, and if the sentence is TRUE or FALSE.

1. The woman is on the counter.

2. The paper is next to the keyboard.

3. The computer is behind the woman.

4. The phone is in front of the woman.

5. The man is next to the board.

6. The keyboard is on the desk.

**B** Work with a partner and use the vocabulary below to make as many sentences as possible about the pictures.

1

2

3

4

| Possible prepositions used | | Possible nouns used | |
|---|---|---|---|
| on | next to | phone | computer |
| in front of | through | platform | board |
| behind | along | counter | woman/man |
| between | | walkway | train |

**C** Look at the following two pictures and the four sentences below. Use prepositions from the box on page 111 to complete the sentences.

**1**    **2**

    **1.** The couple are standing ................ the house.

    **2.** The young girl is riding ................ her father.

    **3.** The man is ................ the woman.

    **4.** They are riding ................ the street.

## 2 Test tactic: Beware of similar sounding words

**A** Many distractors use words that sound similar to key words you can see in the picture. Look at the two sentences below each picture (one correct and one incorrect) and underline any key words which sound similar.

**1**

> The man is pointing at something.
> The man is painting the people.

**2**

> The people are setting the table.
> The people are sitting around the table.

**3**

> The ship is in the harbor.
> The sheep is in the water.

**4**

> The woman is walking along the street.
> The woman is working long hours.

**B** Look at the following two pictures and write two correct sentences about each one. Underline any prepositions you use.

Example: *The woman is cycling through the city.*

**1**  **2**

 **C** Listen to four statements about each picture. After each statement, stop the audio and tell your partner (a) any prepositions you heard and (b) any words that sound similar to words you can see in the picture. Then tick if you think the sentence is correct or wrong.

| | | | | | |
|---|---|---|---|---|---|
| (A) ☐ Correct | ☐ Wrong | | (A) ☐ Correct | ☐ Wrong | |
| (B) ☐ Correct | ☐ Wrong | | (B) ☐ Correct | ☐ Wrong | |
| (C) ☐ Correct | ☐ Wrong | | (C) ☐ Correct | ☐ Wrong | |
| (D) ☐ Correct | ☐ Wrong | | (D) ☐ Correct | ☐ Wrong | |

*Follow up:* Compare with your partner the sentences you first made and the correct sentence.

**Understanding natural English**

English has many words that sound similar. Note the similar words said in each pair below.

He ......... for hours.
He ......... for hours.
The ......... is in the water.
The ......... is in the water.
The man ......... the food.
The man ......... the food.

**3 Tactic practice** 🎧

Use the tactics you have practiced for the next three pictures. You will have one minute to (a) brainstorm vocabulary and (b) predict possible statements with a partner. Then listen to and echo (silently) the answer choices. After you hear each answer choice, tick whether you think it is correct, maybe correct, or wrong.

**1**

| | | |
|---|---|---|
| (A) ☐ Correct | ☐ Maybe correct | ☐ Wrong |
| (B) ☐ Correct | ☐ Maybe correct | ☐ Wrong |
| (C) ☐ Correct | ☐ Maybe correct | ☐ Wrong |
| (D) ☐ Correct | ☐ Maybe correct | ☐ Wrong |

**2**

| | | |
|---|---|---|
| (A) ☐ Correct | ☐ Maybe correct | ☐ Wrong |
| (B) ☐ Correct | ☐ Maybe correct | ☐ Wrong |
| (C) ☐ Correct | ☐ Maybe correct | ☐ Wrong |
| (D) ☐ Correct | ☐ Maybe correct | ☐ Wrong |

**3**

| | | |
|---|---|---|
| (A) ☐ Correct | ☐ Maybe correct | ☐ Wrong |
| (B) ☐ Correct | ☐ Maybe correct | ☐ Wrong |
| (C) ☐ Correct | ☐ Maybe correct | ☐ Wrong |
| (D) ☐ Correct | ☐ Maybe correct | ☐ Wrong |

*Follow up:* Now compare your answers with your partner, explaining your reasons, and what you remember hearing.

 Understanding natural English

Now apply the *Test tactics* at the actual test speed with questions 1–8.

You will have 1 minute 30 seconds to skim the pictures before the first listening starts. After that you will have exactly 5 seconds between each question to mark your answer and focus on the next picture.

1

2

3

4

5

6

7

8

| 1 | Ⓐ Ⓑ Ⓒ Ⓓ | 5 | Ⓐ Ⓑ Ⓒ Ⓓ |
|---|---|---|---|
| 2 | Ⓐ Ⓑ Ⓒ Ⓓ | 6 | Ⓐ Ⓑ Ⓒ Ⓓ |
| 3 | Ⓐ Ⓑ Ⓒ Ⓓ | 7 | Ⓐ Ⓑ Ⓒ Ⓓ |
| 4 | Ⓐ Ⓑ Ⓒ Ⓓ | 8 | Ⓐ Ⓑ Ⓒ Ⓓ |

## **C** ⟶ **Learn by doing: Right or wrong!**

In this game you will take turns reading statements about the pictures below and on page 116.

**Student A:** Look at Activity file 1.4a on page 155. You will ask your partner questions about Set A.

**Student B:** Look at Activity file 1.4b on page 157. You will ask your partner questions about Set B.

Choose one picture from your set, tell your partner the number, then read one of the two statements about it.

For each picture, your partner has the chance to win up to three points:

| | |
|---|---|
| One Point | if they can say if the statement is right or wrong |
| One Point | if they can say what kind of distractor the wrong statement uses (WRONG PREPOSITION or SIMILAR SOUND) |
| One Point | if they can spot (and say!) the wrong prepositions or similar sounds |

The winner is the person with the most points at the end of the game.

### Set A

1

2

3

4

5

6

7

8

9

**Set B**

1

2

3

4

5

6

7

8

9

## D   Further study

Choose a word group from the list a–d. Look up in a dictionary any words you aren't sure of.

Write two sentences using at least two of the words, **plus one preposition**, then choose one of the sentences and make a simple drawing of it.

In your next lesson, show your partner the drawing, read your two sentences and see if they can identify the correct sentence!

| a) bag/big/bug | b) tree/three/flea | c) boy/bay/toy | d) pig/peg/big |
| --- | --- | --- | --- |

Example:
*The bug is in the big bag.*
*The big bug is behind the bag.*

Go to word list and quiz page 179.

# Part 2

# Question-response

**A**

**Strategy:** Be familiar with language used in offers, requests and opinions

Offers, requests and opinions are common in this part of the TOEIC test. This unit will familiarize you with the types of questions and answers choices you will see in this section.

## 1 Language building: Be familiar with language for offers, requests and opinions

**A** Match each question on the left with the two best responses on the right. The first one is done for you. The words commonly used in each category are in **bold**.

### Offers

**1. Would you like** some help with those?

c, e

**2. Do you need** (any) help with setting up the room?

**3. Can/May I** get you anything?

a **Actually**, it's **already** done.

b **No, I've already** eaten.

c Yeah, **could you** take this box?

d A cup of tea **would be lovely**.

e **No, that's alright**. They aren't as heavy as they look.

f **That would be great**. Let's start with the tables.

### Requests

**4. Could/Can you** tell me how to use this machine?

**5. Would you mind if** I opened the window?

**6. May/Can/Could** I borrow your pen for a moment?

g **Actually**, I am a bit cold.

h **I'm afraid** it's not mine.

i **Certainly**, it's pretty easy.

j **Sure**, give it back after class.

k **I'm sorry**, I haven't been trained on it yet.

l No, **go ahead**.

### Opinions

**7. How was** Mr. Smitt's presentation?

**8. What's your opinion of** their price quote?

**9. What would you say is** our greatest weakness?

m **I don't think** we will find a lower one.

n **Frankly**, our sales staff isn't motivated.

o **To tell the truth**, it seemed a bit long.

p **I'd say** we need to lower our prices.

q **Good**. He really is an amusing speaker.

r **It seems** a bit high to me.

**B** Now write one possible answer for each of the following questions.

1. Would you care for a slice of pie? .................................................................

2. Can you tell Ms. Jackson that her parcel has arrived? .................................................................

3. What do you think of your new boss? .................................................................

**Test tip**

Common distractors for this section include use of incorrect grammar, use of the same word/similar sounds, or incorrect meaning

Noticing these types of wrong answer can help you to choose the correct one.

## 2 Test tactic: Identify correct/incorrect offer, request and opinion answers

For the question below, choose the correct answer. Tell your partner why the other choices were wrong: because of incorrect grammar, the same/similar sounding word or incorrect meaning.

1. Is there anything I can do to help with the project?

   a Yes, they finished the project.
   b No, that's fine. It's already taken care of.
   c We could have done it last week.

2. Do you have a calculator I could borrow?

   a Yes, I will call you later.
   b I remember you borrowed it last week.
   c Sorry, I forgot mine at home.

3. How was your test?

   a You have to pass the test to get a license.
   b I think it will be easy.
   c Harder than I expected.

**Test tip**

Repeat each question and answer choice silently after you hear it

This will help you to remember and compare the meanings.

*Follow up:* Now listen to two more questions followed by three answer choices. After each answer choice, stop the audio and repeat what you heard. If it is correct, circle the letter. If not, tick the distractor type(s).

1. (A) ☐ incorrect grammar    ☐ same word/similar sound    ☐ incorrect meaning

   (B) ☐ incorrect grammar    ☐ same word/similar sound    ☐ incorrect meaning

   (C) ☐ incorrect grammar    ☐ same word/similar sound    ☐ incorrect meaning

2. (A) ☐ incorrect grammar    ☐ same word/similar sound    ☐ incorrect meaning

   (B) ☐ incorrect grammar    ☐ same word/similar sound    ☐ incorrect meaning

   (C) ☐ incorrect grammar    ☐ same word/similar sound    ☐ incorrect meaning

**Tactics checklist**

☑ Listen for vocabulary common to offers, requests and opinions.

☑ Listen for and eliminate answers with common distractors.

☑ Repeat each question and answer choice (silently) after you hear it.

## 3 Tactic practice

Use the tactics you have practiced for the next five questions. Stop the audio after each one to allow you to repeat each question and answer choice to your partner.

| 1 | Ⓐ Ⓑ Ⓒ | 4 | Ⓐ Ⓑ Ⓒ |
|---|---|---|---|
| 2 | Ⓐ Ⓑ Ⓒ | 5 | Ⓐ Ⓑ Ⓒ |
| 3 | Ⓐ Ⓑ Ⓒ | | |

*Follow up:* After each question you will have one minute to discuss with your partner which answer you chose and why.

Understanding natural English

**Understanding natural English**

In natural spoken English, sounds are changed, combined and dropped. Listen to these sentences spoken naturally and write in the missing words.

......... carry these books for me?

......... mind showing Mark the system?

## B    Mini-test

Now apply the *Test tactics* at the actual test speed with questions 1–10.

> 🕐 You will have 5 seconds at the end of each item to make your choice. You must then be ready to listen to the next question.

| 1 | Ⓐ Ⓑ Ⓒ | 6 | Ⓐ Ⓑ Ⓒ |
|---|---------|----|---------|
| 2 | Ⓐ Ⓑ Ⓒ | 7 | Ⓐ Ⓑ Ⓒ |
| 3 | Ⓐ Ⓑ Ⓒ | 8 | Ⓐ Ⓑ Ⓒ |
| 4 | Ⓐ Ⓑ Ⓒ | 9 | Ⓐ Ⓑ Ⓒ |
| 5 | Ⓐ Ⓑ Ⓒ | 10 | Ⓐ Ⓑ Ⓒ |

## C    Learn by doing: Offers, requests and opinions

Look at the model conversations below. Practice them with a partner. Then make similar conversations by replacing the words in bold with the words below.

| Offers | Requests | Opinions |
|--------|----------|----------|
| A: Would you like me to **call you a taxi?**<br><br>B: **No, It's not far. Thanks.** | C: Can **I reserve a table for 8:00?**<br><br>D: **Sorry, we are fully booked for this evening.** | E: What do you think about **the changes to the retirement plan?**<br><br>F: **I'm sure a lot of people will be upset.** |
| ... open the door for you?<br><br>... help you with your homework?<br><br>... lend you some money? | ... I borrow 10 dollars till pay day?<br><br>... you give me a hand with this table?<br><br>... you work late this Wednesday? | ... the new sales manager?<br><br>... your new apartment?<br><br>... our chances of getting the contract? |
| No, thanks.<br><br>That would be great.<br><br>Yes, please. I'd appreciate it. | Yes, (of course).<br><br>Sure. (I'd be glad to).<br><br>I'm afraid/sorry, (I can't). | (He) seems (friendly).<br><br>It's great. I'm really pleased.<br><br>Frankly, I think we have an excellent chance./I don't think we will. |

*Follow up:* Make more offer, request and opinion conversations, using your own ideas and words from the unit.

## D    Further study

Think of one offer, request and opinion you have used or heard recently and write them out in English. In the next lesson, say them to your partner, who should respond appropriately.

Go to word list and quiz page 180.

**A**

**Strategy:** Be familiar with polite ways of saying "no"
Listen carefully to the first exchange

Many of the conversations in Part 3 involve requests or inquiries with negative responses. Being familiar with the language and organization common to these types of situations can help to choose the correct answer. It is important to understand the first exchange, as this probably contains the answer to the first question.

**Test tip**

Conversations involving saying 'no' are common in the TOEIC test

Learn to identify denial and refusal phrases and listen carefully to the information that follows them. This information is often the focus of one of the questions.

**1** **Language building: Be familiar with the vocabulary of denial and refusal**

**A** Match the question on the left to the best response on the right. The common words and phrases used for denial and refusal are in **bold**. The first one is done for you.

1. Jane, would you like to join us for drinks tonight? e

2. Could you fix this radio for me?

3. We are going skiing this weekend. Can you and Mary come along?

4. Are we still having the sales meeting after lunch?

5. Is it OK to keep a cat in this building?

6. Do you accept personal checks?

a **We used to, but** we stopped doing it last year.

b **No, I'm sure they wouldn't** allow it. The building owner hates animals.

c **We can, but** I would prefer if we could put it off till tomorrow. I have a lot of other work.

d **I'm afraid we can only** service Tri-sonic units, madam.

e **I'd love to, but** I'm afraid I have to pick up my sister.

f **I don't think we'll be able to** make it. My brother's family is coming on Saturday.

**B** Look at the questions and correct answer choices for the six dialogs above. Write the number of the question/response above that best matches each question and answer below. The first one is done for you.

| | | |
|---|---|---|
| *1* | Why won't the woman go out with her friends? | She has a previous commitment. |
| | What does the man suggest? | Postponing the meeting |
| | Why can't the woman get service? | Her radio is the wrong brand. |
| | What are the speakers discussing? | The store's payment policy |
| | How does the owner feel about pets? | He strongly dislikes them. |
| | What is the man planning for the weekend? | He is entertaining relatives. |

**C** Now listen to three short conversations and answer the following questions.

1. Why can't Eric do what he asks?

   (A) He has to meet a client.

   (B) He needs to prepare some other papers.

   (C) He is leaving the office shortly.

   (D) He will be in a meeting until this evening.

2. How is the man planning on getting to the station?

    (A) He will take the train.

    (B) He will go by bicycle.

    (C) Daphne will drive him.

    (D) He is going to jog.

3. What does the woman say about the man's request?

    (A) They won't be able to press the shirts on time.

    (B) They can clean and press his trousers before 11:00.

    (C) His shirts will need to be repaired.

    (D) His pants need to go to another location.

**Test tip**

**Most Part 3 conversations start with a question or request**

Listen carefully to what the first speaker says, and the response, as this very often relates to the first question.

## 2 Test tactic: Understanding the first exchange

A Match the Part 3 question on the left to the first speaker's question/request on the right. The first one is done for you.

1. What advice does his friend give about trading in his car? b

2. What kind of summer vacation is the man considering?

3. What experience does the man have?

4. How does Mr. Green feel about his request?

a *"Mr. Green, I was wondering if it was OK if I took next Friday off."*

b *"Do you think I should get a new car? It seems to cost me more money in repairs each year."*

c *"I see you are applying for the sales clerk's job. Do you have any experience in sales?"*

d *"What are you doing for your vacation this year, Dario?"*

B Now listen to the full conversations. After each one, stop the audio and repeat as much as you can of the second speaker's response, then choose the answer choice that best matches the response you heard.

    (A) He thinks the time is not good.

    (B) He may be able to save money over time.

    (C) He has done some work in retail sales.

    (D) A low budget one.

## 3 Tactic practice

**Tactics checklist**

☑ Listen for denial/refusal statements and the information that follows them.

Use the tactics you have practiced for the next two conversations. Before you listen to each conversation, stop the audio and use the time to a) predict the context and b) think of other ways to say the answer choices with a partner.

1. What does the first man want to do?

    (A) Buy a house

    (B) Rent somewhere to live

    (C) Go to the beach

    (D) Decorate his bedroom

2. What is the problem?

    (A) The beach is too far away.

    (B) There are no suitable places left.

    (C) It is too expensive.

    (D) He can't see anything.

3. What does the second man offer?

    (A) To show him the bedroom

    (B) To give him a discount

    (C) To show him a different place

    (D) To leave with him

4. What is Jim's problem?

    (A) He hardly knows Bob.

    (B) He only has a little money.

    (C) He wants to lend some money.

    (D) He doesn't have any money.

| | |
|---|---|
| 1 | Ⓐ Ⓑ Ⓒ Ⓓ |
| 2 | Ⓐ Ⓑ Ⓒ Ⓓ |
| 3 | Ⓐ Ⓑ Ⓒ Ⓓ |
| 4 | Ⓐ Ⓑ Ⓒ Ⓓ |
| 5 | Ⓐ Ⓑ Ⓒ Ⓓ |
| 6 | Ⓐ Ⓑ Ⓒ Ⓓ |

**5.** What does Bob do about the situation?

(A) He helps Jim out.

(B) He suggests asking someone else.

(C) He lends him a few dollars

(D) He offers to talk to Darryl.

**6.** What does Bob finally decide?

(A) He will find the wallet.

(B) He will speak to Darryl.

(C) He will not speak to Darryl.

(D) He will make him lunch.

**Understanding natural English**

In natural spoken English, sounds are changed, combined and dropped.
Listen to these sentences spoken naturally and write in the missing words.

I ........ certainly use the exercise.

I was wondering if you ......... drive me there.

## B ▸ Mini-test 🎧

Now apply the *Test tactics* at the actual test speed with questions 1–12.

> 🕐 You will have 30 seconds to skim the questions and answer choices before the first listening starts. After that you will have exactly 8 seconds between each question to mark your answer and focus on the next question.

**1.** What does the woman ask the man?

(A) If he would like to go to the airport

(B) If he can take her to the airport

(C) If he can pick her up by 11:00

(D) If he can drive

**2.** What is the man's response?

(A) He worries he can't cancel his flight.

(B) He refuses her request.

(C) He invites her to play golf.

(D) He agrees to her offer.

**3.** Where is the man going tomorrow?

(A) To the airport

(B) To the office

(C) To the golf course

(D) For a drive

**4.** What was the man's experience of Prestige Air?

(A) He enjoyed it.

(B) He will go next month.

(C) It was commendable.

(D) It wasn't relaxing.

**5.** Why did the man have trouble with the seats?

(A) They didn't fully recline.

(B) There wasn't enough leg room for him.

(C) The seats were too narrow.

(D) There were no footrests.

**6.** What does the man say about the in-flight entertainment?

(A) It met his expectations.

(B) It was too noisy.

(C) It was a cut above the competition.

(D) He was unable to enjoy it.

**7.** What is the caller complaining about?

(A) A tennis racket

(B) A vacuum cleaner

(C) A superstore

(D) An electric train

**8.** What is wrong with the product?

(A) It is too far away.

(B) It is noisy and ineffective.

(C) There is nothing wrong.

(D) It only worked for one day.

**9.** What information does the service representative want to know?

(A) If they can get a replacement

(B) How much the product cost

(C) The date and location of purchase

(D) How far the mall is

**10.** Where does the conversation probably take place?

(A) In a travel agency

(B) In an airplane

(C) In a train station

(D) In a baggage reclaim hall

**11.** What is the woman's problem?

(A) Her luggage has not arrived.

(B) She missed her flight.

(C) She can't find her passport.

(D) She took the wrong flight.

**12.** How does the man help her?

(A) He replaces her documents.

(B) He finds her bag.

(C) He offers to represent her.

(D) He tells her who to speak to.

# C  Learn by doing: Refusing

Practice the following conversations involving a refusal. Then make new conversations by replacing the words in **bold** with the words in the boxes below.

**A:** A group of us are going **bowling** on **Tuesday night**. Would you care to join us?

**B:** I really would, but unfortunately I have **a tennis lesson**.

**A:** Oh, too bad. Maybe another time then?

**B:** Yes, for sure. Thanks for the offer.

**C:** Excuse me. Can I **park my car here**?

**D:** No, I'm afraid not. **This is a no parking zone**.

**C:** Oh, do you know of anywhere around here I can **park**?

**D:** Sorry, I'm afraid I don't.

| | |
|---|---|
| *for Greek food/Wednesday night/to pick up my sister from school* | *cash a check in this shop/We don't accept checks/cash one* |
| *to a movie/Sunday afternoon/to go to a wedding* | *leave my bags here/We can't be responsible/leave them* |
| *to have a barbecue/Saturday/to work* | *use US dollars here/We only take local money/change money* |

*Follow up:* Now make another conversation with a refusal using your own ideas.

# D  Further study

Choose two of the conversations with refusals you made in activity C, write out the dialogs, and write two questions to test your classmates in the next lesson.

Go to word list and quiz page 181.

**Strategy:** Be familiar with re-statements involving "how" and "why" questions
Be aware of same word distractors

Brainstorming vocabulary related to the answer choices can help you identify information in the short talk that restates the answer choices. Be careful of answer choices that use the same words as the recording, as these may be distractors.

## 1 Language building: Brainstorming related words

<u>Underline</u> the word from the list of related words on the right that does NOT match any of the words in the answer choices. The first one has been done for you.

1. How has the change affected business?
   - (A) It has decreased by 50%.
   - (B) The number of potential customers went up.
   - (C) There has been no change.

   fallen, <u>double</u>, dropped, half, slumped

   possible, clients, manager, increased

   stable, increased, the same, constant

2. Why might guests need to dial 9?
   - (A) To contact the concierge
   - (B) To arrange their flight transfers
   - (C) To place a direct call

   hotel staff, speak to, call, chef

   pay, transit, sort out, organize

   ring, telephone, luggage, make

*Follow up:* Now think of a word with a similar meaning for all the underlined words. Example: double → 200%

## 2 Test tactic: Listen for related words and restatements

A Underline the key words in the following questions and answer choices. Then read the tapescript on page 125 and choose the best answers.

1. Why must attendees wear their identification tags?
   - (A) So that people can see their names
   - (B) To get into the presentations
   - (C) Because presentations are starting shortly

2. How can attendees find out about the presenters?
   - (A) By looking at the schedule they were given earlier
   - (B) By checking with the conference organizers
   - (C) By checking the information on their telephones

3. Why do attendees have to use silent mode?
   - (A) To ensure safety
   - (B) To disturb the presentations
   - (C) To avoid bothering the participants

**Tapescript**

*The conference organizers would like to remind attendees that identification tags must be worn at all times, in order to gain entry to the lecture halls. The presentations will be starting shortly, but before that, there are a couple of other announcements to make. Firstly, I would like to remind all conference guests to read the presentation timetable, which includes the names of all the presenters. Secondly, I have to ask all guests to ensure their mobile telephones are on silent mode, so as not to disturb any presentations. OK. That's enough of me, I'll hand you over to your first presenter.*

🎧 **B** Skim the questions and answer choices below and note key words. As you listen, circle any "same words" you hear, then decide if the answer is correct, maybe correct or wrong.

1. Why should customers choose Seymour suits?
   (A) They use high quality cloth but are reasonably priced.　(A) ☐ Correct ☐ Maybe Correct ☐ Wrong
   (B) They are expensive but good quality.　(B) ☐ Correct ☐ Maybe Correct ☐ Wrong
   (C) They are 25% warmer.　(C) ☐ Correct ☐ Maybe Correct ☐ Wrong

2. How can customers tell if their suit is a genuine Seymour suit?
   (A) They use cheaper materials.　(A) ☐ Correct ☐ Maybe Correct ☐ Wrong
   (B) There is a special inner layer.　(B) ☐ Correct ☐ Maybe Correct ☐ Wrong
   (C) It will keep them warm in winter.　(C) ☐ Correct ☐ Maybe Correct ☐ Wrong

3. Why should customers hurry to buy the suits?
   (A) It is winter now.　(A) ☐ Correct ☐ Maybe Correct ☐ Wrong
   (B) They can create the right impression.　(B) ☐ Correct ☐ Maybe Correct ☐ Wrong
   (C) There are limited quantities.　(C) ☐ Correct ☐ Maybe Correct ☐ Wrong

*Follow up:* Compare your answers with your partner, explaining your reasons, and what you remember hearing.

## 3 Tactic practice 🎧

Use the tactics you have practiced for the next two short talks. You will have one minute to a) skim the question and answer choices and identify key words and b) brainstorm related words. Then, listen to the short talks, and select the best answer choices.

1. Why should Mr. Heinrich go to the duty free sales counter?
   (A) To collect his unattended bag
   (B) To make an announcement
   (C) To retrieve an important travel document
   (D) To report a suspicious package

2. Who is told to go to gate number 12?
   (A) Mr. G. Heinrich
   (B) Passengers traveling to Moscow
   (C) All passengers
   (D) Nobody

3. Why should passengers going to Moscow hurry?
   (A) Their flight will leave soon
   (B) There are suspicious packages there
   (C) The Duty Free shop is about to close
   (D) To collect their boarding passes

4. How can guests purchase razors or toothbrushes?
   (A) By placing a call to the hotel front desk
   (B) By dialing 2
   (C) By visiting the housekeeper
   (D) By using a coin-operated machine

**Understanding natural English**

In natural spoken English, sounds are changed, combined and dropped. Listen to these sentences spoken naturally and write in the missing words.

In ........ first year, ........ made a profit of just $25.

These developments are revolutionizing ........ factory.

5. How can outside calls be made?
   (A) By dialing 1
   (B) By contacting the concierge
   (C) By dialing the number, followed by 9
   (D) By dialing 9 first, then the number

6. Why might guests visit the housekeeper on the first floor?
   (A) To get their clothes washed
   (B) To make an inquiry
   (C) To make an outside call
   (D) To purchase toiletries

| 1 | Ⓐ Ⓑ Ⓒ Ⓓ | 4 | Ⓐ Ⓑ Ⓒ Ⓓ |
| 2 | Ⓐ Ⓑ Ⓒ Ⓓ | 5 | Ⓐ Ⓑ Ⓒ Ⓓ |
| 3 | Ⓐ Ⓑ Ⓒ Ⓓ | 6 | Ⓐ Ⓑ Ⓒ Ⓓ |

*Follow up:* Now compare your answers with your partner, explaining your reasons, and what you remember hearing.

 Understanding natural English

## B Mini-test

Now apply the *Test tactics* at the actual test speed with questions 1–12.

> 🕐 You will have 30 seconds to skim the questions and answer choices before the first listening starts. After that you will have exactly 8 seconds between each question to mark your answer and focus on the next question.

1. Who is probably giving this speech?
   (A) A museum visitor
   (B) A soda company executive
   (C) A tour guide
   (D) Samuel Farnestock

2. How was Fizzade usually served until the 1950s?
   (A) From bottles
   (B) From soda fountains
   (C) From cans
   (D) From Vera Mulligan's drugstore

3. How much profit did Dr. Longbotham make in his first year?
   (A) $1900
   (B) $13
   (C) Less than $50
   (D) The speaker doesn't say

4. How will the weather change in the next few days?
   (A) It will get warmer.
   (B) The sun will come out.
   (C) It will get worse.
   (D) There will be a lot of snow.

5. When should people in the DC area hang out their washing?
   (A) At the weekend
   (B) In the afternoon
   (C) In the last few days
   (D) As early as possible

6. Why should drivers be careful?
   (A) The roads may be icy after dark.
   (B) There will be heavy fog.
   (C) The roads moving south are busy.
   (D) The weather is warmer than usual.

7. Who would be particularly interested in this announcement?
   (A) Passengers leaving platform 12
   (B) People traveling to Boston
   (C) People who have refreshments
   (D) Station staff

8. Why was the 12:35 train delayed?
   (A) There was a mechanical problem.
   (B) There was an accident on the line.
   (C) The platform kiosks were closed.
   (D) There was bad weather.

| | | | | |
|---|---|---|---|---|
| 1 | Ⓐ | Ⓑ | Ⓒ | Ⓓ |
| 2 | Ⓐ | Ⓑ | Ⓒ | Ⓓ |
| 3 | Ⓐ | Ⓑ | Ⓒ | Ⓓ |
| 4 | Ⓐ | Ⓑ | Ⓒ | Ⓓ |
| 5 | Ⓐ | Ⓑ | Ⓒ | Ⓓ |
| 6 | Ⓐ | Ⓑ | Ⓒ | Ⓓ |
| 7 | Ⓐ | Ⓑ | Ⓒ | Ⓓ |
| 8 | Ⓐ | Ⓑ | Ⓒ | Ⓓ |
| 9 | Ⓐ | Ⓑ | Ⓒ | Ⓓ |
| 10 | Ⓐ | Ⓑ | Ⓒ | Ⓓ |
| 11 | Ⓐ | Ⓑ | Ⓒ | Ⓓ |
| 12 | Ⓐ | Ⓑ | Ⓒ | Ⓓ |

9. Where should passengers purchase refreshments?

(A) On the platform

(B) In the buffet car

(C) From the café

(D) No refreshments are available

10. Why is lunch going to be delayed?

(A) The last speaker overran.

(B) There was a safety drill this morning.

(C) There was a quick announcement.

(D) People had a lot of questions.

11. How might people know the next speaker?

(A) He attended the previous conference.

(B) He is the number two producer.

(C) He is a revolutionary.

(D) He is the head of Park-Lee industries.

12. What is the topic of the next presentation?

(A) A revolutionary new factory

(B) Fire safety

(C) Innovations in electronics manufacturing

(D) How to conduct a symphony

## C   Learn by doing: Question my answer

**Student A:** Look at Activity file 4.4a "Why" questions on page 153.

**Student B:** Look at Activity file 4.4b "How" questions on page 156.

**A** With your partner check you understand the questions below. Then read out one of the answers for your Activity file. Your partner must read out the matching question to get one point. If they don't choose the correct question, you get a chance to steal the point by guessing the correct question. When all the answers are read out, the player with the highest score is the winner.

**"Why" questions**

1. Why is the manager concerned about sales?

2. Why are travelers advised to avoid the region?

3. Why is there a delay in releasing the new product?

4. Why did the visit have to be rearranged?

5. Why did the President miss the opening address?

**"How" questions**

6. How can guests arrange transport to the airport?

7. How is the new product different from the old model?

8. How will the weather be at the weekend?

9. How does the manager feel about the delay?

10. How can travelers find out about friends or family in the area?

**B** Think of a possible true answer for the following questions. Take turns to read out an answer. Your partner must guess the question.

Why are you taking this course?     How are you different from your father?

How do you usually come to class?     Why do you want to improve your English?

## D   Further study

Look at the "why" and "how" questions in activity C above. Write one more possible answer for each question.

Go to word list and quiz page 182.

**A**

## Strategy: Improve your knowledge of pronouns

Use of pronouns is a common feature tested in Part 5. Being aware of how they are used can improve your score.

### 1 Language building: Subject/object personal pronouns

**A** For each of the following sentences decide whether the missing word is a subject (S) or object (O). The first one has been done for you.

1. Ms. Smithers will attend the function, but her sister will not be coming with ..........     ⓞ

2. The president and his wife argued right in front of us while .......... pretended not to notice.     ☐

3. I bought my wife a watch but she told me .......... didn't fit properly.     ☐

4. When Jack arrived at the meeting, the other members were already waiting for .......... .     ☐

5. While .......... was away at University, Jack's dad wrote to him everyday.     ☐

6. The members were upset that dinner hadn't been arranged for .......... .     ☐

**B** Now choose the best pronoun to fit each blank from the list below, and mark which sentence it best fits. The first one has been done for you.

| Subject Pronouns | | Object Pronouns | |
|---|---|---|---|
| ☐ I | ☐ he | ☐ me | ☐ him |
| ☐ you | ☐ she | ☐ you | ☑ her |
| ☐ we | ☐ it | ☐ us | ☐ it |
| ☐ they | | ☐ them | |

**C** For each of the following sentences decide whether the missing word is a possessive pronoun (P) or a possessive adjective (A). The first one has been done for you.

1. The coat with the red lining is .......... . My mother gave it to me.     Ⓟ

2. Sally had an accident last week and dented .......... car door.     ☐

3. Are you sure that pen is .......... ? I lost one just like it.     ☐

4. They rarely go to restaurants so it is .......... first time to eat Thai food.     ☐

5. I can't find .......... wallet. Could you lend me $10?     ☐

6. John said he left his book in here so I guess this one is .......... .     ☐

**D** Now choose the best pronoun to fit each blank from the list below, and mark which sentence it best fits. The first one has been done for you.

| Possessive Pronouns | | Possessive Adjectives | |
|---|---|---|---|
| ☑ mine | ☐ his | ☐ my | ☐ his |
| ☐ yours | ☐ hers | ☐ your | ☐ her |
| ☐ ours | ☐ its | ☐ our | ☐ its |
| ☐ theirs | (not common) | ☐ their | |

*Follow up:* Compare choices with your partner, then make one or two similar sentences with the pronouns/adjectives you didn't use.

Be aware of indefinite pronoun use tested in the TOEIC

These are some common indefinite pronoun uses tested in the TOEIC.

*Some(-one/-body/-where):* used for sentences with a positive meaning

*No(-one/-body/-where):* used to give a negative meaning to a positive sentence

*Any(-one/-body/-where):* for questions and sentences with a negative meaning

*All, any, both, few, many, more, other, several, some:* used as plural

*Every, each, either, -one:* used as singular

**Tactics checklist**

☑ For personal pronouns decide whether the blank requires a subject or object pronoun.

☑ For possessives decide whether the blank is modifying a noun or replacing it.

☑ Watch for the common uses of indefinite pronouns.

## 2 Test tactic: Indefinite pronouns

Use the tips on common uses of indefinite pronouns in the Test tip to help you choose the answer choice that best matches the sentence. The first one is done for you.

1. ....A.... of the things that local people make would be in high demand on the open market.

2. .......... told me that I had to submit the request three weeks in advance.

   (A) Some
   (B) Another
   (C) Anybody
   (D) Nobody

3. I can't think of .......... else we could find a better location for the new branch.

4. John isn't riding his motorcycle because .......... of its tires are flat.

   (A) either
   (B) someplace
   (C) anywhere
   (D) both

5. Please send .......... of your receipts to the payroll section for speedy repayment.

6. The failed project has left us without .......... working capital for the coming quarter.

   (A) all
   (B) every
   (C) any
   (D) many

## 3 Tactic practice

Use the tactics you have practiced to answer the following questions.

1. Is there .......... around here I can have these documents color printed?
   (A) something
   (B) place
   (C) anywhere
   (D) many place

2. Have you seen the report .......... prepared on the new client?
   (A) her
   (B) she
   (C) hers
   (D) she'll

3. I am sure that coat is Tom's because his mother gave it to .......... for his birthday.
   (A) he
   (B) me
   (C) his
   (D) him

4. I'd love to go, but I don't have .......... money.
   (A) any
   (B) many
   (C) some
   (D) a lot

5. .......... Jane and her new assistant attended the conference.
   (A) Either
   (B) Did
   (C) Both
   (D) Can

6. The list included .......... of the members of the board.
   (A) no one
   (B) either
   (C) any
   (D) each

Now apply the *Test tactics* at the actual test speed with questions 1–12.

 You will have 6 minutes to complete 12 items. To use your time wisely, use the 2-pass method you learnt in Unit 5.1. Spend no more than 30 seconds on each item. If you don't know the answer, guess and move.

1. I'm not sure there was .......... we could have done to get the account.
   (A) something
   (B) what
   (C) anything
   (D) way

2. I don't think the director was very .......... to your ideas for revising our sales approach.
   (A) receivable
   (B) receptacle
   (C) reception
   (D) receptive

3. For some years the management has tried to .......... a low-stress working environment.
   (A) start
   (B) place
   (C) ensure
   (D) give

4. If you hurry, you can probably make it in time to meet .......... plane.
   (A) their
   (B) she's
   (C) air
   (D) a

5. If your car isn't fixed by the weekend you are certainly welcome to borrow .......... to pick up your mother.
   (A) mine
   (B) this
   (C) some
   (D) other

6. Our lawyers have announced that the bank has requested immediate .......... of all outstanding debt.
   (A) borrowing
   (B) repayment
   (C) returning
   (D) loan

7. Our agents have informed us that .......... of the containers were damaged in transit.
   (A) one
   (B) several
   (C) any
   (D) much

8. .......... of the management staff realized the amount of time and effort that had gone into the job.
   (A) Total
   (B) Head
   (C) Few
   (D) Job

9. How long .......... Mr. Parker held his current position in the company?
   (A) did
   (B) can
   (C) will
   (D) has

10. In my opinion .......... of the candidates is particularly suitable for the position.
    (A) neither
    (B) both
    (C) all
    (D) either

11. I am sorry to tell you that we will not be .......... your contract for the coming year.
    (A) requested
    (B) completion
    (C) sign
    (D) renewing

12. The rental contract stated that the customer would be .......... for any dents or scratches found on the vehicle.
    (A) literal
    (B) liable
    (C) limited
    (D) licensed

# C Grammar practice

**A** Pronouns allow us to talk without having to repeat the same words over and over again. Look at the story of Goldilocks and the three bears. Replace the words in brackets with pronouns to make the story sound better.

| it | his | someone | they | she | my | her | their |
|---|---|---|---|---|---|---|---|

**The story of her (*Goldilocks*) and them (*the three bears*)**

Once upon a time, there was a little girl named Goldilocks. One day (Goldilocks) (1) .......... went for a walk in the forest. After a while (Goldilocks) (2) .......... came upon a house. The door was open so (Goldilocks) (3) .......... went in.

On the kitchen table, there were three bowls of porridge. Goldilocks was hungry, so (Goldilocks) (4) .......... tasted the porridge from the first bowl.

"(This porridge) (5) ..........'s too hot!" (Goldilocks) (6) .......... exclaimed.

So, (Goldilocks) (7) .......... tasted the porridge from the second bowl.

"(This porridge) (8) ..........'s too cold," (Goldilocks) (9) .......... said.

So, (Goldilocks) (10) .......... tasted the last bowl of porridge.

"Ahhh, this porridge is just right," (Goldilocks) (11) .......... said happily and ate (the porridge) (12) .......... all up.

Goldilocks was very tired, so (Goldilocks) (13) .......... went to the bedroom. (Goldilocks) (14) .......... lay in the first bed, but (the bed) (15) .......... was too hard. Then she lay in the second bed, but (the bed) (16) .......... was too soft. Then (Goldilocks) (17) .......... lay down in the third bed and (the bed) (18) .......... was just right, so (Goldilocks) (19) .......... fell asleep.

Soon the three bears came home.

"(An unknown person) (20) ..........'s been eating (Papa bear's) (21) .......... porridge," growled the Papa bear.

Then Mama bear saw that (an unknown person) (22) .......... had been eating (Mama bear's) (23) .......... porridge too.

Suddenly Baby bear noticed that (an unknown person) (24) .......... had been eating (Baby bear's) (25) .......... porridge too. "And (the unknown person or persons) (26) .......... ate (Baby bear's porridge) (27) .......... all up!"

(The bears) (28) .......... decided to look around (the bear's) (29) .......... house some more and when (the bears) (30) .......... got upstairs to the bedroom, Papa bear growled, "(An unknown person) (31) ..........'s been sleeping in (Papa bear's) (32) .......... bed."

"(An unknown person) (33) ..........'s been sleeping in (Mama bear's) (34) .......... bed, too" said the Mama bear.

"(An unknown person) (35) ..........'s been sleeping in (Baby bear's) (36) .......... bed and (a female person) (37) ..........'s still there!" exclaimed Baby bear.

Just then, Goldilocks woke up and saw the three bears. (Goldilocks) (38) .......... screamed, "Help!" and ...

**B** How do you think it ends? Finish the story, using pronouns correctly. In the next lesson compare your story with your classmates. How was your ending different?

Go to word list and quiz page 183.

# Part 6

# Text completion

**A** **Strategy:** Choose the correct word: prepositions and conjunctions

Prepositions and conjunctions are a common feature of English writing. Understanding the ways they are used can help you choose the correct answer.

**1** **Language building: Prepositions**

English uses many prepositions to represent time, location, movement/direction and position.

**Time**

**A**  Choose the correct prepositions from the box on the right to complete the text. The first one has been done for you.

> Mr. Sanchez will be arriving ...on... Monday the 25th (1) .......... 5 o'clock. This will be his first visit here (2) .......... April last year, so he hasn't seen our new factory (3) .......... more than nine months. We are keen to show him the new production line, which opened (4) .......... June, so we'll take him there (5) .......... the 27th.

~~on~~
in
on
at
for
since

*Follow up:* Now discuss with your partner how to complete the following statements about time prepositions.

**1.** .......... is used for times of the day.

**2.** .......... is used for days and dates.

**3.** .......... is used for months, years, and seasons.

**4.** .......... is used for lengths of time.

**5.** .......... is used to refer to a point in time in the past.

**Position**

**B**  Three common prepositions of position are *in*, *on* and *at*. Familiarize yourself with some common patterns of usage for these words.

| in | on | at |
|---|---|---|
| She's in the living room. She's in her office. She's in bed. She lives in Manhattan. | They are on the table. They are on the bus. I found them on the floor. | He's at the bank. He's at work. He's at home. Meet me at the corner of 11th and Broadway. |

*Follow up:* Ask and answer the following "where" questions with your partner. Be careful which preposition you choose in your answer.

Where do you usually leave your keys?

Where do you usually meet your friends?

Where do you spend most of your time?

Where do you study English?

**Direction**

C   Choose the correct prepositions from the box on the right to complete the text.
The first one has been done for you.

I walk .o̲u̲t̲. .o̲f̲. my house at 8 o'clock, get (1) .......... my car, and drive
(2) .......... a parking lot, which is about five minutes on foot from my
office. After parking, I walk (3) .......... a short pedestrian street and then
(4) .......... the corner. From there I can see my office (5) .......... the
street. The traffic is always busy, but there is a tunnel that I generally
walk (6) .......... to get to the other side.

~~out of~~
along
through
around
to
into
across

*Follow up:* Now describe your journey from your home/office to where you are now.

**Test tip**

**Compare two halves
of a sentence**

For questions
testing conjunctions,
compare the two
halves and consider
their relationship.
Use this information
to help you choose
the correct
conjunction.

## 2   Test tactic: Conjunctions

A   Conjunctions are used to join two parts of a sentence together and express their
relationship. If the answer choices are conjunctions, look at the two halves of the
sentence before and after the conjunction to help you choose the correct word.

Choose the appropriate conjunction from the box below to complete the following
sentences.

1.   The train journey takes more than an hour    [E]    the train can only reach
25 miles per hour.

2.   He passed the initial interview    ☐    failed the second interview.

3.   You can apply now    ☐    wait until the position becomes
available in future.

4.   In winter the weather is generally cold    ☐    wet.

5.   It is not polite to wear shoes in the house    ☐    to blow your nose loudly.

A   and       B   nor       C   but       D   or       E   because

B   Other conjunctions occur in natural pairs. Learn to recognize these patterns to
help you identify the correct choices quickly. Study the list on the left for thirty
seconds. Then answer the questions on the right as quickly as possible.

*both ... and*

*not only ... but also*

*either ... or*

*neither ... nor*

*whether ... or*

1.   We have the service to suit you, .......... you want to
travel in luxury, or arrive as soon as possible.

(A)  not only

(B)  whether

(C)  both

2.   Entering the building requires not only a keycard, ..........
a fingerprint scan.

(A)  but also

(B)  or

(C)  and

3.   We will .......... have to take the bus, or get a taxi in order
to reach the office in time.

(A)  neither

(B)  both

(C)  either

**Tactics checklist**

☑ Eliminate wrong prepositions quickly.

☑ Compare the two parts of a sentence to choose conjunctions.

**3** **Tactic practice**

Use the tactics you have practiced to answer the following questions. Read the questions, and quickly eliminate any definitely wrong answers before choosing the correct answer choice.

**Questions 1–4** refer to the following letter.

---

Dear Mr. Anderson,

Thank you very much for the letter you sent ............... us on September 17th, inquiring about the

    **1.** (A) to
       (B) with
       (C) of
       (D) from

availability of replacement parts for the CX232 fan heater. Please accept my apology for being unable to give you a definitive answer ............... this time.

    **2.** (A) at
       (B) on
       (C) by
       (D) with

Unfortunately, our principle supplier of this part, HX Industries, was badly affected by a fire at one of their main manufacturing plants, ............... this has left us with a deficit of replacement parts.

    **3.** (A) but
       (B) and
       (C) because
       (D) whether

We are currently seeking an alternative supplier, and hope to be able to conclude a deal ............... the end of the month. We will request immediate delivery of all parts required then.

    **4.** (A) until
       (B) in
       (C) on
       (D) by

We will be happy to notify you as soon as we receive information to confirm this. Thank you for your continued interest in our company.

Yours sincerely,

*Hamilton S. Williams*

Hamilton S. Williams

CEO Fantech

---

## B  Mini-test

Now apply the *Test tactics* at the actual test speed with questions 1–12.

 You have 6 minutes to complete 12 items. To use your time wisely, use the 2-pass method you learnt in Unit 5.1. Spend no more than 30 seconds on each item. If you don't know the answer, guess and move on.

**Questions 1–4** refer to the following article.

---

Travelers ............... the Tei Kai region have long been impressed by its towering mountains to the north,

    **1.** (A) visiting
        (B) to visit
        (C) visited
        (D) visit

and desert plains to the south. Long known as an economically backward region, it has, ............... the last fifty

    **2.** (A) while
        (B) since
        (C) for
        (D) in

years, undergone something of a transformation. The construction of the Wan Hei dam enabled engineers to channel the waters of the Gang River for agricultural purposes. The result has been an ever expanding corridor of greenery spreading ............... the once barren land, and a subsequent rise in the population and wealth

**3.** (A) through
    (B) to
    (C) along
    (D) without

of the region. The benefits to ............... may, however, spell bad news for some former residents, as falling

    **4.** (A) environment
        (B) industry
        (C) agriculture
        (D) investment

numbers of the rare Eastern desert fox in the last ten years have shown the effects on local wildlife.

---

GO ON TO THE NEXT PAGE ▶

Questions 5–8 refer to the following article.

Ineffective hiring practices lead to customer dissatisfaction. In order to improve the quality of the applicants being hired, managers can take a number of staffing decisions ............... each stage of the hiring process.

     **5.** (A) for
        (B) at
        (C) by
        (D) in

1) Having a clear job description is critical as it provides the necessary information ............... which staffing decisions are based.

**6.** (A) around
   (B) for
   (C) upon
   (D) with

2) ............... the recruiting process begins recruiters need to consider the possible

   **7.** (A) As long as
      (B) During
      (C) Before
      (D) While

sources of recruits, including databases of previous qualified but not selected applicants.

3) During the pre-screening stage recruiters should consider using telephone interviews to make decisions regarding which applicants to consider further. It is also essential to ............... applicants' professional references.

     **8.** (A) follow up on
        (B) take care of
        (C) look out for
        (D) give out

Following these simple guidelines can have considerable impact on the efficiency and effectiveness of employee hiring.

**From:** Hank Jennings
**To:** Arnault Pascale
**Subject:** Visit to QMG

Dear Arnault,

This is just a quick note to explain the agenda for your upcoming visit to QMG, ................ March 27th.

**9.** (A) at
(B) on
(C) in
(D) around

On the first day, you'll be met ................ the airport and taken to your hotel. I hope you like the place

**10.** (A) at
(B) on
(C) from
(D) by

we found for you. On the second day, we'll bring you into the office, and show you around the new production line. ................ you leave, I'll make sure you have a chance to talk to

**11.** (A) While
(B) During
(C) Before
(D) Since

our production line manager, Jim Tavarey, as he is the man we'll be sending to Orleans next month to help you set up your factory.

I am looking forward ................ next week. I hope you have a pleasant flight over.

**12.** (A) to talk to you
(B) meeting you
(C) our meeting
(D) to meeting you

Hank

Read the following email and fill the gaps with either prepositions or conjunctions from the boxes on the left. Be careful – there are two extra words in each box. Compare your choices with a partner in the next lesson.

| | |
|---|---|
| on | |
| for | in |
| to | at |
| as | by |

| | |
|---|---|
| at | about |
| outside | around |
| before | through |

| | |
|---|---|
| so | next to |
| or | around |
| because | before |

**To:** Hernando Gonzales
**Re:** upcoming trip to Dallas

Dear Mr. Gonzales,

We are very much looking forward to finally meeting you next week. We are all excited to hear about your proposals (1) ................ the solar electric generator at the developers' conference (2) ................ the 25th. (3) ................ I believe this is your first trip (4) ................ Dallas, I will be sending my assistant, Colin, to meet you (5) ................ the airport.

I understand your flight is due to arrive (6) ................ around 4:30 p.m. It should take (7) ................ 30 minutes to get (8) ................ customs and immigration, so I have asked Colin to meet you (9) ................ the arrivals gate by 5:00.

We have arranged a hotel and evening meal for you, (10) ................ you can relax when you arrive. Don't feel that you need to bring a tuxedo (11) ................ other formal wear. We'll take you to somewhere (12) ................ the corner from the office, where you can get a taste of the real Dallas.

If you have any questions (13) ................ you leave, then don't hesitate to contact me.

Paul McCawley

Go to word list and quiz page 183.

**A**  **Strategy:** Learn how to answer questions dealing with charts, tables, forms and double texts

Charts, tables, forms and double texts are common question types that require a slightly different approach from the other questions found in Part 7. This unit will familiarize you with the format of these questions and how to find the correct answers.

**Test tip**

**Understand parts of charts, tables and forms**

Specific information questions are most common with these texts. Try to identify what different parts of the text refer to in order to locate answers as quickly as possible.

**Test tip**

**Find information quickly**

Skim the questions and identify which part of the text is referred to. Then compare the answer choices to that part of the chart, table or form.

## 1  Test tactic: Dealing with charts, tables and forms

**A**  Look at the following table, and try to identify the different features included.

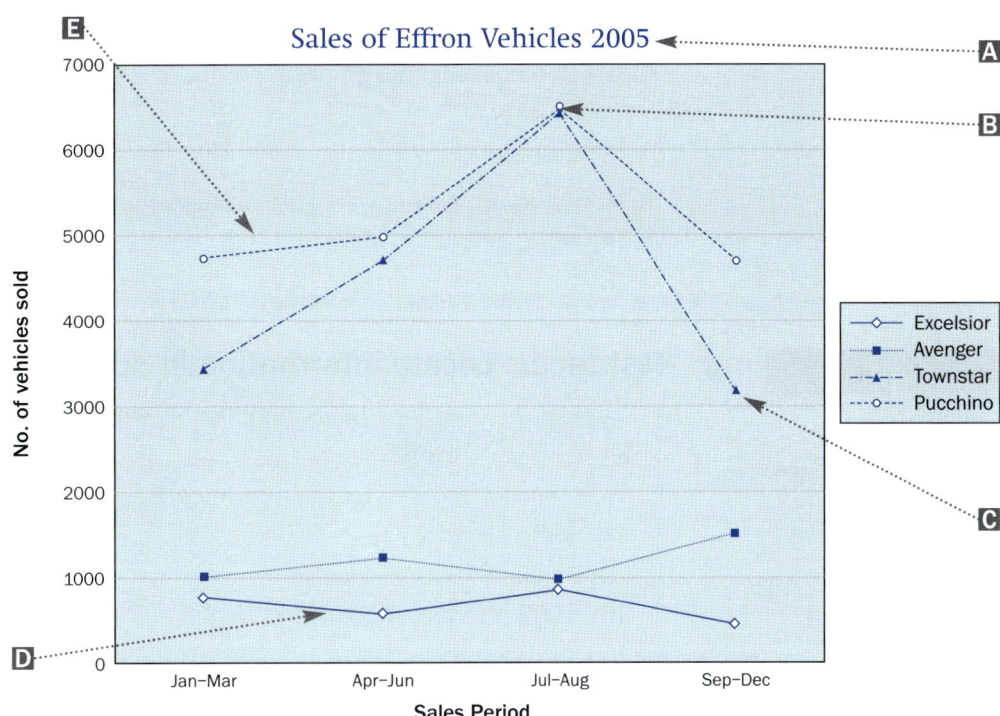

**B**  Match the letters A–E from the charts above to the following questions.

1.  What does the chart represent?  | A |
2.  In which sales period was the smallest number of Townstars sold?
3.  Which model sold the greatest number overall?
4.  Which was the most successful period for sales of the Pucchino?
5.  Which model sold the smallest number?

UNIT 7.4  **139**

---

The table in the image:

| Sales of Effron Vehicles 2005 | | | | | |
|---|---|---|---|---|---|
|  | Jan–Mar | Apr–Jun | Jul–Aug | Sep–Dec | Total Sales |
| Excelsior | 756 | 598 | 899 | 465* | 2718 |
| Avenger | 1024 | 1245 | 995 | 1523 | 4787 |
| Townstar | 3484 | 4756 | 6498 | 3156 | 17894 |
| Pucchino | 4735 | 4986 | 6512 | 4720 | 20953 |

*model discontinued in November

**C**   Now choose the best answer as quickly as possible.

1. What does the chart show?
   (A) The number of vehicles sold by one manufacturer.
   (B) The rising and falling sales of Townstars.

2. In which sales period were the smallest number of Townstars sold?
   (A) Jul-Aug
   (B) Sep-Dec

3. Which model sold the greatest number overall?
   (A) Avenger
   (B) Pucchino

4. Which was the most successful period for sales of the Pucchino?
   (A) Jul-Aug
   (B) Jan-Mar

5. Which model sold the smallest number?
   (A) Avenger
   (B) Excelsior

6. How many Excelsiors were sold in December?
   (A) 465
   (B) 0

## 2   Test tactic: Locate information in double text questions

**A**   Look at the questions below and identify which text on page 141 you should look at to find the answer.

1. How much is the rent for the apartment?                 ☐ text 1   ☐ text 2
   (A) $985 all inclusive
   (B) Almost $1000 minus bills
   (C) $985 plus gas, electric and water

2. Why does Kelvin want to move to a new apartment?         ☐ text 1   ☐ text 2
   (A) To be nearer the middle of town
   (B) To get a bigger place
   (C) To live in a furnished apartment

3. How many rooms are there in the apartment?               ☐ text 1   ☐ text 2
   (A) 2
   (B) 6
   (C) 5

4. When is the earliest Kelvin and his fiancé can move in?  ☐ text 1   ☐ text 2
   (A) Monday
   (B) Mid-March
   (C) Whenever they want to

5. Which of the following does Kelvin NOT ask for?          ☐ text 1   ☐ text 2
   (A) Instructions on how to find the apartment
   (B) Information about pets
   (C) Photographs of the interior

**Questions 1–5** refer to the following advertisement and email.

Text 1

## Apartment for rent

- Modern studio apartment located 10 mins from shops and subway
- 2 bedrooms, kitchen, living/dining room, bathroom, balcony
- Centrally heated (gas)
- Suit young couple or professional type
- Part furnishing can be arranged
- Rent $985 p.c.m. plus utilities
- Deposit + 1 month's rent in advance
- No pets
- Available mid-March

Contact Karim on 555 2345
Email: karim98@s_mail.com

Text 2

**To:** karim98@s_mail.com
**Cc:**
**From:** Kelvin Adams (kelheart2@s_mail.com)

I saw your advertisement in the local newspaper. I'm very interested in the apartment, for myself and my fiancé. We are currently living in Westside, but are looking for something closer to the town center, and I think your place would be ideal. I was hoping to be able to arrange a visit sometime next week. Monday would be the best day for us, but we can be flexible and fit into your schedule.

In the ad, you mentioned that the place could be part-furnished. We have a small amount of furniture ourselves, but probably not enough for a two-bedroom place. Could you possibly tell us what inventory is likely to be included with the apartment?

I would also really appreciate it if you could possibly send us a couple of pictures of the bedroom and living/dining room, as well as some directions as to how to get there. Thank you very much in advance.

Yours

Kelvin Adams

*Follow up:* Compare your ideas with your partner.

**B** Now, look at the answer choices and choose the best answer.

### 3 Tactic practice: Charts, tables, forms and double texts

Use the tactics you have practiced for the following questions.

**Questions 1–3** refer to the following chart.

**Tactics checklist**

☑ Quickly check what different parts of the form refer to.

☑ Skim questions to identify where to look for answers.

☑ Be careful of the "small print".

## Price comparisons of major supermarkets 2002-2004

| 2002 | Eggs (dozen) | Bread (sliced medium loaf) | Tomato sauce (500 ml) | Potato chips (Salted, 25 g) | Frozen peas (500 g) |
|---|---|---|---|---|---|
| Floor Mart | $1.25 | $0.95 | $1.95 | $0.55 | $1.25 |
| 5-9 Stores | $1.29 | $1.15 | $1.90 | $0.60 | $1.45 |
| Leavinson's | $1.35 | $1.35 | $2.55 | $0.65 | $1.95 |
| VFG | $1.20 | $0.90* | $2.05 | $0.50 | $1.25 |

| 2003 | Eggs (dozen) | Bread (sliced medium loaf) | Tomato sauce (500 ml) | Potato chips (Salted, 25 g) | Frozen peas (500 g) |
|---|---|---|---|---|---|
| Floor Mart | $1.26 | $1.05 | $1.99 | $0.55 | $1.29 |
| 5-9 Stores | $1.35 | $1.15 | $1.95 | $0.65 | $1.45 |
| Leavinson's | $1.39 | $1.45 | $2.55 | $0.70 | $2.05 |
| VFG | $1.25 | $0.95 | $2.10 | $0.55 | $1.23 |

| 2004 | Eggs (dozen) | Bread (sliced medium loaf) | Tomato sauce (500 ml) | Potato chips (Salted, 25 g) | Frozen peas (500 g) |
|---|---|---|---|---|---|
| Floor Mart | $1.26 | $1.10 | $1.99 | $0.55 | $1.25 |
| 5-9 Stores | $1.40 | $1.20 | $1.99 | $0.65 | $1.40 |
| Leavinson's | $1.45 | $1.40 | $2.45 | $0.75 | $2.05 |
| VFG | $1.30 | $1.10 | $2.10 | $0.60 | $1.22 |

\* This food item was introduced in October of the noted year.

1. Which company sold the cheapest bread throughout 2002?
   (A) Floor Mart
   (B) 5-9 Stores
   (C) Leavinson's
   (D) VFG

2. What happened to the price of eggs at Floor Mart from 2002 to 2004?
   (A) They stayed largely unchanged.
   (B) They dropped slightly.
   (C) They rose dramatically.
   (D) They matched their competitors.

3. Which company reduced their price of frozen peas each year?
   (A) Floor Mart
   (B) 5-9 Stores
   (C) Leavinson's
   (D) VFG

# Suntours holidays

Experience the welcoming culture of the Greek islands. Suntours holidays offers you the once in a lifetime opportunity to visit the unspoiled island of Kefalonia. Stay at the recently renovated Casa Stanoupolos Hotel, a mere five minutes from the beautiful blue waters of the Aegean. Each room has a balcony with a view of the beach, and a private bathroom. The hotel has two pools and a Jacuzzi, as well as its own highly-rated restaurant, where you can enjoy some of the island's more traditional meals.

Holidays include all flights and transfers, as well as a choice of two exciting tours, including a boat trip to nearby Turkey, a chance to scuba dive in the pristine waters, or a visit to one of the local villages, where life continues much as it has for the past few hundred years. Call now on 555 143 4873 for more information on this fascinating vacation opportunity.

132B, West Bayside
San Francisco
CA
24<sup>th</sup> August 2006

Dear sir,

I am writing to complain about a recent trip I took with Suntours. I originally signed up for a two week trip to the island of Kefalonia, as advertised in Newsmonth magazine, and was looking forward to enjoying the holiday immensely. Unfortunately, I felt that a number of things spoiled the holiday for me. Firstly, I was led to believe that all rooms in the hotel had a balcony with a view of the beach. However, my room not only did not have a balcony, but it faced away from the sea. Secondly, only one of the hotel's pools was open, the other was still under construction, and the promised Jacuzzi was not there at all. The hotel's restaurant was excellent, but it was closed two nights a week, meaning that my family had to walk about two miles into the nearest town to eat, as there was no evening bus service. Finally, we took the tour to Turkey, but were left on the boat, as nobody reminded us to bring our passports along.

I feel very disappointed about the trip, and would appreciate some compensation.

Yours truly,

*Dave Clayman*

Dave Clayman

4. How far is the hotel from the beach?
   (A) 5 minutes
   (B) 2 miles
   (C) 1 hour
   (D) 100 meters

5. Which of the following is available on the vacation?
   (A) A suite room
   (B) A private beach
   (C) A chance to visit a second country
   (D) A chance to visit historic ruins

6. How does Mr. Clayman feel about his trip?
   (A) He enjoyed himself immensely.
   (B) He is angry about the quality of the restaurant.
   (C) He is complaining about the size of the Jacuzzi.
   (D) He feels the advertisement misrepresented the hotel.

7. Which of the following was the customer NOT disappointed about?
   (A) The view from his window
   (B) The quality of the food in the restaurant
   (C) The tour to Turkey
   (D) The lack of a bus service

8. What does Mr. Clayman hope to receive from Suntours?
   (A) A free vacation
   (B) Some money back
   (C) An apology
   (D) A new catalogue

**B** **Mini-test**

Now apply the *Test tactics* at the actual test speed with questions 1–12.

> You have 12 minutes to complete 12 items.

**Questions 1–2** refer to the following bill.

---

# La Traviata Restaurant
### Cole Road,
### Baton Rouge, LA

---

| | | |
|---|---|---|
| Spaghetti Vongole | | $14.95 |
| Spaghetti Carbonara | | $15.95 |
| Pizza Quattro Staggione | | $16.95 |
| Pizza Formaggio Grande | | $18.95 |
| Sparkling Mineral Water | 2 @ $03.50 = | $07.00 |
| Red Wine – house carafe | 2 @ $12.85 = | $25.70 |
| Gelato | | $03.99 |
| Zabaglione | 2 @ $05.99 = | $11.98 |
| Tartufo | | $04.50 |
| Cappuccino | 4 @ $04.95 = | $19.80 |
| | | ———— |
| Sub Total | | $139.77 |
| Tax @ 12.5% | | $17.47 |
| Total | | $157.24 |

Service not included

---

**1.** What can be inferred from this bill?

   (A) Pasta is more expensive than pizza.

   (B) All of the customers drank mineral water.

   (C) Four people ate a meal.

   (D) The guests didn't leave a tip.

**2.** What was the single most expensive item on the bill?

   (A) Spaghetti Vongole

   (B) Cappuccino

   (C) House Red Wine

   (D) Pizza Formaggio Grande

**GO ON TO THE NEXT PAGE**

## Holiday Booking Form

| Mr/Mrs/Ms | Initial | Surname | Dep. Date (M/D/Y) | From | To | Class | Holiday insurance |
|---|---|---|---|---|---|---|---|
| Mr | SW | Fletcher | 4/25/06 | London | Barbados | Economy | Ⓨ/ N |
| Mrs | YF | Fletcher | 4/25/06 | London | Barbados | Economy | Ⓨ/ N |
| | | | | | | | Y / N |
| | | | | | | | Y / N |
| | | | | | | | Y / N |

| Hotel | Room type | No. of rooms | No. of nights | Meals (Full/Half/BnB) | Check in (M/D/Y) | Check out (M/D/Y) |
|---|---|---|---|---|---|---|
| Montego Bay | Twin | 1 | 9 | Full | 4/26/06 | 5/5/06 |

| Special Requests | | Contact details: |
|---|---|---|
| balcony, private bath | | Address: 3, The Hawthorns, Park Lane, Hampton |
| | | Tel: (0255) 555 1566          Email: fletcher_s@apex.com |

| For office use only | Agent's initials: JBT | Package code: | A | 1 | 2 | 3 | C | |
|---|---|---|---|---|---|---|---|---|

3. What kind of room do the guests wish to stay in?
   (A) A double room with a balcony
   (B) A twin room with a shared bathroom
   (C) A twin room with a balcony
   (D) A double room with a private bathroom

4. Which of the following could be the name of the agent?
   (A) Sam William Fletcher
   (B) Jane Brenda Thompson
   (C) Yvonne Fiona Fletcher
   (D) John Peter Andrews

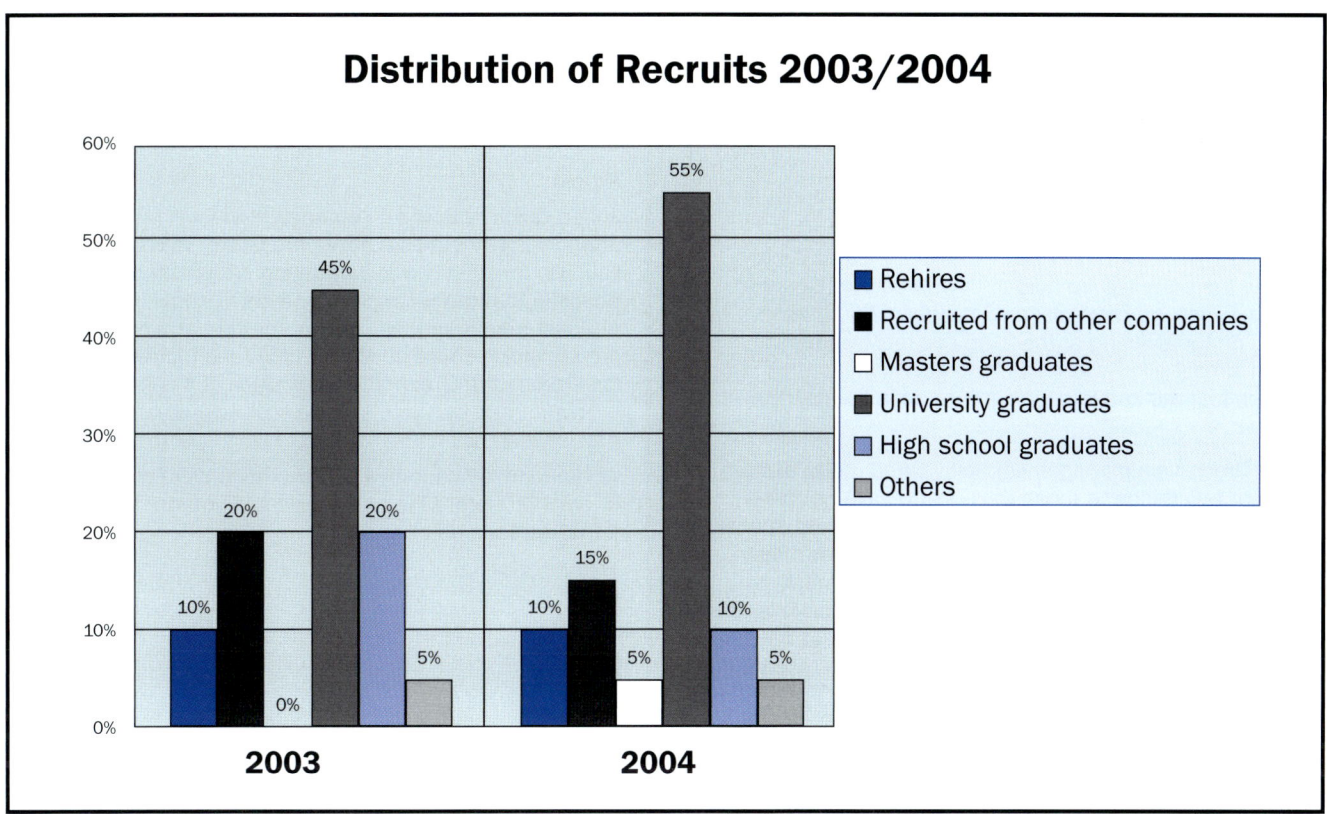

**Distribution of Recruits 2003/2004**

Legend:
- Rehires
- Recruited from other companies
- Masters graduates
- University graduates
- High school graduates
- Others

5. Which group provided the largest number of new employees over the two years?
   (A) University graduates
   (B) Recruits from other companies
   (C) High school graduates
   (D) Former employees

6. Which of the following groups showed an increase in percentage from 2003 to 2004?
   (A) Rehires
   (B) High school graduates
   (C) Masters graduates
   (D) Others

7. Which of the following is NOT true?
   (A) The percentage of university graduate recruits increased.
   (B) The percentage of rehires remained constant.
   (C) The percentage of recruits from other companies dropped.
   (D) In 2003 most recruits were high school graduates.

GO ON TO THE NEXT PAGE

## MEMORANDUM

**To:** All members of the sales department

**Re:** Christmas party

**From:** Arnold Derringer

This is just a quick note to let you all know the arrangements for next week's Christmas party. As you know the party will be held at the Green Vale Country Club, which we have reserved between 7:30 and 10 p.m. on the evening of the 21st. I've received replies from almost all of you confirming attendance, but if you haven't let me know yet, please do so in the next day or two.

The Green Vale management have asked me to explain one or two things to those of you who have not been there before. Basically, there is sufficient parking space for only 100 vehicles, so they would like to ask those of you planning to drive to try to car-pool as much as possible. Also, the number of lockers available is limited, so guests should try to keep belongings to a minimum.

Thanks in advance, and here's to a successful party.

---

**To:** Arnold Derringer

**cc:**

**From:** Kyle Berwick

Arnold

Just a quick note to let you know that I will be able to attend the Christmas party at the Green Vale Country Club on the 21st. I was wondering if it would also be possible to bring a couple of guests? I know it is a bit of a last minute request, but my brother and his wife are planning to visit us at that time, and I know they'd love to see the Green Vale clubhouse. If it is not a problem, then can you let me know how much I should pay for their tickets?

I'll be in my office until the 17th, then I have a couple of days off before the party, so could you get back to me as soon as possible?

Thanks a lot

Kyle

---

8. What is the purpose of the memorandum?

(A) To explain the arrangements for a special event

(B) To encourage people to car-pool

(C) To ask for help arranging a Christmas Party

(D) To thank people for a successful party

9. Which of the following is NOT true about the Green Vale Country Club?

(A) It has limited parking.

(B) It is closed in the evening.

(C) There are only a few lockers.

(D) It can be rented for private functions.

10. Why did Kyle Berwick contact Arnold Derringer?

(A) To ask about the price of movie tickets

(B) To excuse himself from attending the party

(C) To confirm his attendance and make a request

(D) To ask him if he would be able to attend the party

11. What information does Kyle Berwick require?

(A) The date of the party

(B) How to get to the Green Vale Country Club

(C) The price of tickets

(D) Who to ask in order to car-pool

12. When does Kyle need the information by?

(A) The 21st

(B) The next day or two

(C) The 17th

(D) Christmas Day

# Reading in action

**A** Read the following advertisements, then discuss the questions below.

## Position Available

High-level secretary required for firm located in central Los Angeles. Applicants should have good communication skills, reasonable computer skills and be able to type 80 wpm.

Ability to speak French and Spanish an advantage.

3–5 years experience with at least 2 years as secretary to top management a must.

Applicants should be prepared to work with high-level contacts whilst maintaining a calm and pleasant nature.

Send resumé and cover letter together with two references to RTS International, Box 1244, Los Angeles, CA.

## Job Opening

Secretarial position available starting March. Working for an independent film producer based in Los Angeles. You should be enthusiastic and knowledgeable about the movie business.

Minimum 2 years' experience required, secretarial skills, word processing, etc.

Send resumé and cover letter to Fanfilms, Box 1553, Los Angeles, CA

1. What kind of jobs are on offer?
2. How much experience is required?
3. What special skills are needed?
4. What are the differences between the two job offers?

**B** Now read the following reply to the first advert on page 149. Does this person fit the position? Complete the cover letter for a person applying for the second job using the words in the box below. Be careful, two of the expressions are not required.

---

RTS International
Box 1244
Los Angeles CA
April 1 2005

Dear Mr. Williams

I am writing in reply to your advertisement for a secretarial position, which I saw in the Gazette on Monday.

After my graduation from secretarial school, I worked for a number of local companies for around four years, and developed my secretarial skills. I can type at 100 wpm, and I speak good Spanish, as well as basic French, which I am keen to improve. For the last two years I have been the personal assistant of the president of QBC, an internet shopping company. I enjoy my work, but am looking for more of a challenge. I'm sure your company can provide me with that challenge.

I look forward to hearing from you.

Yours sincerely

*Miriam Masters*

Miriam Masters

---

Fanfilms
Box 1553
Los Angeles CA
April 2 2005

Dear Sir or Madam

(1) ................ to your advertisement in Movie Weekly. I was (2) ................ about the position.

I have been working as (3) ................ for the past three years, during which time I (4) ................ for writing letters, answering the telephone and other (5) ................ .

I am (6) ................ and have some experience with simple spreadsheets. I am also half Mexican, so I am bilingual in English and Spanish.

I feel that (7) ................ , coupled with (8) ................ the movie industry, make me an ideal candidate for this job. I look forward to hearing from you.

Yours faithfully

*Consuela Peruzzi*

Consuela Peruzzi

---

| | |
|---|---|
| secretarial duties | a secretary |
| would like to | have been responsible |
| good at word processing | my knowledge of |
| my enthusiasm for the job | very good typist |
| I am writing in reply | very excited to hear |

---

 **D**     # Further study

Find an advertisement in an English magazine or newspaper, and think of two or three questions to test your classmates.

Go to word list and quiz page 185.

# Activity files

## Activity file 2.1

**Student B**

You are Barton Donovan, the Director of Seimex Watches America.
You just sent the following fax to your New York office.
You will get a call from Mr. Carson, as there are some parts of the fax he cannot read.

**Task**

- Read the fax now and confirm with your partner that you understand what it says.
- Then take Mr. Carson's call and answer any questions he may have.

---

### Fax Message

**Important**

**Re: August 14 meeting**

Mr. Carson,

I am writing to let you know that I will be arriving on Tuesday August 13. I am flying with United Airlines and my plane is scheduled to land at 9:15 p.m. Could you arrange my hotel for me?

The main purpose of my visit is the problem with our Accuron Line of watches. We have had many complaints about water damage. We must discuss how we can deal with the problem. Please invite Paul Smith and Mary Davis also.

Barton Donovan.

---

## Activity file 1.2a

When your partner chooses a number, make a sentence to describe the picture. When it's your turn, choose a number and listen carefully to your partner. If they say one of the words on your bingo card you can mark it off. The first person to get all the words marked off is the winner.

**Bingo card 1**

| B | I | N | G | O |
|---|---|---|---|---|
| holding | opening | sitting | wearing | shining |

## Activity file 1.2b

When your partner chooses a number, make a sentence to describe the picture. When it's your turn, choose a number and listen carefully to your partner. If they say one of the words on your bingo card you can mark it off. The first person to get all the words marked off is the winner.

**Bingo card 1**

| B | I | N | G | O |
|---|---|---|---|---|
| standing | getting into | walking | enjoying | pushing |

## Activity file 4.2a

Read your partner the following news report.

| **Your news report** |
|---|
| FHL Electronics announced its sales figures for the last financial year. |
| The president explained that the decrease in orders would lead to the closure of three factories. |
| The president blamed the disappointing results on increasing labor costs in Asia. |
| He apologized to his shareholders for the company's debts and promised that next year would be a much better one. |

## Activity file 3.3a

With your partner take turns reading one sentence at a time. They will try to guess the correct job, location or activity.

1. Sorry, I have to go to Boston on Tuesday. Could we make it for next Monday? (activities – **changing an appointment**)

2. Please open your books to page 20 and look at Unit 1. (jobs – **teacher**)

3. Would you like anything to drink with your meal? (locations – **restaurant**)

4. If you want to go to Bramston, you have to change at Union station to the central line. (jobs – **train conductor**)

5. This picture was painted by Samuel Evans just before his death in 1934. (locations – **art museum**)

6. Could you tell me how to get to the Miller building? (activities – **asking for directions**)

## Activity file 1.3a

When your partner chooses a square read one of the questions from the same number square below. They must say whether it is "Correct" or "Wrong". If they are right, they get the square.

| 1. | 2. | 3. |
|---|---|---|
| A. The photographer is carrying the camera. (**Wrong**)<br>B. They are filming a scene. (**Correct**) | A. The man is holding the dog. (**Wrong**)<br>B. The dog is standing near the cowboy. (**Correct**) | A. The chef is cooking. (**Correct**)<br>B. The woman is cleaning the kitchen. (**Wrong**) |
| 4. | 5. | 6. |
| A. The machine is making a hole. (**Correct**)<br>B. The worker is digging. (**Wrong**) | A. The boat is tied to the pier. (**Correct**)<br>B. The ship is sailing across the bay. (**Wrong**) | A. The woman is making a bookshelf. (**Wrong**)<br>B. She is reading. (**Correct**) |
| 7. | 8. | 9. |
| A. The truck is plowing the road. (**Correct**)<br>B. The road is clear of snow. (**Wrong**) | A. The man is using the restroom. (**Wrong**)<br>B. The worker has stopped cleaning. (**Correct**) | A. The firemen are having a break. (**Correct**)<br>B. The dog is standing near the truck. (**Wrong**) |

## Activity file 4.4a

Read out one of the following answers. Your partner must identify the question that best matches it. If they do, they score 1 point. If not, you have a chance to steal their point. Continue to take turns reading out all the answers.

**Answers to "why" questions**

(A) Governments are worried about their safety.

(B) They have decreased in the last few months.

(C) There was a clash with the annual general meeting.

(D) His plane took off late.

(E) The latest model is still under development.

## Activity file 4.2b

Read your partner the following news report.

| Your news report |
|---|
| A huge earthquake struck central Togassa at 5 o'clock this morning. |
| Most people were still sleeping when the first tremor struck. |
| The earthquake damaged many homes and buildings and destroyed the main bridge leading to the city. |
| The destruction of the bridge means that emergency supplies must be flown in by helicopter. |

## Activity file 3.3b

With your partner take turns reading one sentence at a time. They will try to guess the correct job, location or activity.

1. The acting was good but there wasn't much action. – (activities – **talking about a movie**)

2. What time does the pool close this evening? – (locations – **sports club**)

3. Yes, we have one with the same heel, but in brown leather. – (jobs – **shoe salesman**)

4. How much is a pound of tomatoes? – (locations – **supermarket**)

5. I'm not sure I like the color and the sleeves are a bit short. – (activities – **buying clothes**)

6. Can you help me copy these? I have a meeting in 15 minutes. – (jobs – **office worker**)

# Activity file 1.4a

1.  [PREPOSITION]
    A. The man is <u>on top of</u> the car.
    **B. The man is leaning <u>against</u> the car.**

2.  [SIMILAR SOUND]
    **A. The woman's <u>hand</u> is touching the box.**
    B. The woman is turning the <u>handle</u>.

3.  [SIMILAR SOUND]
    **A. The <u>flight</u> attendant is wearing a red jacket.**
    B. The door is very <u>light</u>.

4.  [SIMILAR SOUND]
    A. The man is <u>re-sitting</u> the test.
    **B. The man is <u>sitting</u> next to the control panel.**

5.  [ PREPOSITION]
    A. The man is <u>behind</u> the computer.
    **B. The keyboard is <u>in front of</u> the computer.**

6.  [SIMILAR SOUND]
    A. The <u>bride</u> is on the sidewalk.
    **B. The girl <u>rides</u> her scooter.**

7.  [ PREPOSITION]
    **A. The children are <u>on</u> the grass.**
    B. They are <u>in front of</u> each other.

8.  [ PREPOSITION]
    A. The skiers are <u>under</u> the snow.
    **B. People are <u>on</u> the chair lift.**

9.  [SIMILAR SOUND]
    A. The woman <u>looks</u> at the doors.
    **B. There are <u>locks</u> on the doors.**

## Activity file 1.3b

When your partner chooses a square read one of the questions from the same number square below. They must say whether it is "Correct" or "Wrong". If they are right, they get the square.

| 1. | 2. | 3. |
|---|---|---|
| A. Two men are standing near the camera. (**Correct**)<br>B. They are watching a film. (**Wrong**) | A. The dog is running near the tires. (**Wrong**)<br>B. The man is kneeling near the dog. (**Correct**) | A. The chef is working in the kitchen. (**Correct**)<br>B. The kitchen is very dirty. (**Wrong**) |
| **4.** | **5.** | **6.** |
| A. The worker is watching the digging. (**Correct**)<br>B. The man is fixing the machine. (**Wrong**) | A. There is a lot of equipment on the pier. (**Correct**)<br>B. The ship is leaving the water. (**Wrong**) | A. The woman is holding many books. (**Wrong**)<br>B. She is standing near the shelf. (**Correct**) |
| **7.** | **8.** | **9.** |
| A. The truck is pushing the snow. (**Correct**)<br>B. It is snowing heavily. (**Wrong**) | A. The man is washing the sink. (**Wrong**)<br>B. The worker is holding the mop. (**Correct**) | A. The firemen are sitting on the truck. (**Correct**)<br>B. The dog is watching the men. (**Wrong**) |

## Activity file 4.4b

Your partner will read out one of the following answers. You must identify the question that best matches it. If you do, you score 1 point. If not, your partner has the chance to steal your point. Next it is your turn to read out an answer. (Check the key on page XX of the Key and Tapescripts to make sure.) Continue to take turns reading out all the answers.

**Answers to "how" questions**

(F) By contacting the concierge.

(G) Much the same as today.

(H) There are a lot of innovations.

(I) By contacting the emergency number.

(J) It is a potential problem.

## Activity file 1.4b

1. [SIMILAR SOUND]
   A. **The cookies are on the <u>counter</u>.**
   B. The boy is <u>counting</u> the cookies.

2. [PREPOSITION]
   A. **The student is leaning <u>against</u> the locker.**
   B. The student is looking <u>inside</u> her locker.

3. [SIMILAR SOUND]
   A. The man is <u>shipping</u> some food.
   B. **The customer is <u>shopping</u> for food.**

4. [SIMILAR SOUND]
   A. The man <u>tastes</u> the food.
   B. **The man <u>tests</u> the soil.**

5. [SIMILAR SOUND]
   A. The people <u>hide</u> behind the building.
   B. **The people <u>hold</u> umbrellas.**

6. [SIMILAR SOUND]
   A. **The <u>diners</u> sit around the table.**
   B. Their <u>dinner</u> is on the table.

7. [PREPOSITION]
   A. The scientist is <u>on</u> the table.
   B. **The student is <u>in</u> the laboratory.**

8. [PREPOSITION]
   A. **The people walk <u>along</u> the sidewalk.**
   B. The commuters are <u>between</u> the buses.

9. [SIMILAR SOUND]
   A. **The man is by a <u>sign</u>.**
   B. The man is going to <u>resign</u>.

# General glossary of terms

## Terms used in instructions

| | |
|---|---|
| **brainstorm (v)** | To think of many ideas on a topic quickly and creatively |
| **focus (n)** | The main or most important thing or things |
| **key words (n)** | The most important words in terms of meaning, usually nouns, verbs, adjectives and adverbs |
| **paraphrase (v)** | To restate something in other, usually simpler words |
| **predict (v)** | To say what is going to happen in the future. In the TOEIC test this usually means to guess what you are going to hear in the listening section |
| **related (adj)** | Connected in some way to an idea |
| **scan (v)** | To read quickly in order to pick out specific information (e.g. looking for a name in a phone book) |
| **similar (adj)** | Having some things in common but not completely identical (e.g. African elephants are very similar to Indian elephants) |
| **skim (v)** | To read quickly in order to get a general idea of the contents (e.g. quickly going over a movie review to see if it is worth watching) |
| **tactic (n)** | A method or technique used to achieve an immediate goal |

## Test related terms

| | |
|---|---|
| **answer choices (n)** | The four possible answers (A, B, C, D) you can choose from in the TOEIC test |
| **context (n)** | The background events or situation within which something belongs or takes place |
| **denial (n)** | A negative response to a request |
| **distractor (n)** | An incorrect option in a multiple-choice question |
| **implied (v)** | Something which can be understood or is suggested without being directly stated |
| **infer (v)** | To use context or related information to understand something that isn't directly stated |
| **refusal (n)** | A statement of an unwillingness to do something |
| **response (n)** | Something said or written in reply to a question or statement |
| **similar sounds (n)** | A common type of test distractor which uses a word or words which sounds similar to a possible correct answer |

## Grammar terms

| | |
|---|---|
| **noun (n)** | A word which is used as the name of a person, place or thing (e.g. *John*, *Canada*, *pencil*) |
| **verb (v)** | A word that is used to show an action, or state (e.g. *run*, *is*) |
| **adjective (adj)** | A word that describes a noun or pronoun (e.g. *big*, *happy*), or gives extra information about them |
| **adverb (adv)** | A word that adds more information about place, time, manner, cause, or degree to a verb, an adjective, a phrase or another adverb (e.g. *look carefully*, *incredibly fast*) |
| **subject (s)** | A grammatical word describing the noun or noun phrase that performs the action in a sentence (e.g. **Cats** eat fish – "*Cats*" is the subject). Or in a passive sentence, the noun that is affected by the action of the verb (e.g. **The tree** *was blown over by the strong wind*.) |
| **object (o)** | A grammatical word describing the noun or noun phrase that is being acted upon or affected by the verb in a sentence (e.g. Cats eat **fish** – "*fish*" is the object) |
| **preposition (prep)** | A word which is used to indicate position, or movement in time or space (e.g. The ball is **in** the box, It finishes **at** 9:00, He is going **into** the store) |
| **pronoun (pron)** | A word that takes the place of a noun (e.g. *I*, *you*, *it*) |
| **subject pronoun** | A word that takes the place of a subject noun (e.g. *he*, *they*) |
| **object pronoun** | A word that takes the place of a noun (e.g. *him*, *us*) |
| **indefinite pronoun** | A pronoun that doesn't refer to any specific person or thing (e.g. *something*, *anything*) |
| **suffix** | A group of letters added at the end of a word that affects the meaning or use (e.g. "-ed" in "*amused*", "-ly" in "*slowly*") |
| **prefix** | A group of letters added at the beginning of a word that affects the meaning or use (e.g. "*bi-*" in "*bicycle*", "*pre-*" in "*predict*") |

# Word list and Quizzes

## Unit 1.1

**covered** (adj)  to put something over the whole top of something else
*The trees are covered in snow.*
*The car was completely covered in thick dust from the trip.*

**discuss** (v)  to talk about a subject with other people
*The couple are discussing something.*
*I would like to discuss our summer sales plans.*

**green** (n)  the grassy area near a golf hole
*The golfers are walking on the green.*
*The pro hit his ball onto the green with his first shot.*

**incredible** (adj)  very surprising or difficult to believe, very good
*The mountain view is incredible.*
*He was an incredible piano player and had won several awards.*

**keyboard** (n)  a set of keys used to type on a computer or word processor
*His new computer came with a wireless keyboard.*
*While he was typing his essay, he accidentally spilled coffee on his keyboard.*

**oar** (n)  a long wooden pole with a flat end used to move a boat through the water
*There is an oar by his right side.*
*He pulled hard on the oars to make the boat go faster.*

**tie** (v)  to make a knot in a rope or string to hold something
*She is tying her shoe.*
*Her hair was tied back with a silk ribbon.*

**wave** (v)  to move something back and forth
*The man is waving his arms.*
*The soldier waved the flag to signal the attack.*

## Unit 2.1

**arrange** (v)  organize or make plans for something
*Could you arrange my hotel for me?*
*My secretary will arrange the meeting time.*

**arrangement** (n)  a plan that has been made for an event
*What are the arrangements for tomorrow?*
*We made the arrangement by telephone.*

**bother** (v)  to disturb or interrupt someone
*I'm sorry to bother you Mr. Donovan, but I'm afraid we couldn't read your fax properly.*
*I couldn't sleep as the noise from next door was bothering me.*

**cheap** (adj)  low price, not expensive
*Where can I buy a cheap air conditioner?*
*Airlines offer cheap prices to attract new customers.*

**complaint** (n)  a spoken or written statement expressing dissatisfaction with a product or service
*We have had many complaints about water damage.*
*The customer service department deals with all complaints.*

**customer** (n)  a person paying for goods or services
*My customers live in Boston.*
*Why did the customer cancel his contract?*

**decide** (v)  to choose to do something after thinking about it carefully
*I haven't decided yet.*
*I decided not to visit the conference this year.*

**discuss** (v)  to talk about something and try to reach a decision
*We must discuss how we can deal with the problem.*
*The managers are discussing the current proposals.*

**get along (with)** (v)  have a good relationship, be friendly with
*I didn't get along with the boss.*
*My sister and I got along with each other when we were children.*

**goods** (n)  items produced by a company that are available for sale
*There's a range of goods.*
*We plan to expand our range of goods in the next two years.*

**(give someone a) lift** (n)  a ride in someone's car or other vehicle to a particular place
*Mary gave me a lift.*
*I asked my father to give me a lift to the station.*

**notice** (n)  a sign displayed publicly giving information to a group of people
*Have you seen the notice about the sheep?*
*The notice asked people not to smoke in the kitchen area.*

**overtime** (n)  work done in addition to regularly scheduled hours
*How much overtime have you done this month?*
*Overtime is paid at a higher rate than regular pay.*

**parcel** (n)  a package, usually wrapped in paper, to be delivered by mail
*What company did you use to ship the parcel?*
*The mailman delivered the parcel at 2 o'clock this afternoon.*

**profit** (n)  money made (usually by a business) above the money they spent
*Has the sale improved profits?*
*The new product caused a profit rise of ten percent.*

**(be) receive(d)** (v)  the way people react to something
*How were her findings received?*
*His presentation was very well received.*

**recently** (adv)  in the near past
*Why does Irving look so tired recently?*
*I recently passed my driving test, so I want to get a car.*

**repairs** (n)  work done to fix something that was broken
*How much are the repairs going to cost us?*
*The building needed a lot of repairs following the storm.*

**terrible** (adj)  very bad, or shocking
*Traffic can be terrible in this city.*
*The food at that restaurant is terrible.*

**vacation** (n)  a holiday, or a trip taken during a holiday period
*What are you doing for your vacation?*
*I went to Guam for my vacation last summer.*

7 I don't really ................... with Giles. I don't like his sense of humor.
   (A) discuss
   (B) arrange
   (C) get along

8 Let's sit down and ................... your plans for the retirement fund.
   (A) receive
   (B) discuss
   (C) complain

## 2 Read the definitions and write the words.

1 items produced by a company (*doogs*)    g...................
2 a holiday (*cavtoina*)    v...................
3 a package (*epracl*)    p...................
4 a person who buy things (*erctusom*)    c...................
5 a sign (*entoci*)    n...................
6 work done in addition to scheduled work (*tmoviere*)    m...................
7 work done to fix something (*sparier*)    r...................
8 in the near past (*ylercnte*)    r...................
9 a low price (*eaphc*)    c...................
10 very bad (*ritrelbe*)    t...................
11 choose to do something after thinking carefully about it (*eeidcd*)    d...................
12 make plans to do something (*rrganae*)    a...................

## Unit 3.1

**adapter** (n) a device used to change the power from a socket to match the requirements of the appliance
*You can run it with an AC adapter.*
*You'll need an international adapter to use your hairdryer overseas.*

**appointment** (n) an arranged meeting, usually for some business purpose
*He has to rush to a previous appointment.*
*I made an appointment to see the dentist next Thursday.*

**appreciate** (v) to be thankful for something
*I'd appreciate the company.*
*We appreciate your help.*

**appreciation** (n) the feeling of thanks for something
*I wish he would show his appreciation.*
*We'd like to offer our appreciation for all your work.*

**auction** (n) a public sale where the goods are sold to the person who makes the highest offer
*Are you by any chance driving down to the auction tomorrow?*
*I bought it at an auction.*

**block** (v) to place an object or stand in a way that nothing can get past
*You are blocking the emergency exit for the theatre.*
*The boxes blocked access to the emergency exit.*

**branch** (n) one of several offices or shops belonging to a larger group
*She is at the wrong branch.*
*The bank has branches all over the country.*

**buckle** (n) a metal fastener, used especially in belts, to keep them closed
*The buckle is damaged.*
*It is a leather belt with a buckle made of silver.*

**company** (n) having another person with you
*I'd appreciate the company.*
*You can come with me to keep me company.*

**courier** (n) a person, working for a delivery company, who is paid to take letters and packages from one place to another
*The courier is going to pick them up in 15 minutes.*
*The fastest way to deliver items is to use a courier.*

**criticize** (v) to say what you think is wrong with something
*What did some trainees criticize?*
*His approach was criticized for being too aggressive.*

**feedback** (n) information to let people know about their performance, usually at work
*What kind of feedback did you get from the trainees?*
*The boss doesn't give us feedback very often.*

**improvement** (n) something that is better than a previous situation or version
*It's an improvement on their previous one.*
*He has shown a steady improvement in the quality of his work.*

**included** (adj) part of the contents of a package, not separate, not requiring additional purchase
*The adapter isn't included.*
*Batteries are included.*

**label** (n) a note attached to a product explaining some detail (e.g. the price)
*The label is incorrect.*
*You can find the washing instructions on the label.*

**loan** (v) to lend money, usually charging an amount
*...for Harry to loan him some money.*
*The bank will loan us the money for this project.*

**participant** (n) a person taking part in an event
*Comments from the participants...*
*3000 participants completed the marathon this year.*

**pleased** (adj) happy or satisfied with something
*What isn't Harry pleased with?*
*I was very pleased with the Christmas present I received.*

**plug (it) into/in** (v) to connect an electrical item to a socket
*You can plug it into a socket.*
*Where can I plug my laptop in?*

**practical** (adj) having a real and clear use
*It doesn't have any practical value.*
*The training showed lots of practical ways to use the application.*

**previous** (adj) before now, in the past
*He has to rush to a previous appointment.*
*My previous job was working for an IT company.*

**purchase** (v) to buy something
*Purchase an adapter.*
*You can purchase tickets online.*

**replacement** (adj) used in place of the original
*...give a replacement part.*
*Since Tony left we haven't been sent a replacement worker.*

**socket** (n) the place you plug electronic items into the wall in order to provide them with power
*You can plug it into a socket.*
*He plugged the television into the socket and switched it on.*

**stock** (n) the number or amount of a product available to sell to customers
*Check the parts stock.*
*I'm afraid we don't have any of those in stock at the moment.*

**theoretical** (adj) based on ideas rather than experience; opposite of practical
*It was too theoretical.*
*The lecture was very theoretical, but seemed to make sense.*

## Quiz 3.1

### 1 Use the definitions to find the words to complete the puzzle.

**Clues**
1 to lend money
2 to connect an electrical item to a socket
3 to buy something
4 a person who is paid to take letters and packages
5 something that is better than it was before
6 one of several offices or shops
7 the amount of goods available
8 something you use instead of something else
9 to feel thankful to someone
10 a person who takes part in an event
11 a public sale where things are sold to the person who will pay the most

## 2 Complete the sentences with the following words.

> adaptor appreciation block buckle
> company criticized feedback
> included label pleased practical
> previous socket theoretical

1  The cost of post and packing isn't ................... in the price.
2  If your computer isn't working, check the ................... . Sometimes people forget to switch it on!
3  There isn't a(n) ................... on this package. I don't know who it's for.
4  Please don't ................... the entrance to the hospital.
5  The ................... on this bag is broken. Can you replace it?
6  I didn't get the job, but they didn't tell me why. I'm going to ask for some ................... .
7  I'd like some ................... when I go to Singapore. I don't want to travel alone.
8  Don't forget to take your international ................... to Japan. You'll need it for your laptop.
9  They showed their ................... of the employee by giving him more money.
10 The director is ................... with the company's improved performance.
11 A lot of people have ................... plans for a new supermarket in the area. They don't think it's needed.
12 This bag isn't very ................... . It's too small.
13 My ................... manager always listened to my suggestions, but my new manager isn't interested.
14 The ................... part of the exam requires a good knowledge of the highway code.

## Unit 4.1

**apologize** (v) to say sorry for an action
*We apologize for any inconvenience.*
*He apologized for being late.*
**assist** (v) to help with something
*Can you assist with the project?*
*The staff assisted us with our luggage problem.*
**boost** (v) to cause something to become better, larger or greater
*We aim to boost our sales in this segment.*
*The good exchange rates have really boosted exports.*
**cancel** (v) to request that an order or reservation be stopped
*Service to Darby has been canceled for the foreseeable future.*
*I canceled my subscription to the newspaper as I didn't have enough time to read it.*
**circumstance** (n) a situation or the way in which it happened
*Make specific note of any special circumstances.*
*Do not open the door in any circumstance.*
**complimentary** (adj) offered without charge
*We will shortly be serving complimentary tea.*
*The saunas are offered as a complimentary service to all guests.*

**deadline** (n) the final date a piece of work has to be completed by
*The deadline for the Q-com project has been moved forward by a week.*
*I need to ask for an extension to the deadline to allow me time to do more research.*
**deter** (v) to encourage someone not to do something
*The rugged coral reefs deterred pirates.*
*The lights and alarms are designed to deter burglars.*
**disposal** (n) the throwing away of waste products or garbage
*Improper disposal of hazardous materials can cause pollution.*
*The garbage disposal men come every Thursday.*
**foremost** (adj) leading, top, ahead of other people or events
*It is one of the world's foremost maritime events.*
*He is one of the foremost spokespeople on this topic.*
**gains** (n) increases in sales or profits
*Impressive gains were made by our budget priced EL101.*
*Our stock prices have made steady gains in this financial period.*
**getaway** (n) a short holiday or place where you can make a holiday
*A perfect spot for a tropical getaway.*
*We bought ourselves a little getaway in the Bahamas.*
**hazardous** (adj) dangerous to life
*Improper disposal of hazardous materials can cause pollution.*
*People were asked to remain indoors due to the threat of hazardous waste.*
**in the meantime** (expression) for now, until something else happens
*In the meantime we are arranging for a shuttle bus.*
*We'll wait to see what happens in the meantime.*
**inconvenience** (n) something that causes trouble or a problem for other people
*We apologize for any inconvenience.*
*The road works caused a lot of inconvenience to commuters.*
**injuries** (n) harm or damage done to a person, often in an accident or fight
*First of all, check for injuries.*
*He only suffered minor injuries in the fall.*
**interrupt** (v) to cause something to be stopped, to break into someone's conversation suddenly
*Service has been interrupted due to the weather.*
*I'm sorry to interrupt your meeting, but there's an urgent call on line one.*
**involve** (v) to cause someone to become part of an activity or event
*We hope you are never involved in an accident.*
*She tried to involve us in her meeting.*
**isolate** (v) to separate something from other things
*Normally, our system would have isolated the virus.*
*The islanders were isolated from civilization for thousands of years.*
**landscape** (n) everything that can be seen when you look out at a (usually undeveloped) area
*They want to describe its landscape.*
*The landscape is beautiful around the town.*

**organic** (adj) made or grown without the use of artificial elements
*Only use organic waste bags.*
*Organic vegetables are becoming more popular in US supermarkets.*
**patience** (n) an ability to wait without becoming frustrated or annoyed
*Thank you for your attention to this matter and your patience.*
*His patience was rewarded.*
**pleasantly** (adv) nicely, enjoyably
*We were pleasantly surprised.*
*The evening passed pleasantly.*
**reduction** (n) a change from a larger to a smaller number or amount
*Sales showed a reduction in overall volume.*
*Workers had to accept a reduction in salaries due to poor sales figures.*
**refund** (n) money paid back to a customer for an unsatisfactory product or service
*Passengers are being refused a refund.*
*We promise all our customers will be satisfied or we'll give you a full refund.*
**refuse** (v) to not agree to do something
*Passengers are being refused a refund.*
*He refused to accept being transferred to Mongolia.*
**rugged** (adj) (of landscape) covered with rocks, very difficult to cross
*The rugged coral reefs deterred pirates.*
*The rugged mountains have attracted sightseers for years.*
**secluded** (adj) (of an area) hidden from sight, away from populated areas
*It has miles of secluded beaches.*
*The secluded bay provides a perfect place for nesting sea turtles.*
**tremendous** (adj) very good, or a very large amount
*It has a tremendous wealth of powdery soft beaches.*
*It was a tremendous effort to build the factory in such a short space of time.*
**typo** (n) an error in a typed document, usually made unconsciously
*Check the documents for any typos.*
*Make sure there are no typos in company documents before sending them out to the customers.*

## Quiz 4.1

### 1 Choose the correct word.

1  The ................... is Friday. Applications will not be considered after this date.
   (A) getaway
   (B) disposal
   (C) deadline

2  Unfortunately, there has been a(n) ................... in profits over the last few months.
   (A) inconvenience
   (B) reduction
   (C) refund

3  Tina has got special ................... which means she doesn't have to go on the trip.
   (A) typos
   (B) gains
   (C) circumstances

4 The plane will be delayed by three hours. Thank you for your ................... .
(A) inconvenience
(B) patience
(C) circumstances

5 The train has been ................... due to an earlier problem on the track.
(A) interrupted
(B) cancelled
(C) refused

6 I'm sorry to ................... your conversation, but the director would like to see you.
(A) apologise
(B) interrupt
(C) assist

7 I ................... to work on Saturday. I already have plans.
(A) deter
(B) cancel
(C) refuse

8 I'm not ................... by hard work. I like a challenge.
(A) assisted
(B) deterred
(C) refused

9 The company is trying to ................... its profits this year.
(A) boost
(B) involve
(C) refund

10 The director wants to ................... everybody in the decision.
(A) refuse
(B) isolate
(C) involve

11 The new manager has made a ................... effort to be friendly.
(A) tremendous
(B) organic
(C) rugged

12 Ships are not allowed to leave ................... waste in the sea.
(A) secluded
(B) hazardous
(C) foremost

## 2 Read the definitions and write *true* or *false*.

1 *Inconvenience* means having an easy time.
2 If you get a *refund* you get your money back.
3 A *getaway* is a type of aeroplane.
4 *Landscape* is a type of holiday.
5 A *typo* is an error in a document.
6 *Gains* is the opposite of losses.
7 *Injuries* is the damage done to a person after an accident.
8 *Disposal* means the throwing away of garbage.
9 *Apologize* means to be angry with someone.
10 *To assist* means to help.
11 If a beach is *secluded* it is very crowded.
12 If something is *complimentary* it's expensive.
13 If your house is *isolated* you don't live near other people.
14 If a person is *foremost* it means he or she is ahead of other people in a subject.

15 *Rugged* means covered in rocks.
16 If something is *organic* it's made artificially.
17 *Pleasantly* means horribly.
18 *In the meantime* means until something else happens.

## Unit 5.1

**accommodation** (n) a place to live or stay
*The director was unhappy with the quality of his accommodations.*
*I'm looking for new accommodation, as my current place is too small.*

**advantage** (n) something that gives you a better chance than another person of success
*Graduating from a famous university is an advantage for job hunting.*
*His ability to speak French gave him an advantage over the other applicants.*

**aid** (v) to assist people in need of help, especially by giving money
*The fund collects donations to aid local underprivileged citizens.*
*The government tries to aid refugees as much as possible.*

**bankruptcy** (n) the state of being bankrupt (see glossary 4.2), not having enough money to pay debts
*Due to his father's bankruptcy, he couldn't enter university.*
*He filed for bankruptcy.*

**complexity** (n) the level of difficulty or detail
*The complexity of modern economic systems makes them far from predictable.*
*The complexity of the design makes it difficult to copy.*

**(be) considered** (v) thought by many people
*Adam Smith is considered to be an important philosopher.*
*He was considered to be the best choice for the job.*

**courier** (n) a person, working for a delivery company, who is paid to take letters and packages from one place to another
*The courier is going to pick them up in 15 minutes.*
*What time does the courier come in the evenings?*

**credit** (n) money available to borrow from banks or other financial institutions
*Careless use of credit can lead trouble sooner than you expect.*
*Can I get this on credit?*

**distribution** (n) the way goods are delivered from the factory to the shops
*We can increase our sales margin by streamlining our distribution system.*
*The distribution of goods takes only a day or two.*

**downturn** (n) a change for the worse, usually of a country or company's economic situation
*Small downturns in the US economy can have a global impact.*
*The financial situation has taken a bit of a downturn.*

**emergency** (n) a sudden and serious situation
*In an emergency, press the red alarm button.*
*Keep enough money to make a phone call in case of emergency.*

**immediate** (adj) without hesitation, connected to now
*...there was an immediate need to improve costs.*
*Is there any immediate action to be taken?*

**impact** (n) the effect one thing has on another
*Small downturns in the US economy can have a global impact.*
*The gowth of the tourist industry has a tremendous impact on the environment.*

**margin** (n) the difference between money spent and profits made
*We can increase our sales margin by streamlining our distribution system.*
*We are operating on pretty small margins here.*

**optimistic** (adj) having a positive feeling about something
*The dates we were quoted are too optimistic.*
*They were optimistic about the outcome of the negotiations.*

**outraged** (adj) very angry about something.
*He was outraged over the charges of misuse of company property.*
*I was outraged at the state of the hotel.*

**philosopher** (n) a person that thinks about and tries to understand life or other basic matters
*Adam Smith was a philosopher of the 18th century.*
*I'm not a philosopher, so I'll probably never understand.*

**reach** (v) to contact someone by telephone
*Please dial "9", then the number you wish to reach.*
*I've been trying to reach him all day.*

**recommendation** (n) a suggestion, something thought to be a good idea
*I don't think the consultant's recommendation will help the situation.*
*What is your recommendation for the main course?*

**retirement fund** (n) money kept for workers to be paid a regular allowance after they become too old to continue working
*The company saves money for workers in a retirement fund.*
*All employees are invited to join the retirement fund.*

**streamline** (v) to make a business more efficient and use money more carefully
*We can increase our sales by streamlining our distribution system.*
*We need to streamline our operations to avoid bankruptcy.*

**underprivileged** (adj) the poor, those with less money than they require to live a normal life
*The city welfare fund collects donations to aid local underprivileged citizens.*
*Charity should target the underprivileged.*

**welfare** (n) money paid by the government to help those unable to help themselves
*The city welfare fund collects donations to aid local underprivileged citizens.*
*Welfare payments account for 25% of all taxes.*

**1 Complete the sentences with the following words.**

accommodation   advantage
complexity   considered   credit
distribution   downturn   immediate
impact   margin   recommendations
welfare

1 The latest project is ................... to be our most ambitious.
2 Our company has a(n) ................... fund that collects money for elderly people.
3 The use of ................... when making purchases is convenient but should be used carefully.
4 We hope there won't be a(n) ................... in the economy over the next few months.
5 The recent bad weather has had a(n) ................... on the profits of many travel companies.
6 The company needs to increase its profit ................... significantly.
7 The ................... of the situation means the project is going to take a long time to complete.
8 The director wants more people to receive our goods, so is planning to improve our ................... service.
9 Mr. Green felt there was a(n) ................... need to start a new project.
10 This ................... isn't in a convenient location for our employees.
11 Simon has made several ................... that the director has agreed with.
12 Speaking several languages is a(n) ................... when working in the travel industry.

**2 Read the definitions and write *true* or *false*.**

1 A *retirement fund* is an amount of money used to help workers with health costs.
2 An *attorney* is a businessman.
3 *Underprivileged* families have very little money.
4 *Bankruptcy* is the result of a large increase in profits.
5 If you *aid* somebody, you give them help.
6 A *philosopher* is a thinker.
7 To *streamline* means to make something simpler, or more efficient.
8 If you want to *reach* somebody, you want to get in touch with them.
9 If you are *outraged* you are very happy about a situation.
10 A *courier* is a type of transport.
11 A company that is *optimistic* is worried about its future.
12 An *emergency* is a dangerous or very difficult situation.

## Unit 6.1

**audit** (n) a financial review of a company, checking how much money or capital is present
*Next week will be the annual expenses audit.*
*The audit discovered some financial irregularities.*

**behalf** (n) done in place of another person
*I am writing on behalf of one of our clients.*
*I can't speak on his behalf.*

**complain** (v) to express a feeling of dissatisfaction with something
*I am writing to complain about the above noted large diesel generator.*
*We have to listen carefully when our customers complain.*

**confirm** (v) to state that something is definitely correct
*I am just writing to confirm…*
*I would like to confirm my attendance at next weeks meeting.*

**consignment** (n) a large amount of goods to be delivered
*This vessel was carrying a consignment for our client.*
*We ordered a consignment of paper, but it has not yet arrived.*

**customer** (n) a person paying for goods or services
*They often play golf with their customers.*
*Our policy is that the customer is always right.*

**evaluate** (v) to assess or decide the value of something or someone
*They will evaluate our travel and entertainment expenses.*
*It is hard to evaluate the success of the new campaign.*

**foreman** (n) the person in charge of a group of workers, especially on a construction site
*The workers stood around waiting for the foreman to arrive.*
*The foreman will explain the plans to the workers.*

**influential** (adj) having a great effect on other people
*He was one of the most influential scientists of the century.*
*His ideas were both brilliant and influential.*

**install** (v) place something in the correct place, often used for computer software or hardware
*The generator must be installed by the end of the week.*
*He installed a new hard disk to replace the broken one.*

**invention** (n) a product or idea that nobody else has thought of before
*His invention, the steam converter, was an important discovery.*
*His invention was patented and made him a millionaire.*

**licensing** (n) getting permission to produce another company's design
*We would like to discuss licensing of your design.*
*We are licensing our design to a Chinese company.*

**monument** (n) a building constructed to remind people of a person or event
*The city is building a monument to this great man.*
*The monument is in need of some repair work.*

**penalty** (n) money that must be paid for failing to do something
*You will be held responsible for any late delivery penalties.*
*He was given a penalty for parking illegally.*

**prompt** (adj) done very quickly
*A prompt reply would be appreciated.*
*He gave me a prompt response to my letter.*

**specification** (n) how something is described, especially a technical product
*The brackets were longer than our design specifications said.*
*We build all our products to the highest specifications.*

**thief** (n) a person that takes items (usually valuable ones) from another without their permission
*While we were sleeping the thieves broke into our house.*
*Thieves stole cash and jewelry from the store.*

**tidy** (adj) clean and well organized
*He lived in a small, tidy, very average house.*
*The desk is very tidy.*

**vital** (adj) extremely important
*It is vital that we receive these parts by Tuesday.*
*New capital is vital to our future success.*

**1 Choose the correct word.**

1 I'd like to ................... about the poor service I received last week.
   (A) evaluate
   (B) complain
   (C) confirm

2 Please would you ................... that the parts will be available next Tuesday?
   (A) install
   (B) complain
   (C) confirm

3 We were pleased to receive a ................... reply from the company.
   (A) prompt
   (B) vital
   (C) tidy

4 Ms. Lloyd is very ................... . She has changed the director's mind about many issues.
   (A) influential
   (B) tidy
   (C) prompt

5 The director would like to ................... the success of our department.
   (A) evaluate
   (B) install
   (C) complain

6 They are going to decide about ................... our premises next week.
   (A) licensing
   (B) licensed
   (C) license

7 A new air conditioning system ................... today.
   (A) is installed
   (B) is being installed
   (C) has installed

8 Mr Rawson's desk is usually very
.................... , but today it's covered in
papers.
(A) prompt
(B) vital
(C) tidy

9 It is ................... that the generator is
repaired immediately.
(A) prompt
(B) influential
(C) vital

## 2 Match the words with the definitions.

| audit consignment customer foreman |
| :-: |
| invention on behalf monument |
| penalty specification thief |

1 a formal examination of a company's
accounts
2 punishments for not doing something
3 a large amount of goods which are
delivered to somebody else
4 do something in the interest of someone
5 a description of something especially
something technical
6 a person that buys something
7 a new creation or discovery
8 something which is built in memory of
somebody
9 a person who steals things from houses
and offices
10 a person who is in charge of a group of
workers

## Unit 7.1

**administrative** (adj) associated with the
running of the company, especially
organization of documents
*He took an administrative position after
graduation.*
*I'll show you your administrative duties after
you have met everyone.*
**anticipate** (v) to think about how
something will happen
*We anticipate complaints from our customers
due to late delivery.*
*We couldn't have anticipated the demand for
our products.*
**applicant** (n) a person that sends their
information to a company to try to get a
job there
*Due to the large number of highly qualified
applicants we have already filled the position.*
*Interested applicants should follow the
procedure below to promptly receive their
library card.*
**appropriately** (adv) correctly, properly
*The weather can be very cold, so please
dress appropriately.*
*Be appropriately polite when addressing the
Duke.*
**assist** (v) to give help with something
*To assist customers, we offer a special 50%
discount on Express costs.*
*The staff assisted us with our luggage
problem.*
**barcode** (n) a series of small black lines
that, when read by a machine, give
product details

*You will receive a library barcode number via
email (enabling you to place reservations).*
*The barcode scanner is broken.*
**benefit** (v) to receive an advantage or help
from something
*Who will benefit from this?*
*Local residents will benefit from increased
job opportunities.*
**certification** (n) official documents
*...use this website if your payment is related
to sewer certification.*
*He provided certification to prove his
qualification.*
**complaint** (n) a spoken or written
statement expressing dissatisfaction with
a product or service
*We anticipate complaints from our customers
due to late delivery.*
*I'd like to make a complaint about the poor
in-flight service.*
**consignment** (n) a large amount of goods
to be delivered
*...concerning the delay to your shipment,
consignment number SD1278.*
*This vessel was carrying a consignment for
our client.*
**enable** (v) to give someone or something
the ability to do something
*You will receive a library number enabling
you to place reservations.*
*The extra money enabled them to buy a new
car.*
**facility** (n) a building or piece of equipment
used for a particular purpose
*Follow the procedure below to make use of
the full range of facilities.*
*The venue provides facilities for disabled
visitors.*
**failure** (n) lack of success
*We are not responsible for failure to meet
delivery schedules...*
*His failure to produce an alibi made the
detective suspicious.*
**inquiry** (n) a question or request asking for
information
*All general inquiries should be addressed to
the Information Section.*
*The receptionist handles all basic inquiries.*
**intend** (v) to plan or mean to do something
*If your payment is intended for past-due
sewer charges...*
*How long do you intend to stay in Australia?*
**intended** (adj) planned
*Who is the intended recipient of this letter?*
*Who is this shipment intended for?*
**intention** (n) what someone plans or
means to do
*Please let us know as soon as possible about
your intentions.*
*He did it with the best of intentions.*
**nominate** (v) to make a decision and name
it/them
*Your card will be available at the branch
library you have nominated.*
*He nominated Johnson as his successor.*
**nonpayment** (n) not paying for something
*If your door has been tagged for
nonpayment, you must call 555-0874 to stop
termination of water service.*
*Nonpayment of bills will result in the
telephone being disconnected.*
**potential** (adj) possible
*Who would not be a potential customer for
this company?*
*It is a potential problem.*

**promptly** (adv) done quickly or as soon as
possible
*Follow the procedure below to receive your
library card promptly.*
*He responded promptly.*
**recipient** (n) the person who receives
something, often mail
*Who is the intended recipient of this letter?*
*The lucky recipient of the golden ticket will
get a free cruise around the Caribbean.*
**reservation** (n) an agreement that a hotel
room, restaurant table, etc. is kept for the
person who orders it
*You will receive a library barcode number via
email (enabling you to place reservations)*
*Reservations can be cancelled up to 24
hours in advance.*
**responsible (for)** (adj) being a person's job
or duty
*I'm responsible for the overall running of the
section.*
*Who is responsible for the maintenance of
the company vehicles.*
**suitably** (adv) enough, to an appropriate
extent
*He is suitably qualified.*
*I hope you are suitably impressed with our
operation, Mr. Bond.*
**tag** (v) to attach a label to something
*If your door has been tagged for
nonpayment, you must call 555-0874*
*Tagged items should be taken to the cash
register for removal of the devices.*
**termination** (n) stopping something or
bringing it to an end
*If your door has been tagged for
nonpayment, you must call 555-0874 to stop
termination of water service.*
*The termination of his contract was due to
unsatisfactory performance.*

## Quiz 7.1

### 1 Find ten words in the puzzle. Match them with their meanings.

| R | E | S | E | R | V | A | T | I | O | N |
|---|---|---|---|---|---|---|---|---|---|---|
| C | R | U | O | S | B | D | I | F | N | T |
| E | Q | C | U | R | D | E | B | A | M | E |
| R | U | E | S | N | G | O | E | I | Y | R |
| T | D | A | E | E | G | D | I | L | N | M |
| I | A | T | C | U | O | E | N | U | E | I |
| F | N | I | E | C | B | S | A | R | L | N |
| I | E | N | R | A | O | E | R | E | T | A |
| C | I | A | A | N | E | S | U | I | E | T |
| A | B | C | N | A | K | S | R | E | N | I |
| T | I | N | Q | U | I | R | Y | A | B | O |
| I | E | F | A | C | I | L | I | T | Y | N |
| O | F | R | E | C | I | P | I | E | N | T |
| N | O | N | P | A | Y | M | E | N | T | M |

1 the person that receives something
2 something that is built or installed to serve
a particular purpose
3 when something is ended
4 the opposite of success
5 the group of spaces, bars and numbers on
something that are used to identify it

6 when something hasn't been paid
7 when something is kept back for somebody
8 giving something official recognition
9 requests for information
10 to plan to do something

## 2 Complete the sentences with the following words.

administrative anticipate
applicants appropriately assist
benefit complaint consignment
enable intended intention
nominate potential promptly
responsible suitably tag

1 Please .................... somebody for *The employee of the year* award.
2 All .................... for the post of foreman should complete the following form.
3 My .................... is to ask for a refund.
4 All employees will .................... from the marketing course.
5 A credit card will .................... you to buy things more freely.
6 We .................... a rise in profits due to successful sales.
7 We can .................... employees with their moving costs abroad.
8 I don't think I'm a(n) .................... candidate for the job as I don't have enough experience.
9 The package didn't arrive at its .................... destination. It went to Singapore instead.
10 The marketing director is .................... for the problems we've had this year.
11 If we leave .................... , we should arrive on time.
12 If your property has a .................... on it, please take it to reception where it will be removed.
13 A new .................... of goods arrived yesterday.
14 I'd like to make a(n) .................... about a colleague.
15 You must speak .................... to the director.
16 John is .................... qualified for the job in France. He speaks French fluently.
17 The order was placed twice due to .................... errors.

## Unit 1.2

**camp** (v) to stay temporarily in a tent
*The family are camping.*
*We enjoy camping in the mountains.*
**collect** (v) to gather things together and keep or bring them somewhere
*The woman is collecting their cups.*
*He collects old swords and displays them in his living room.*
**customer** (n) a person (or company) who buys goods or services
*He's pouring some beer for the customer.*
*Marshall Steel is one of our largest customers.*
**dock** (n) a place alongside water where ships can load and unload
*The skyscrapers stand near the docks.*
*He tied his boat alongside the dock so he could unload the supplies.*

**freeway** (n) a toll-free highway
*They're driving along the freeway.*
*My car broke down on the freeway, miles from the nearest garage.*
**guardrail** (n) a rail acting as a safety barrier at the side of a road, or other dangerous area
*The guardrail divides the highway.*
*His mother told him to hold tightly to the guardrail along the steep mountain path.*
**hold** (v) to keep, carry or temporarily support something
*The woman is holding a glass of wine.*
*Can you hold this light for me while I fix the engine?*
**lie (on something)** (v) to be positioned on a flat horizontal surface
*The snow lies deeply on the farmer's field.*
*I think I saw your hat lying on the bed.*
**monitor** (n) a video device used to view data or images from a computer
*The computer monitors cover the wall.*
*My new computer has a 19 inch flat screen monitor.*
**overpass** (n) a road that crosses over another road
*The overpass casts a shadow on the road.*
*The police car waits under the overpass to catch speeding cars.*
**passenger** (n) someone traveling in a vehicle that is not the driver or a crew member
*The passenger is getting out of the taxi.*
*The passengers of the boat were unhappy about the poor food.*
**pour** (v) to make something (especially a liquid) flow in a stream
*He is pouring some beer for the customer.*
*Pour the milk into the tea.*
**revise** (v) to study before an exam; also, to change something in order to correct, update, or improve it
*The students met to revise their notes before the exam.*
*Her manager asked her to revise the report before the meeting.*
**shine** (v) to be very bright or reflect light
*The sun was shining over the lake.*
*The stars were shining so brightly we could walk without lights.*
**skyscraper** (n) a building that is extremely tall.
*The skyscrapers stand near the docks.*
*The bank built a 50-story skyscraper for its head offices.*
**tent** (n) a portable fabric shelter used for camping
*The tent sits on the beach.*
*After the earthquake, many of the people had to live in tents for several months.*
**withdraw** (v) to take money out of a bank account
*The woman is withdrawing her money.*
*I would like to withdraw $20 from my savings account.*

## 1 Choose the correct word.

1 A(n) *overpass / freeway* is a road that passes over another road.
2 A *monitor / skyscraper* is a very tall building.
3 A *customer / passenger* is somebody who travels.
4 A *dock / tent* is an area where there are boats.
5 To *hold / collect* means to gather things together.
6 To *pour / lie* means to make liquid flow.
7 To *revise / withdraw* means to study before an exam.

## 2 Complete the sentences with the following words.

customer freeway guardrail
holding lie monitor shining
tent withdraw

1 I need to .................... some money for my holiday.
2 It's a dangerous road and should have a .................... .
3 I'm tired and I need to .................... down.
4 The screen on my .................... is dirty. I can't read the information properly.
5 He drove too fast along the .................... .
6 The .................... asked for coffee, but the waiter brought him tea.
7 The sun was .................... so we went for a walk.
8 The man was .................... a bag and an umbrella.
9 I enjoyed sleeping in a .................... when we were on holiday even though it was cold.

## Unit 2.2

**available** (adj) free to do something (for people), or be used for some purpose (for objects)
*Did she say when she would be available?*
*Are there any seats available on the flight?*
**briefcase** (n) a kind of bag, usually made of leather and carried by business people to hold their documents
*This is your briefcase, isn't it?*
*I left my briefcase on the train and had to go to the lost and found to claim it.*
**certain** (adj) sure about something, having no doubts about it
*I can't be certain.*
*I am certain he is the man that attacked me.*
**custom** (n) a tradition or habit, usually associated with a country or region
*Yes, it's an old custom.*
*The custom still continues in local areas.*
**depart** (v) to leave a location, usually by some form of transportation
*No, he's departing tomorrow.*
*My flight departs at 3 p.m. so I have to be at the airport by 1 p.m.*
**detailed** (adj) including a lot of information
*Yes, it was very detailed.*
*He gave me a detailed description of the product.*

**drive** (v) to operate a motorized vehicle
*Can you drive?*
*I learned to drive when I was 17 and I have never had an accident.*

**forget** (v) to be unable to remember
*No, I forgot to ask her.*
*I forgot to bring a pen, so can I borrow one from you?*

**handy** (adj) convenient, or very useful
*I thought it was very handy.*
*The cell phone is a handy tool for keeping in touch when on the move.*

**invite** (v) to ask guests to attend a party or other function
*Everyone has been invited.*
*I am going to invite some of my friends to dinner tomorrow night.*

**member** (n) a person who has joined an organization or group
*No, he's not a member.*
*I was a member of my school's soccer team.*

**mind** (v) to feel strongly that something is not acceptable
*Do you think they would mind if I came along?*
*I don't mind the heat, but I do mind the humidity.*

**prefer** (v) to like one thing more than another
*I prefer pop music.*
*Would you prefer to drink tea or coffee with breakfast?*

**prepare** (v) to get something ready to be used
*Could you help Laura to prepare the documents?*
*The men are preparing dinner in the kitchen.*

**probably** (adv) likely to be true, also used to express an opinion in a more polite manner
*You should probably call them first.*
*He'll probably arrive on the next train.*

**rearrange** (v) to make an alteration to a plan or schedule
*Could you rearrange the venue for me?*
*We can rearrange the meeting for next Tuesday, if that is convenient.*

**(read/go) through** (adv) read or say something from beginning to end
*You read through the notes, didn't you?*
*He went through the process to show us how it worked*

**top** (n) an item of clothing worn on the upper body
*Yes, it's a new top.*
*Which top should I wear with my new skirt?*

**understand** (v) to know the meaning of something and be able to follow it
*Yes, but I couldn't understand them.*
*I understood the announcement.*

**unfortunately** (adv) causing someone to feel regret, or express sadness or disappointment
*Unfortunately, he can't join us because he's on holiday then.*
*We bought tickets, but unfortunately we didn't win anything.*

**upstairs** (n) the floor above where the speaker currently is
*I think he's upstairs.*
*The bathroom is upstairs, next to the master bedroom.*

**venue** (n) the place where an event is to be held
*Could you rearrange the venue for me?*
*The venue for this year's general meeting had to be changed at the last minute.*

## Quiz 2.2

### 1 Choose the correct word.

1 I've got a new, black, leather ................... .
(A) briefcase
(B) venue
(C) custom

2 I bought a ................... to go with my new outfit.
(A) top
(B) venue
(C) briefcase

3 I need to ................... a report for tomorrow's meeting.
(A) forget
(B) drive
(C) prepare

4 I don't ................... doing overtime sometimes, but I don't like working every weekend.
(A) prefer
(B) mind
(C) understand

5 What kind of music do you ...................?
(A) mind
(B) prefer
(C) rearrange

6 I ................... to buy some milk. Could you get some on your way home?
(A) prepared
(B) minded
(C) forgot

7 Could we ................... the meal? I'm busy this evening.
(A) prefer
(B) rearrange
(C) understand

8 I don't ................... what you're saying. Could you repeat it?
(A) forget
(B) understand
(C) mind

9 I'm not ................... what you mean. Could you explain it a bit more?
(A) certain
(B) available
(C) detailed

10 ................... the company hasn't done well this year.
(A) Through
(B) Unfortunately
(C) Neither

11 Let's ................... the document together after work.
(A) go through
(B) do through
(C) be through

12 It's a ................... in our office not to wear a tie on Fridays.
(A) briefcase
(B) custom
(C) top

### 2 Use the definitions to find the words to complete the puzzle.

**Clues**
1 leave
2 operate a vehicle
3 on a floor above
4 ask someone to a party
5 likely to be true
6 useful
7 a person belonging to a group
8 including a lot of information
9 a place where an event is held

## Unit 3.2

**argument** (n) a disagreement that often involves people getting angry with each other
*It turned into a major argument.*
*They haven't been able to settle their argument.*

**attend** (v) to go to or be present at a function (usually formal)
*Why didn't George attend the meeting?*
*I attended my sister's wedding.*

**carelessness** (n) not taking care of what you should be doing
*A worker's carelessness.*
*Carelessness in the factory causes accidents.*

**content** (adj) happy, more than satisfied with the state of something
*He is content in his job.*
*I am content to wait for a chance to be promoted.*

**cover** (v) offer or agree to pay the costs of something
*He will cover all the costs since it was his fault.*
*He is unable to cover the bill.*

**definitely** (adv) certainly, surely, having no doubts
*I definitely plan on staying with the company.*
*It's definitely not an easy test.*

**demanding** (adj) for people, frequently asking for attention, usually unreasonably so; for jobs, very difficult
*My boss is very demanding.*
*It is a demanding job.*

**disagreement** (n) a difference of opinion between people (not as strong as an argument)
*There was a disagreement between attendees.*
*There is still disagreement about what caused the dinosaurs to die out.*

**discount** (n) a reduction in price
*I would like a discount.*
*Can I get a discount if I pay by cash?*

**document** (n) a piece of paper that contains important information
*Who filed these documents?*
*I'll need those documents on my desk first thing tomorrow morning.*

**drastically** (adv) change by a large amount, a sudden and marked difference
*Stubbs wants to drastically cut back on the sales staff.*
*Sales of the product dropped drastically following the recall.*

**exceed** (v) to become greater than
*Don't exceed the speed limit.*
*The results exceeded our expectations.*

**file** (v) to place documents in their correct order in a cabinet
*He hates filing documents.*
*We must finish filing these reports before we go home.*

**graduate** (v) to leave university, school or college with a successful qualification
*He has worked there since he graduated.*
*He graduated top of his class.*

**inexperienced** (adj) new to a job or activity, not having much knowledge about it
*The people she works with are inexperienced.*
*Inexperienced divers should be accompanied at all times.*

**inquire** (v) to ask about
*...inquiring about the man's relative.*
*Can I inquire as to how you became a doctor?*

**mileage** (n) the amount of gas used by a vehicle to operate
*The gas mileage is very low.*
*Compact cars tend to get very good mileage.*

**pushy** (adj) often making other people do what he/she wants them to do, usually unreasonably so
*My new boss is very pushy.*
*I don't like pushy people telling me what to do.*

**receipt** (n) a printed record of a cash transaction, used to prove purchase
*He needs to see the receipt.*
*You'll need to provide the receipt in order to get a refund.*

**recent** (adj) happening in the near past
*To discuss a recent argument with employees.*
*The company has had several recent resignations.*

**refund** (n) money paid back to a customer for an unsatisfactory product or service
*The woman can have a refund.*
*We promise all our customers will be satisfied or we'll give you a full refund.*

**relative** (n) a family member, including uncles, cousins, and more distantly connected people
*...inquiring about the man's relative.*
*Some of my relatives live in Canada.*

**satisfied** (adj) happy with a situation, reasonably content
*I am not satisfied with it.*
*I was satisfied with our sales last year, but I think we can do even better this year.*

**seminar** (n) a class or lesson where a group of people discuss a topic
*It was a seminar on natural resources.*
*The management seminar will be held in room 202 this afternoon.*

**shipping** (n) money paid for delivery of goods
*Free shipping.*
*Shipping is not included in the price.*

**shortcut** (n) a quick route between two places other than the normal route
*I know a shortcut.*
*There's a shortcut over the fields.*

**situation** (n) what happens or happened to you
*I was in the same situation with my dad.*
*We will try to avoid that situation if possible.*

**suggest** (v) to offer your idea on how to do something
*What does the man suggest?*
*I suggest we wait until tomorrow before completing this project.*

**turnover** (n) the amount of money made by a company; for people, the number of people leaving and replaced by the company
*Her company has high employee turnover.*
*The company makes a turnover of $3 million.*

**unappreciated** (adj) not thanked or given credit for ability or actions
*He thinks he is unappreciated.*
*The cleaning staff are an often unappreciated, but very important part of the company.*

## Quiz 3.2

### 1 Read the definitions and write the words.

1 money you get back when you return an item (furedn)  r....................
2 to be present at a function (ndtaet)  a....................
3 to place documents in their correct order (efli)  f....................
4 to ask about (uiinqer)  i....................
5 a family member such as an uncle (tarelvie)  r....................
6 the kind of person who makes others do what he/she wants (usyhp)  p....................
7 a reduction in price (cidsuont)  d....................
8 happy (tecnont)  c....................
9 offer to pay the costs of something (recvo)  c....................
10 a printed record of a transaction (ecirtpe)  r....................

### 2 Find nine words in the puzzle. Then match them with their definitions.

| D | I | S | A | G | R | E | E | M | E | N | T |
|---|---|---|---|---|---|---|---|---|---|---|---|
| E | S | S | T | H | U | S | W | U | L | E | I |
| T | H | E | U | E | T | Y | M | C | S | S | T |
| P | I | E | E | G | W | N | A | I | W | A | U |
| O | P | X | J | A | G | C | A | L | R | T | R |
| U | P | C | W | Q | Y | E | E | N | S | I | N |
| G | I | E | T | M | A | E | S | N | C | S | O |
| L | N | E | U | I | E | R | S | T | T | F | V |
| A | G | D | T | O | A | E | O | N | H | I | E |
| V | E | T | U | N | I | T | E | H | C | E | R |
| A | E | N | I | D | I | C | D | E | O | D | H |
| I | E | M | R | S | E | A | O | M | E | Q | P |
| U | E | W | E | R | B | U | T | I | P | U | I |
| S | D | O | C | U | M | E | N | T | E | B | D |

1 a class or lesson where a group of people discuss a topic
2 a difference of opinion between people
3 money paid for delivery of goods
4 the amount of money made by a company
5 a piece of paper that contains company information
6 to offer an idea about something
7 happening not long ago
8 to become greater than
9 happy with a situation

### 3 Complete the sentences with the following words.

> argument  carelessness  definitely
> demanding  drastically  graduated
> inexperienced  mileage  shortcut
> situation  unappreciated

1 Our manager is in a very difficult .................... because he agrees with the workers' complaints.
2 He knows a lot about the company, but he's very young and .................... .
3 There was a big .................... at the union meeting last night.
4 .................... is dangerous in a factory.
5 I'm .................... going to apply for the job as foreman. I'm ready for a change.
6 We took a .................... and arrived an hour earlier than everybody else.
7 I .................... in English twenty years ago.
8 The .................... on our new car isn't very good, so we use a lot of gas.
9 The director is holding a party to show that nobody is .................... in this office.
10 Being a department manager is very .................... sometimes.
11 Staff were .................... reduced last year when the company's profits fell.

## Unit 4.2

**bankrupt** (adj) of companies or individuals, to not have enough money to pay expenses or debts
*After years of bad sales, the company was bankrupt.*
*It is a bankrupt organization.*

**boast** (v) to proudly talk about one's achievements
*We are also proud to boast two junior regional champions.*
*He always boasts about his new car.*

**closure** (n) the act of closing a factory, shop or other business
*The closure of factories led to rising unemployment.*
*We will need to increase profits to avoid branch closures.*

**cordless** (adj) not connected by any cables
*It has a cordless telephone handset.*
*The cordless speakers work by using radio technology.*

**debt** (n) money that is owed to another person or, often, a bank or other financial institution
*He was unable to pay his debts.*
*The company accumulated large debts by unwisely expanding.*

**delighted** (adj) very happy
*I'm delighted to be able to report that sales are up.*
*He was delighted with his birthday gift.*

**depressing** (adj) likely to cause someone to feel unhappy or disappointed
*It is one bright spot on an otherwise depressing afternoon.*
*These are depressing sales figures.*

**double** (v) to become twice as large
*We almost doubled the number of customers.*
*The price has doubled since last year.*

**elderly (people)** (adj) of people, old
*There is a home for elderly people near my house.*
*Society has a responsibility to take care of the elderly.*

**expand** (v) to increase in size·
*Last year we expanded our field of operations.*
*The number of internet users expanded rapidly in the late twentieth century.*

**gesture** (n) something done to express your feelings, often to express thanks
*It would be a nice gesture to get him something for his birthday.*
*It was a generous gesture to donate your prize to charity.*

**laden** (adj) carrying a large amount of something
*It is almost impossible for trucks laden with aid to get through.*
*The grandparents arrived, laden with presents.*

**landslide** (n) a large amount of earth or rocks that falls down the side of a mountain or hill
*The heavy rains led to landslides in some areas.*
*The road to the village was blocked by a landslide.*

**mention** (v) to tell someone a piece of news, often in casual conversation
*Don't mention this to him.*
*John mentioned that he was thinking of moving to New York.*

**overall** (adj) total, complete, related to the whole thing
*It will improve your overall fitness.*
*Although not as cheap as some models, this one has the best overall features.*

**politician** (n) a government official, chosen by the people
*The politicians will meet to discuss the new tax laws.*
*Our local politician will be visiting the hospital this week.*

**remarkable** (adj) amazing, incredible, different to normal (generally used to express a positive feeling)
*It was remarkable.*
*It is in remarkable condition.*

**renovate** (v) to repair something to a condition as good as new
*It was totally renovated just six months ago.*
*The house really needs to be renovated.*

**respond** (v) to do something to meet another person's needs or request
*You will need to be able to respond to customer needs.*
*I'd like you to respond to this inquiry.*

**responsible (for)** (adj) being a person's job or duty
*I'm responsible for the overall running of the section.*
*Who is responsible for completing the annual sales report?*

**runner up** (n) the person, team or group that finishes a competition in second place
*He was the national runner up.*
*The runner up got the silver medal.*

**shareholders** (n) people that own stocks or shares of a company
*Each shareholder receives a percentage of the company's profits.*
*There is a shareholders' meeting next week.*

**spacious** (adj) large, wide, having lots of space
*The kitchen is quite spacious.*
*There is a spacious office with a view of Manhattan.*

**struggle** (v) to find something difficult to do or complete
*Workers are struggling to deliver aid to the more remote villages.*
*I struggled to get into university.*

**tremor** (n) an earth movement caused by an earthquake
*Although the earthquake was 200 miles away, we could feel the tremors here.*
*Strong tremors shook the city in the early morning.*

**unfavorable** (adj) not to someone's advantage, bad
*Sales were affected by unfavorable exchange rates.*
*We were unable to ski, due to unfavorable weather conditions.*

**venture** (n) a new business project, often one considered risky
*This venture has been very successful.*
*We'll need some financial assistance with this venture.*

**venture capitalist** (n) a person that invests in new businesses, expecting to make money in return
*We approached some venture capitalists about support for developing our prototype.*
*Without venture capitalist money, the project would never have been successful.*

## Quiz 4.2

### 1 Choose the correct word.

1 I think it would be a nice .................... to buy James a leaving present.
(A) closure
(B) gesture
(C) venture

2 The .................... of the factory resulted in strikes.
(A) tremor
(B) debt
(C) closure

3 The heavy rains caused a .................... .
(A) landslide
(B) tremor
(C) venture

4 The company .................... last year which means more people will be employed.
(A) renovated
(B) expanded
(C) struggled

5 I am proud to .................... a huge increase in profits for the company.
(A) boast
(B) expand
(C) double

6 A good manager .................... to the requests of his or her workers.
(A) boasts
(B) responds
(C) struggles

7 I need to .................... the fact there will be some job losses next year.
(A) mention
(B) respond
(C) renovate

8 Our offices are small. We need something more .................... .
(A) delighted
(B) laden
(C) spacious

9 There were a few problems, but .................... the meeting went well.
(A) overall
(B) delighted
(C) remarkable

10 The ships were .................... with goods.
(A) responsible
(B) spacious
(C) laden

11 Our sales figures for last year were .................... . They need to improve.
(A) depressing
(B) remarkable
(C) favorable

12 Simon is .................... for the new project.
(A) depressing
(B) responsible
(C) overall

### 2 Read the definitions and write true or false.

1 A *venture* is a new business project.
2 A *runner up* usually comes first in a competition.
3 If you *struggle* to do something you find it difficult to do.
4 If a price *doubles* it goes down by half.
5 A *politician* is a government official.
6 *Venture capitalists* are people that invest in new businesses.
7 *Shareholders* usually receive the whole of a company's profits.
8 A *debt* is money owed to somebody.
9 A *tremor* is an earth movement during an earthquake.
10 If a company is *bankrupt* it doesn't have enough money to continue.
11 To *renovate* means to improve the way somebody looks.
12 *Elderly* people are old.
13 If something is *unfavorable* it isn't to someone's advantage.
14 *Remarkable* means amazing.
15 If something is *cordless* it is connected by cables.
16 If you are *delighted* with something you are very happy with it.

## Unit 5.2

**advanced** (adj) including recent technology
*I wish I had bought a more advanced model.*
*The machines are the most advanced ones available.*

**advise** (v) to tell someone what you think they should do
*I advised her to invest in steel.*
*He advised me not to buy now.*

**alternative** (adj) being a further choice, or a different option
*Union leaders agreed to discuss an alternative proposal.*
*We need to find an alternative route to the station.*

**applicant** (n) a person that sends their information to a company to try to get a job there
*The applicant lied about his previous experience in the field.*
*There are at least fifty applicants for each job.*

**careless** (adj) lacking in attention (Also see glossary 3.2, **carelessness**)
*Most workplace accidents are due to careless practices.*
*He was charged with careless driving by the police.*

**commercial** (adj) connected with the buying or selling of goods to make a profit
*The product was not a commercial success.*
*It is a commercial operation.*

**demand** (v) to make a very clear request using direct language
*I demanded to speak to the manager.*
*If it is not possible, then I demand to know why.*

**entrée** (n) the main course of a meal in a restaurant
*I waited more than thirty minutes for my entrée to arrive.*
*Would you like meat or fish for your entrée?*

**evidence** (n) something used to connect a person with a crime
*The police are searching for new evidence.*
*There is no evidence to link him to the robbery.*

**gradually** (adv) at a slow pace, not quickly
*Black and white television sets were gradually replaced.*
*He is gradually recovering from his injuries.*

**illegal** (adj) something done against the rules of the country
*...to protect data from illegal attacks, the systems section installed anti-virus protection.*
*His suitcase contained several illegal items.*

**impression** (n) how something makes you feel, your initial feeling about it
*I get the impression he is not interested in the project.*
*You will make a good impression at the conference next month.*

**limousine** (n) a long, luxury car, used to take (usually rich) passengers from one place to another
*The President's limousine should be here soon.*
*We can send a limousine to meet you at the airport.*

**principal** (adj) main, most important
*It appears that our principal rivals are considering our proposal.*
*The principal reason is that customers traditionally stay at home on that day.*

**prior to** (prep) before
*Passengers must complete an immigration questionnaire prior to arrival.*
*I ate dinner prior to coming here today.*

**protection** (n) defense against some kind of attack
*...to protect data from illegal attacks, the systems section installed anti-virus protection.*
*Wear a hat as a basic form of protection from the suns rays.*

**questionnaire** (n) a series of written questions to determine a person's opinions, status or habits
*Passengers must complete an immigration questionnaire.*
*Can I ask you to help me with this questionnaire?*

**receptionist** (n) the person in an office or hotel that greets visitors or answers the telephone
*The receptionist offered to take a message for me.*
*She is my new receptionist.*

**regret** (v) to feel bad about something you have done in the past; to wish something had been done differently
*I regret not buying a more advanced camera.*
*Do you regret leaving your previous job?*

**resent** (v) to be angry about something
*The first applicant seemed to resent the questions.*
*I resent the fact that he was promoted ahead of me.*

**rivals** (n) competitors, those trying to achieve the same goal as an individual or company
*Our business rivals strongly oppose our takeover proposal.*
*Following the takeover, there were no real rivals in their business.*

**takeover** (n) when one company buys another company
*Our principal rivals may be considering a takeover proposal.*
*We will resist any attempts at a takeover.*

**variety** (n) choice, selection, many different things
*During winter many people enjoy a variety of winter sports.*
*There was a wide variety of wines available.*

## Quiz 5.2

### 1 Choose the correct word.

1 I .................... see the director immediately.
   (A) demanded
   (B) demanded to
   (C) advised to

2 They .................... not spending more money on advertising last year.
   (A) demanded to
   (B) regretted to
   (C) regretted

3 The foreman .................... him to leave the company.
   (A) advised
   (B) resented
   (C) demanded for

4 Everybody .................... being at the meeting.
   (A) resented to
   (B) resented
   (C) resented of

5 Unfortunately our .................... applicant can't come for an interview today.
   (A) principal
   (B) advanced
   (C) careless

6 Our company is planning a .................... early next year.
   (A) takeup
   (B) takein
   (C) takeover

7 The new model is more .................... than our last one.
   (A) advanced
   (B) illegal
   (C) careless

8 There will be a light lunch .................... to the meeting.
   (A) advanced
   (B) commercial
   (C) prior

9 The accounts department made some .................... mistakes.
   (A) careless
   (B) illegal
   (C) principal

10 The workers aren't interested in the proposal, so the foreman is going to discuss some .................... ideas.
   (A) prior
   (B) principal
   (C) alternative

### 2 Read the definitions and write *true* or *false*.

1 A *questionnaire* is an interview with somebody.
2 An *applicant* is a manager.
3 A *limousine* is a type of car.
4 Police need *evidence* to catch criminals.
5 A *receptionist* talks to the public, answers the phone, takes messages, etc.
6 If something is permitted, it's *illegal*.
7 If something is *commercial* it's for profit.
8 People who do a *variety* of jobs have more than one responsibility.
9 If your computer has *protection*, it won't get a virus.
10 Your *rivals* usually get along with you.
11 You would normally eat an *entrée* at the end of a meal.
12 If you make a good *impression*, people like you.
13 If something happens *gradually,* it happens very quickly.

## Unit 6.2

**attentively** (adv) paying close attention to what someone is saying
*John never listened attentively in class.*
*The audience listened to the presentation attentively.*

**cautiously** (adv) carefully, without taking any risks
*...to begin cautiously moving up the south ridge.*
*Drive cautiously in bad weather.*

**comfortable** (adj) pleasant or nice to the touch
*Your new chair looks very comfortable.*
*Our suits are both comfortable and hard-wearing.*

**consistently** (adv) without changing
*Our sales have been consistently good in the last three months.*
*He has been consistently late since he started.*

**eager** (adj) wanting to do something very much
*He seems eager, but in two weeks he has been late twice.*
*The new employees are eager to learn the job.*

**emerge** (v) to come out of something
*They emerged from their tents...*
*The politicians emerged from the meeting at 3 a.m. looking very sleepy.*

**endurance** (n) the ability to survive extreme conditions or very hard work
*...and the limits of human endurance.*
*Marathon runners try to develop their endurance by a combination of training and diet.*

**enforced** (adj) made to do something according to the rules
*I have had to caution him about the strictly enforced policy on safety.*
*There is an enforced speed limit on this section of highway.*

**grueling** (adj) hard, taking a long time and requiring a lot of effort
*They reached the summit after a grueling climb.*
*The Hawaii Iron-man is a grueling race.*

**harshness** (n) rough and unpleasantness
*Their struggle against the harshness of Mother Nature...*
*The harshness of his words surprised me.*

**meticulously** (adv) with great attention to detail
*I spent weeks meticulously planning every detail.*
*The artists paint each flower meticulously by hand.*

**restore** (v) to repair something to its previous condition
*The original prints have been restored to modern digital standards.*
*Painting damaged in the fire were restored by expert artists.*

**serious** (adj) not to be taken lightly
*We have serious problems in our Tokyo office.*
*The board had a serious discussion to decide the direction of the company.*

**strictly** (adv) without exception, in one way only
*I have reminded workers about our strictly enforced policy on safety.*
*He is strictly vegetarian.*

**struggle** (n) a fight against something, to not give up
*Their struggle against the harshness of Mother Nature...*
*It is a struggle to save enough money each month.*

**timely** (adj) done just in time, or at exactly the right time
*The defender made a timely interception to prevent the goal.*
*We aim to deliver our products in a timely manner.*

**triumph** (n) a great achievement, a wonderful result
*Hillary's climb of Mount Everest was a triumph of courage and spirit.*
*England's triumph in the 1966 World Cup has never been forgotten by the English.*

## Quiz 6.2

### 1 Complete the sentences with the following words.

> comfortable  consistently  eager
> emerged  enforced  grueling
> meticulously  restored
> serious  timely

1 They .................... planned the details of the journey.
2 Paul's .................... . He started work at 6 o'clock this morning.
3 The company has strictly .................... security rules.
4 Rising prices are a .................... problem at the moment.
5 The beds in the hotel are very .................... .
6 Ms. Howard's work performance has .................... improved.
7 It was a .................... three-day journey.
8 His arrival was .................... . We were just about to discuss a subject he's very experienced in.
9 The damaged piano has finally been .................... .
10 When we finally .................... from the meeting, we went to lunch.

### 2 Choose the correct word.

1 The difficult climb tested the men's .................... .
(A) triumph
(B) struggle
(C) endurance

2 They stopped climbing because of the .................... of the weather conditions.
(A) harshness
(B) struggle
(C) triumph

3 The successful takeover was a .................... for the company.
(A) harshness
(B) triumph
(C) comfortable

4 The long journey was a .................... for everybody.
(A) triumph
(B) struggle
(C) harshness

5 The project is difficult, so we'll continue .................... .
(A) cautiously
(B) timely
(C) eagerly

6 It's .................... no smoking in the restaurant.
(A) attentively
(B) consistently
(C) strictly

7 I listened .................... to what my colleague said.
(A) attentively
(B) strictly
(C) timely

## Unit 7.2

**alumnus** (plural **alumni**) (n) previous student (usually of a university) that has graduated
*A student alumni magazine*
*He is one of our more famous alumni.*

**anticipate** (v) to think about how something will happen
*We couldn't have anticipated the demand for our products.*
*I was unable to confirm the anticipated launch date.*

**application** (n) a formal request, usually written, for something
*We are now open for membership applications.*
*The university accepted applications from over one hundred different countries.*

**bulletin** (n) a newsletter distributed freely, especially within a company
*A community services bulletin.*
*This month's bulletin doesn't contain any interesting articles.*

**campaign** (n) carefully planned actions or a series of actions leading to a final goal
*We are expecting to confirm a well-known model for the campaign shortly.*
*The President's campaign took him to each of the states.*

**cancellation** (n) asking a reservation or order to be stopped
*The effective date of the cancellation is the date the withdrawal notice is received by the center.*
*We must try to prevent the cancellation of contracts.*

**cardiovascular** (adj) related to the heart and blood vessels
*This new gym features a range of cardiovascular equipment.*
*You need to improve your cardiovascular system before attempting a marathon.*

**complaint** (n) a spoken or written statement expressing dissatisfaction with a product
*The customer service department deals with all complaints.*
*We received a complaint about improper garbage disposal.*

**comprehensive** (adj) complete, without anything missing, very detailed
*The exercise studio will offer a comprehensive program of dance...*
*The software comes with a comprehensive manual.*

**criticism** (n) a negative opinion of something stated aloud or in writing
*Weather forecasters soon faced criticism for failing to predict...*
*Criticism of the movie centered on the weak plot and lack of laughs.*

**disposal** (n) the throwing away of waste products or garbage
*Improper disposal of waste materials can cause pollution.*
*We received a complaint about improper garbage disposal.*

**driftwood** (n) waste pieces of wood that have been left on the shore by the tide
*Along the south coast, damage to yachts was extensive and a famous pier was even reduced to driftwood.*
*He built a fire from driftwood to keep himself warm.*

**extensive** (adj) a large amount, a wide area, a lot
*Damage to yachts and boat yards was extensive.*
*He owns an extensive property.*

**fail** (v) to not succeed to do something
*I failed my driving test three times.*
*Weather forecasters soon faced criticism for failing to predict the severity of the weather.*

**feature** (v) to be included
*It's a great film and features the best Hollywood actors.*
*This new Muscles Gym features a fully stocked workout gym.*

**forecaster** (n) a scientist that predicts the weather
*Forecasters incorrectly assumed that the weather system would...*
*According to the forecasters, tomorrow will be fine.*

**freak** (adj) out of the ordinary, not normal, usually in a bad way
*Damage caused by freak natural occurrences.*
*The freak wave caused the ship to capsize and sink.*

**further** (adv) additional, more
*I look forward to discussing this sales opportunity with you further.*
*We walked further than last week.*

**impending** (adj) coming in the very near future, usually referring to something bad
*News didn't mention the impending storm.*
*The workers went on strike to protest against the impending merger.*

**improper** (adj) not correct, not suitable, impolite
*We received a complaint about improper garbage disposal.*
*He used improper language.*

**inaccuracy** (n) mistakes, errors
*The inaccuracy of some weather forecasts.*
*The inaccuracy of his work cost the company thousands of dollars.*

**infer** (v) how someone understands something based on their reasoning
*What can be inferred about the New Health product line?*
*It can be inferred that the company was not performing well.*

**medical** (adj) to do with medicine, doctors or treatment
*If there is a medical reason for the request...*
*He requires urgent medical treatment.*

**memorandum** (n) a written note or message without the formal address of a

letter, usually distributed within a company
*He left a memorandum on your desk.*
*Did you read the latest memorandum?*

**occurrence** (n) something that happens, usually unexpectedly
*Damage caused by freak natural occurrences.*
*There were more occurrences later that month.*

**onwards** (adv) continuing from
*From the second lesson onwards,...*
*From that day onwards, his reputation was assured.*

**opportunity** (n) a chance
*This is a once in a lifetime opportunity.*
*I look forward to meeting you and discussing this sales opportunity with you further.*

**participant** (n) a person taking part in an event
*The effective date of the withdrawal, regardless of the date the participant stopped attending the class.*
*3,000 participants completed the marathon.*

**pier** (n) a long thin structure attached to the land that stands in the sea and that boats can be secured to
*Along the south coast, damage to yachts was extensive and a famous pier was even reduced to driftwood.*
*There used to be a theater on the end of the pier.*

**predict** (v) to imagine how something will happen in the future
*Weather forecasters soon faced criticism for failing to predict the severity of the weather.*
*I predict that next year will be our most successful yet.*

**refund** (n) money paid back to a customer for an unsatisfactory product or service
*Refunds for fitness programs will not be processed until...*
*The woman can have a refund.*

**regardless** (adv) without consideration of something
*The effective date is the date..., regardless of when the participant...*
*Anyone can do it, regardless of age or experience.*

**remittance** (n) payments for goods or merchandise (a formal word)
*Cash/Check remittances will be refunded by check.*
*All remittances must be made by the end of the month.*

**severity** (n) how serious something is
*Weather forecasters faced criticism for failing to predict the severity of...*
*The severity of the fire was clear from the number of fire trucks summoned.*

**strategy** (n) planning or way of doing something
*I will be coming to London to discuss our pricing strategies in more detail.*
*His strategy is to wait for his opponent to attack, then counter quickly.*

**swathe** (n) a long area of land
*...instead it cut a swathe right across the south of the country.*
*The army took another swathe of land.*

**unattended** (adj) not participating, not attending
*The way to obtain refunds for unattended courses.*
*The gasoline pumps were unattended.*

**unprecedented** (adj) referring to something that has never happened before
*A 'storm' caused unprecedented damage.*
*It was an unprecedented fourth successive title for Anderson.*

**withdrawal** (n) decision to stop taking part in some event
*The effective date of the withdrawal is the date the withdrawal notice is received by the center.*
*His withdrawal from the race...*

**yacht** (n) a kind of boat, usually small and powered by sails; also used to describe large motorboats
*Along the south coast, damage to yachts was extensive and a famous pier was even reduced to driftwood.*
*The dinner party was held aboard his luxury yacht.*

## Quiz 7.2

**1 Use the definitions to find the words to complete the puzzle.**

**Clues**
1 bits of wood you find in the sea and on beaches
2 you can walk on this; it stretches over the sea
3 to make guesses about the future
4 if something isn't done correctly, it's i....
5 an unusual happening such as in the weather
6 a person who talks about the future of the weather
7 the money you get back if your return something to a shop
8 a written message or reminder
9 the opposite of succeed
10 a way of doing something
11 a sailing boat

## 2 Complete the sentences with the following words.

> alumni  applications  bulletin  campaign  cancellation  cardiovascular  complaints  criticism  occurrences  participants  remittance  swathe  withdrawal

1  There has been a long .................... by the union to improve working conditions.
2  There have been three .................... from the class and one person never attended.
3  There was a(n) ...................., so I was able to get a seat on an earlier flight.
4  There were seven .................... in the company football match.
5  There have been several .................... this month from unhappy customers.
6  He got a small .................... for his train ticket and other expenses.
7  There was a(n) .................... reunion at the university.
8  The weekly .................... gives information about staff benefits.
9  We have had six .................... for the job of foreman.
10  I usually do .................... exercise at the gym.
11  There has been a lot of .................... of the new retirement plan.
12  A .................... is a long area of land.
13  There have been several unusual .................... recently, including a storm.

## 3 Read the definitions and write *true* or *false*.

1  If a meeting is *unattended* it means a lot of people were there.
2  If you *infer* something you say something clearly.
3  When you *anticipate* something, you expect it to happen.
4  To *feature* means to include.
5  *Impending* means expected to happen soon.
6  *Medical* relates to doctors and hospitals.
7  If a program is *comprehensive*, it's incomplete.
8  If something is *unprecedented* it's very unusual.
9  *Extensive* means a lot.
10  The meaning of *severity* is serious.
11  *Inaccuracy* means that something has been done perfectly.
12  If you do something *regardless* you aren't worried about any potential problems.
13  *Onwards* means in the past.
14  If you want to discuss something *further* you haven't finished talking.
15  An *opportunity* is a chance.
16  *Disposal* is rubbish.

## Unit 1.3

**backpack** (n)  a large sturdy bag, worn on the back by hikers and travelers
*The backpack is being filled.*
*John's backpack was so heavy he could barely lift it.*

**bored** (adj)  uninterested or having little to do
*The man looks bored.*
*John soon became bored with life on the farm and moved back to the city.*

**chef** (n)  a professional, usually trained cook
*The chef is standing by the grill.*
*The restaurant was popular because of its famous chef.*

**cry** (v)  to shed tears or make a loud noise usually as a result of strong emotion
*The woman is crying on the bed.*
*The boy cried for days after his dog died.*

**diagram** (n)  a usually simple drawing or chart used to explain something
*The man is drawing a diagram.*
*I just couldn't understand the diagram in the instruction sheet.*

**discuss** (v)  to talk on a particular subject with two or more people
*They are discussing the TV program.*
*I would like to discuss our sales figures for May.*

**draw** (v)  to make a picture with pens, pencils or anything other than paint
*The man is drawing a diagram.*
*The children drew funny faces on their notebooks.*

**figurine** (n)  a small, often pottery or wood figure used for decoration
*The wooden figurines are on sale.*
*He bought his mother a lovely figurine of a dancing girl.*

**fix** (v)  to repair something that is broken
*They are fixing the boy's bicycle.*
*I sent the damaged radio back to the company to be fixed.*

**focused** (adj)  concentrated attentively on one thing
*The man is focused on his work.*
*His goals were focused on completing the project by the target date.*

**forest** (n)  an area of land covered with trees
*A forest grows in the valley.*
*I love to go hiking through the forest in the spring.*

**grill** (n)  a flat metal or barred plate used for cooking
*The chef is standing by the grill.*
*The cook was cooking bacon and eggs on the grill.*

**hang** (v)  to suspend something from above, e.g. from a hook or string
*The clothes hang in the closet.*
*The monkey was hanging from the tree by its tail.*

**hiker** (n)  someone who walks in the hills or countryside for recreation
*The hiker is sitting on the ground.*
*The mountain trail was packed with hikers enjoying the nice weather.*

**kneel** (v)  to rest or support oneself on the knees
*The man is kneeling near the dog.*
*I had to kneel down to see under the bed.*

**pier** (n)  a long thin structure attached to the land that stands in the sea and that boats can be secured to
*The boat is tied to the pier.*
*I used to fish off the end of the pier.*

**plain (view)** (adj)  clearly visible, simple
*The signs are in plain view.*
*The design of the new car was plain but attractive.*

**plow** (v)  to clear or cut a path through something
*The truck is plowing the road.*
*The farmer plowed his fields every spring.*

**popular** (adj)  well known or liked by a large number of people
*The seaside is popular today.*
*Barry Glimmer used to be a popular singer.*

**ruin** (v)  to damage something beyond repair
*The jacket has been ruined.*
*His chances of getting the job were ruined by his arrest for drunk driving.*

**scene** (n)  a section of a movie or play
*They are filming a scene.*
*I liked the scene where the detective explains the crime.*

**seaside** (n)  land on or close to the sea
*The seaside is popular today.*
*The couple bought a small cottage near the seaside.*

**stack** (v)  to arrange things into a pile
*Logs are stacked in the yard.*
*Can you stack these cans in the display by the entrance?*

**steep** (adj)  with a sharply rising or falling slope
*The mountain is steep.*
*The chart showed a steep drop in sales for the month.*

**tie** (v)  to make a knot in a rope or string to hold something
*She is tying her shoe.*
*The boat is tied to the pier.*

**trawler** (n)  a boat used to catch fish using a large net
*The trawler goes out to sea.*
*In the summer, Jake worked on a tuna trawler.*

**valley** (n)  an area of low land often between mountains
*A forest grows in the valley.*
*The bottom of the valley featured a fast river.*

**weight** (n)  the amount that somebody/thing weighs
*The woman is checking her weight.*
*The weight of the prize winning pig was over 2000 pounds.*

**wooden** (adj)  made of wood
*The wooden figurines are on sale.*
*Wooden canoes are heavier than fiberglass ones.*

**yard** (n)  an area of ground used for a particular purpose
*Logs are stacked in the yard.*
*He parked his truck in the storage yard next to the factory.*

## Quiz 1.3

### 1 Choose the correct word.

1  After dinner the children .................... all the dishes in the kitchen.
  (A) ruined
  (B) fixed
  (C) stacked

2  Please .................... your coat in the cupboard in the hall.
  (A) stack
  (B) hang
  (C) draw

3 Could you please check this
.................... ? The charts have been
incorrectly labelled.
(A) diagram
(B) weight
(C) yard

4 The path to the top of the mountain was
too .................... , so we were unable to
reach the summit.
(A) steep
(B) plain
(C) popular

5 Please don't interrupt. I'm ....................
an important contract.
(A) discussing
(B) crying
(C) drawing

6 During exam week the students were
.................... their revision.
(A) focused on
(B) focused to
(C) focused with

7 Our day out to the .................... was
fantastic – we swam and walked along
the beach.
(A) forest
(B) seaside
(C) valley

8 The .................... enjoyed cooking on an
open fire when they reached the
campsite.
(A) trawlers
(B) figurines
(C) hikers

9 The Golden Temple is very .................... ;
more than half a million visitors go there
every year.
(A) wooden
(B) bored
(C) popular

## 2 Choose the correct word to complete the definition.

1 A *chef / hiker* is a professionally trained
cook.
2 A *valley / forest* is an area of low land
between mountains.
3 A *grill / weight* is a flat metal plate that you
can cook things on.
4 If you *ruin / fix* something you cannot repair
it.
5 A person who is *bored / wooden* is no
longer interested in what he or she is doing.
6 If you *draw / discuss* something you need a
pencil and some paper.
7 To *plow / stack* is something that a farmer
does to the land before planting seeds.
8 To *kneel / hang* means to you are resting
on your knees.
9 To *plow / tie* something means to hold
something with a rope.

## 3 Complete the sentences with the following words.

| backpack cry figurine fixed |
| forest pier plain scene trawler |
| weight wooden yard |

1 The results of the survey are very .................... :
everyone wants to pay less tax.
2 My grandfather made this old ....................
chair from a tree that fell down in the
garden.
3 My watch is not working properly; I must get
it .................... .
4 I'm going to get a new .................... for my
trip to the Rocky Mountains.
5 We have to move the old desks into the
.................... because new office furniture
is arriving tomorrow.
6 Hikers are not allowed to light fires in the
.................... at any time of year.
7 The maximum .................... for an airmail
package to Europe is 2,000 grams.
8 They put the pottery .................... on the
shelf next to the other decorations.
9 This fish is taken straight from the
.................... to the fish market.
10 The little girl had hurt her knee badly, but
she didn't .................... .
11 Let's go down to the .................... to watch
all the boats come in.
12 In the film there's a really scary
.................... in the woods late at night.

## Unit 2.3

**actually** (adv)  in fact, really, in truth
*Actually, we don't have any plans.*
*I don't actually know.*

**bank** (n)  a place where customers can save
and withdraw money, as well as getting
help with other financial services
*Could you tell me where a bank is?*
*I have to get some money from the bank
before we go out tonight.*

**block** (n)  an area of town marked by streets
on all sides
*If you go across the street and turn left you
should see a Chinese restaurant about a
block down.*
*The bus stop is three blocks from here.*

**boardroom** (n)  a room in a company used
to hold important meetings, especially
those involving the president and top
executives
*How do I get to the boardroom?*
*The boardroom is not available this
afternoon.*

**cafeteria** (n)  a kind of restaurant where
customers choose their food from a
counter and bring it to the table
themselves
*Down the hall, turn left and it's just across
from the cafeteria.*
*The food in the cafeteria is quite good.*

**chair** (v)  to be in charge of a meeting
*I have to chair a meeting.*
*The president usually chairs the meetings,
but he is not here today.*

**crash** (v)  of computers, to stop working
suddenly without warning, often temporarily
*My laptop crashed and I lost all the data I
was working on.*
*It seems to have crashed.*

**cupboard** (n)  a cabinet with doors, usually
in the kitchen, used to keep cups, plates,
dishes and other items. Also used to
describe a very small storage room
*The chairs are locked in the cupboard.*
*Put the dishes in the cupboard when you
have finished.*

**deliver** (v)  to take something to give to
someone
*The package was delivered about an hour
ago.*
*My paper wasn't delivered this morning.*

**drawer** (n)  part of a piece of furniture
(e.g. a desk) that can be pulled open to
reveal a box into which items can be
placed
*In the drawer, as usual.*
*The knives and forks go in the top drawer.*

**enter** (v)  to go into something
*The staff enter together.*
*You can't enter the office until the security
alarm has been switched off.*

**hospital** (n)  a place where sick or injured
people receive treatment to help them
recover
*Could you show me the way to the hospital?*
*He was in hospital for a month after the car
accident.*

**journey** (n)  a trip (usually long) from one
place to another
*How long did the journey take?*
*The journey takes twelve hours by plane.*

**(be) kept** (v)  be placed in a particular
location
*Where is the A4 paper kept?*
*The transport claim forms are kept in the
bottom drawer.*

**(be) ordered (to do something)** (v)  be
made to do something by another person
*Yes, they were ordered to do it.*
*We were ordered to leave the building by the
police.*

**package** (n)  an item, usually wrapped in
paper or in a box, to be delivered by mail
*When did the package arrive?*
*There is a package from head office on your
desk.*

**polite** (adj)  displaying good manners
*It's not polite to stare.*
*The waiter was not very polite to the
customers.*

**refrigerator** (n)  a large kitchen appliance
used to keep food chilled and fresh
*It's in the refrigerator behind the vegetables.*
*There is no milk in the refrigerator.*

**several** (adj)  more than one or two
*She's been working here for several months.*
*There are several ways to get to the airport.*

**stare** (v)  to look very directly at something
or someone
*It's not polite to stare.*
*She is staring at the goods on display.*

## Quiz 2.3

### 1 Complete the sentences with the following words.

| actually  bank  blocks  cafeteria |
| cupboard  drawer  kept  ordered |
| polite  several |

1 Walk down three .................... and turn
right into 39th Street.
2 The holiday request forms are kept in the
top .................... of the filing cabinet.
3 The paper is stored in the stationery
.................... next to the photocopier.

4 You can use your credit card to withdraw foreign currency at the .................... .
5 Following the health inspection they were .................... to close the kitchen immediately.
6 Let's have lunch in the .................... ; it's quicker than going to a restaurant.
7 I can't find the key to storeroom. Do you know where it is .................... ?
8 We have .................... new products going on the market this season.
9 We live in the center of town, .................... , not the suburbs.
10 It is .................... to greet your neighbors when you see them.

## 2 Read the definitions and write *true* or *false*.

1 You keep food warm in a *refrigerator*.
2 You can send a *package* by mail.
3 The *boardroom* is where staff can enjoy cheap meals.
4 A *hospital* is a place for sick and injured people.
5 To *deliver* something means to pick it up from the Post Office.
6 When your computer *crashes* it freezes and stops working.
7 To *enter* a building means to leave it.
8 If you *chair* a meeting you are in charge of it.
9 A *journey* is a kind of magazine.
10 To *stare* means to listen to someone very carefully.

## Unit 3.3

**amusing** (adj) funny, likely to make people laugh
*He really is an amusing speaker.*
*It was amusing.*
**available** (adj) free to do something (for people), or be used for some purpose (for objects)
*Did she say when she would be available?*
*The special is only available until 1:30 p.m.*
**calculations** (n) the process of working to find the answer to a mathematical problem
*Your team is already half way through the calculations.*
*I think there is a mistake in your calculations.*
**catch** (v) take a bus, train or other form of public transport
*You better catch a taxi.*
*If you don't catch the next train you'll be late.*
**coach** (adj) standard class on American trains
*Coach class is fine.*
*We traveled coach class.*
**deposit** (n) the act of placing money into a bank account (opposite of withdrawal)
*Deposits can be made between 9 a.m. and 3 p.m.*
*I'd like to make a deposit, please.*
**desperate** (adj) wanting, or needing to do something very much
*He's desperate to work overseas.*
*The local people are desperate to leave the region.*

**heel** (n) the back part of the foot, furthest from the toes, or the similar place on a shoe
*We have one with the same heel.*
*I banged my heel against the door when I was walking out of the room.*
**initially** (adv) in the beginning, to begin with
*What does the woman initially think?*
*Initially, I thought he was from the USA, but it turns out he is Canadian.*
**license** (n) a document that allows the owner to do something otherwise restricted or controlled by law
*You have to pass the test to get a license.*
*Could you show me your driving license?*
**nuisance** (n) something that causes you to become annoyed
*It turned out to be a bit of a nuisance.*
*The baby crying throughout the performance was something of a nuisance.*
**package** (n) an item, usually wrapped in paper or in a box, to be delivered by mail
*When did the package arrive?*
*There is a package from head office on your desk.*
**rare** (adj) uncommon, or limited in number
*I think it's quite rare.*
*Pandas are now very rare in the wild.*
**remarkable** (adj) amazing, incredible, different to normal (generally used to express a positive feeling)
*It was remarkable.*
*We had a remarkable time on our Egyptian vacation.*
**reservation** (n) an agreement that a hotel room, restaurant table, etc. is kept for the person who orders it
*You will receive a library barcode number via email (enabling you to place reservations).*
*I'm sorry, but there is no record of your reservation.*
**right away** (adv) immediately, without pause or hesitation
*If you get started right away, it shouldn't be too much of a problem.*
*If we want to get there by six, we'll have to leave right away.*
**sleeves** (n) the arms of a shirt, jacket or other upper body item of clothing
*The sleeves are a bit short.*
*Is it possible to get the sleeves adjusted?*
**stadium** (n) a large building, with seating all around it, where sporting events are held
*The track finals will be held at the stadium later tomorrow.*
*The marathon runners finish their route at the Olympic stadium.*
**unreasonable** (adj) not acceptable, unfair
*He sometimes sets unreasonable deadlines.*
*Their quote was unreasonable given the amount of work needed.*
**vacancies** (n) empty rooms in a hotel, guest house or trip etc.
*Do you have any vacancies for tonight?*
*We have only a few vacancies left on tomorrow's excursion.*
**withdrawal** (n) the act of taking money out of a bank account (opposite of deposit)
*The largest withdrawal that can be made in one day is $1000.*
*Can I make withdrawals from other companies' ATMs?*

## 1 Choose the correct word.

1 The safari was a(n) .................... experience – we'll never forget it.
  (A) remarkable
  (B) desperate
  (C) amusing

2 Receiving junk mail from the Internet can be a .................... .
  (A) withdrawal
  (B) nuisance
  (C) reservation

3 The museum section of the library has a special collection of .................... books.
  (A) available
  (B) rare
  (C) unreasonable

4 The earthquake victims were .................... ; they didn't have enough food, water or medicine.
  (A) remarkable
  (B) rare
  (C) desperate

5 I've booked two tickets .................... class to New York.
  (A) reservation
  (B) available
  (C) coach

6 The car hire company needs to see your driving .................... and a form of ID.
  (A) license
  (B) vacancy
  (C) reservation

7 I'd like to make a .................... my savings account.
  (A) deposit from
  (B) deposit into
  (C) deposit around

8 Special weekend rates are .................... on all rooms – call today to make a reservation.
  (A) available
  (B) remarkable
  (C) vacancies

9 I couldn't stay at the same hotel because they didn't have any .................... .
  (A) vacancies
  (B) calculations
  (C) withdrawals

10 There is a .................... for you in this morning's mail.
  (A) package
  (B) deposit
  (C) heel

11 The jacket almost fits, but the .................... are a bit too long.
  (A) calculations
  (B) heels
  (C) sleeves

## 2 Match the words with the definitions.

> amusing  calculations  catch  heel
> initially  reservation  right away
> stadium  unreasonable  withdrawal

1 the process of solving a mathematical problem
2 to take public transport
3 immediately
4 funny, makes people laugh
5 large sporting events are held here
6 at first
7 taking money out of a bank account
8 not acceptable, unfair
9 an booking agreement; for example, for a hotel room, or a plane ticket
10 the back part of a foot

## Unit 4.3

**adjust** (v)  change the settings of how something works or appears
*You can adjust the level of resistance.*
*If the picture is not clear, try to adjust the aerial.*

**ambitious** (adj)  something done on a large scale, usually confidently
*It is our most ambitious yet.*
*We have ambitious plans for the European market.*

**background** (n)  information about the past of a person, object or event
*I would like to give you some background on Bill Gates.*
*We need some more background information.*

**delighted** (adj)  very happy
*We are delighted that he has agreed to speak to us.*
*He was delighted with his birthday gift.*

**feature** (v)  to be included (usually in a movie, show or other production)
*Indigo Heart, a new movie featuring Andy Vega.*
*It's a great movie that features some of the hottest new Hollywood talent.*

**hand you over** (v)  transfer a conversation from one person to another, usually on the telephone
*I'll hand you over to her.*
*If you could hold the line, I'll hand you over to our customer service department.*

**handling** (n)  money paid to delivery people, (often used together with shipping, see 3.2)
*Only $29.99 plus shipping and handling.*
*How much are the handling costs?*

**impact** (n)  the effect one thing has on another
*The fabrics will have an impact on our sales.*
*The weak dollar should have limited impact on exports.*

**innovation** (n)  a new invention, or idea
*The Springblade is a new innovation in personal fitness training.*
*Our company has always tried to be a leader in innovations.*

**keen** (adj)  interested and excited, very much wanting to do something
*I am sure you will all be keen to attend.*
*I'm keen to hear more about your ideas.*

**latecomer** (n)  a person that arrives late for an event
*Latecomers had better take public transit.*
*The conference was held up for thirty minutes to allow latecomers to find their seats.*

**on the lookout for** (expression)  to be actively searching for someone or something
*Be on the lookout for James Cheeby.*
*I'm on the lookout for a new computer. Do you know anyone that is selling theirs?*

**optimistic** (adj)  having a positive feeling about something
*We are very optimistic that her eye for detail and understanding of...*
*The financial forecast is quite optimistic.*

**particular** (adj)  more than usual, special
*Officers on patrol on 5th street should be on particular alert.*
*Take particular care when signing your name, not to write outside the box.*

**realize** (v)  to understand something (often suddenly)
*I realize that this is a non-working day.*
*The staff realized the amount of time that had gone into the job.*

**salvage** (v)  to save or recover something, e.g. a ship or building, from destruction
*The ship was recently salvaged from Jamestown harbor.*
*We can try to salvage this deal.*

**schedule** (v)  to arrange an event on a timetable
*There are three plenary discussions scheduled for Saturday.*
*We should try to schedule a meeting next week.*

**spectator** (n)  a person watching an event
*Spectators should try to get down to the Jamestown marina early.*
*Ten thousand spectators watched the finals.*

**support** (v)  to provide help or assistance to others
*He did a lot of things to support the members of his group.*
*New employees can expect the support of their colleagues.*

**vicinity** (n)  in the area of, nearby
*...around the vicinity of the Buena Vista Pool Hall.*
*Are there any banks in the vicinity?*

**vigilant** (adj)  keeping a close watch on something
*Officers should be vigilant in the vicinity of the Buena Vista Pool Hall*
*Be vigilant for pickpockets around the markets.*

## Quiz 4.3

### 1 Find ten words in the puzzle. Match them to their definitions.

| I | N | N | O | V | A | T | I | O | N |
|---|---|---|---|---|---|---|---|---|---|
| T | W | E | T | I | W | O | Y | E | M |
| D | E | L | I | G | H | T | E | D | G |
| E | T | H | A | I | P | K | O | I | E |
| R | Q | S | P | L | I | O | P | R | T |
| T | H | C | O | A | R | I | U | U | S |
| C | A | H | I | N | E | T | L | Y | A |
| S | P | E | C | T | A | T | O | R | L |
| A | T | D | U | E | L | U | M | T | V |
| I | P | U | F | U | I | Y | N | R | A |
| P | U | L | Y | Y | Z | T | B | E | G |
| E | F | E | T | T | E | F | G | S | E |
| O | T | I | M | I | S | T | I | C | A |

1 very interested and wanting to do something
2 having a positive feeling about something
3 a person watching an event
4 keeping a close watch on something, being careful
5 a new idea or invention
6 a timetable
7 very happy
8 to recover something that is badly damaged
9 to understand
10 to be included in a film

### 2 Complete the sentences with the following words.

> adjust  ambitious  background
> hand over  impact  latecomers
> lookout  particular  support
> vicinity

1 The shops in this .................... are very convenient, and they are all within walking distance.
2 Does this model have any .................... advantages over the others?
3 The police are on the .................... for an escaped prisoner.
4 They are trained to be .................... ; they all want top jobs.
5 Once the concert has begun, .................... cannot enter the auditorium until the interval.
6 The engineering department provides technical .................... and maintains all the machinery.
7 I'm going to .................... you .................... to the person who normally deals with sales enquiries.
8 If you want to .................... the volume, simply press here.
9 What kind of .................... do you think the new policy will have on single-parent families?
10 Is there any .................... information on this company? We're thinking of buying some shares.

## Unit 5.3

**bankrupt** (adj) of companies or individuals, to not have enough money to pay expenses or debts
*That company went bankrupt.*
*After paying the legal expenses he was bankrupt.*

**co-supervise** (v) two or more people taking responsibility for a project or department
*Jake Thomson and Phil Greene co-supervise the project.*
*I co-supervise the sales team.*

**criticize** (v) to say what you think is wrong with something
*The strategy was criticized for being too aggressive.*
*Jon's boss would often loudly criticize him.*

**dependence** (n) reliance, needing something in order to survive
*The company's dependence on a single supplier caused problems.*
*Our dependence on imported parts is costing us a lot of money.*

**devastate** (v) to cause a great deal of damage to something
*Officials worry that the hurricane will devastate the coastal areas.*
*The area was devastated by the tornado.*

**disconnect** (v) to detach something from its power source, to remove (especially a telephone) from the network
*The phone company came to disconnect his line.*
*You should disconnect the printer before switching the power on.*

**document** (n) a piece of paper that contains company information
*He hates filing documents.*
*He realized he had left a key document on his desk at home.*

**identify** (v) to find and name someone or something
*A consultant was hired to identify the company's main weaknesses.*
*I couldn't identify the man, as he was wearing a mask.*

**impatient** (adj) to be annoyed or frustrated due to an inability to wait
*I often get very impatient if there is heavy traffic when I am in a hurry.*
*I am impatient to hear the result of the election.*

**intercom** (n) an electronic device used to communicate with people inside and outside of a room
*There is an intercom in each room.*
*Call me on the intercom and I'll let you in.*

**internship** (n) a period of work where students are given professional supervision
*Doing an internship is a good way for students to get work experience.*
*Law students usually look for an internship during their final year at college.*

**investigation** (n) an organized way to find out information about how something happened
*The stockholders want an investigation to find the money.*
*The investigation will take at least a week.*

**mishear** (v) to fail to hear something correctly
*Sorry, I think I misheard you.*
*I misheard the announcement and went to the wrong gate.*

**non-refundable** (adj) not possible to receive money back for something purchased
*Since the gift was on sale it was non-refundable.*
*All sale items are non-refundable.*

**overpaid** (adj) given too much money for doing a job
*Many people believe that lawyers are overpaid.*
*I don't believe that miners are overpaid; they work very hard.*

**renovate** (v) to repair something to a condition as good as new
*The house needs to be renovated.*
*The company spent millions to renovate its main office.*

**repetitiveness** (n) the feeling of something being done the same way many times
*Many people dislike the repetitiveness of working in a factory.*
*I didn't mind the repetitiveness of the work.*

**resurface** (v) replace the outer layer of something, especially a road
*After the crash they needed to resurface the damaged runway.*
*We need to resurface the driveway.*

**soften** (v) to make something soft
*Cyclists often use pads to soften the seat for long-distance rides.*
*Add extra water to soften the mixture.*

**subdivide** (v) to make a whole into separate smaller pieces
*His department was subdivided into many smaller sections.*
*The company is subdivided into three regional sections.*

**unwrap** (v) to remove the paper layer from a parcel or gift
*The children couldn't wait to unwrap their presents.*
*Don't unwrap the parcel until Christmas.*

## Quiz 5.3

### 1 Match the words with the definitions.

> bankrupt  criticize  dependence
> document  impatient  intercom
> internship  investigation
> non-refundable  repetitiveness

1  trying to find out the truth about something
2  doing the same thing again and again
3  a two-way communication system that uses a microphone and a loudspeaker
4  a file of some kind
5  a person or a company that has terrible financial difficulties that can't improve
6  easily annoyed or irritated
7  when you can't get your money back
8  a period of work done by a student that is supervised by professionals
9  rely on somebody or something to help you
10 the opposite of praise

### 2 Choose the correct word.

1  I'm sorry, but we've ................... you. Could you return the money?
   (A)  unwrapped
   (B)  disconnected
   (C)  overpaid

2  We've ................... the problem. It's bad management in the accounts department.
   (A)  criticized
   (B)  identified
   (C)  renovated

3  It's a beautiful old building, but it would cost a lot of money to ................... it.
   (A)  devastate
   (B)  resurface
   (C)  renovate

4  The storm has ................... many coastal areas.
   (A)  devastated
   (B)  subdivided
   (C)  resurfaced

5  I must ................... these new hiking boots. They hurt my feet.
   (A)  soften
   (B)  unwrap
   (C)  mishear

6  We've ................... the company into small departments.
   (A)  renovated
   (B)  softened
   (C)  subdivided

7  The two managers are currently ................... the takeover.
   (A)  disconnecting
   (B)  co-supervising
   (C)  mishearing

8  The committee are planning to ................... the road.
   (A)  resurface
   (B)  renovate
   (C)  disconnect

9  I must have ................... John. I thought he said he was leaving the company, but he isn't.
   (A)  co-supervised
   (B)  misheard
   (C)  criticized

10 They ................... our electricity because we forgot to pay the bill.
   (A)  identified
   (B)  criticized
   (C)  disconnected

11 The director is going to ................... his leaving present. I wonder what they brought him.
   (A)  unwrap
   (B)  disconnect
   (C)  identify

## Unit 6.3

**abandoned** (adj) left alone, by parents or owners
*...PAWS has rescued, protected and provided a home for thousands of abused and abandoned animals...*
*The abandoned building quickly fell victim to vandals.*

**abused** (adj) someone or something treated badly
*...PAWS has rescued, protected and provided a home for thousands of abused and abandoned animals...*
*The home for abused women provides help for hundreds of women.*

**accuse** (v) to say that another person is guilty of doing something wrong
*Union officials are claiming that this will result in a loss of over 2000 jobs for Milltown area and have accused Beeton of closing the plant...*
*Smith was accused of driving without a license.*

**chairman** (n) the head of a company or the leader of a meeting
*I'm meeting the chairman are 3:00.*
*The chairman called for any questions.*

**claim** (v) to state something is what you believe
*Union officials are claiming that this will result in a loss of over 2000 jobs for Milltown area...*
*The police claim that nobody was hurt in the riot.*

**closure** (n) the act of closing a factory, shop or other business
*They have promised strikes and protests in all Beeton factories unless the closure is canceled.*
*The sales staff hadn't been paid for several months, prior to the closure.*

**damage** (n) harm done to something
*This year they hope to repair the damage caused to the fence...*
*There wasn't much obvious damage done.*

**denounce** (v) to criticize something or state that you do not accept it
*Several religious groups have denounced the court decision.*
*The politician denounced his former party.*

**dispute** (n) a disagreement, for example between workers and management
*The company failed to resolve a six-month long labor dispute.*
*We have been in dispute with them over ownership of the design.*

**employ** (v) to give somebody a job, to pay somebody to do a job
*How long have you been employed at your present company?*
*The company employs more than two thousand people.*

**equipment** (n) items used to achieve a particular purpose, for example a hobby or job
*He helped secure the loan on the new equipment for the farm last year.*
*Ski equipment can be rented on site.*

**extremely** (adv) very
*You have been extremely kind to my family and me.*
*It is an extremely long journey.*

**facility** (n) a building or piece of equipment used for a particular purpose
*Costs at the facility had been rising for some time.*
*The laboratory has all the latest facilities.*

**famed** (adj) famous, known by a lot of people
*The famed orchestra will be giving a one night performance.*
*The town's famed clock tower is the first place tourists visit.*

**foreign** (adj) from another country
*The agricultural board will increase taxes on foreign imports.*
*We are looking to expand into foreign markets.*

**fundraising** (n) trying to gather money for charitable purpose
*The Animal Welfare Society is having its annual fundraising dinner.*
*The fundraising achieved its goal of ten thousand dollars.*

**inconvenience** (n) something that causes trouble or a problem for other people
*We apologize for any inconvenience.*
*I'm sure I'll quickly get tired of the inconvenience and long travel times.*

**invoice** (n) an official receipt of payments, usually given to a company
*The shipping agent said he will change the cargo invoices.*
*We keep all our invoices for tax-calculation purposes.*

**lack** (n) to be without something or to be in need of it
*The annual conference has been cancelled this year due to lack of money.*
*We lack experience in this area.*

**livestock** (n) animals on a farm
*This year they are hoping to repair the damage caused to the fence in the large livestock run...*
*Livestock arrives at the market every day.*

**loan** (n) an amount of money borrowed from a bank or other financial institution
*He helped secure the loan on the new equipment for the farm last year.*
*We could take out a loan to pay for it.*

**negotiation** (n) a discussion to come to an agreement between two sides with different opinions
*The minister of the war-torn country stated on TV that they won't start negotiations until the rebels have renounced violence.*
*We are in negotiations with the film studio about a movie adaptation of the best-selling book.*

**opportunity** (n) a chance
*This is a once in a lifetime opportunity.*
*We may not have many opportunities to do this later.*

**originally** (adv) in the beginning, to start with, before
*Recently I have come into a bit of money and will be able to afford the return to school earlier than I had originally thought possible.*
*He was originally born in Scotland, but his family emigrated to Canada.*

**outline** (n) a basic description without much detail
*He hasn't seen the new outlines yet.*
*Have the design team draw up an outline?*

**pronounce** (v) to say a word with the correct sounds
*Kenji had never heard the word pronounced.*
*Some African languages are extremely difficult to pronounce.*

**protest** (n) a complaint, often made by a group
*They have promised strikes and protests in all Beeton factories unless the closure is canceled.*
*The president listened to the protests and decided to act on them.*

**raise** (v) to collect money, usually for a charity
*This year they are hoping to raise $4500 to repair the damage*
*The telethon raised more than three million last year.*

**rare** (adj) uncommon, one of only a small number
*Fans of classical music are in for a rare treat in December.*
*It was a rare sight to see him in the office on time.*

**recently** (adv) in the near past
*Recently I have come into a bit of money.*
*I recently passed my driving test.*

**refuse** (v) to not agree to do something
*I have to refuse your offer of a job for the coming year.*
*Our rivals refused our offer to merge.*

**religious** (adj) connected with a belief in a god or gods
*Several protesting religious and social groups have denounced the court decision.*
*The prince and princess decided against having a religious ceremony for their wedding.*

**renounce** (v) to give up a previously held belief
*They won't start negotiations until the rebels have renounced violence and surrendered their weapons.*
*He renounced his support of communism.*

**repair** (v) to fix something so that it works again
*This year they are hoping to raise $4500 to repair the damage.*
*I had to send my watch back to the factory to be repaired.*

**report** (v) to tell people, usually in an official manner
*John Leighton reported that costs at the facility...*
*The representative in Manila reported that the factory had not been hit too badly in the earthquake.*

**rescue** (v) to save something or move it from a dangerous situation
*For over 25 years PAWS has rescued... thousands of abused and abandoned animals...*
*Aid workers are trying to rescue hundreds of people trapped by landslides.*

**resolve** (v) to come to a decision, e.g. in a dispute
*...recent talks had failed to resolve a six-month long labor dispute.*
*Today's meeting aims to resolve our negotiations.*

**retirement** (n) the period of life after someone has stopped working, usually from around 60 years old
*I am looking forward to my retirement.*
*Vasily Krampfstein has announced his retirement.*

**secure** (adj) safe, out of danger
*The abused dog was placed in a secure and loving home.*
*Government bonds are a secure and practical way to save money.*

**secure** (v) to make sure a loan is covered by other assets, to keep something safe
*We wouldn't have been able to secure the loan...*
*We were able to secure the doors.*

**situation** (n) what happens or happened to you
*I'm afraid since we spoke, my situation has changed.*
*We will try to avoid that situation if possible.*

**social** (adj) relating to society, people or culture
*Several protesting religious and social groups have denounced the court decision.*
*Homelessness is only one of several social problems the government has ignored.*

**strike** (n) when workers refuse to work because they are unhappy with their conditions or pay
*They have promised strikes and protests in all Beeton factories unless the closure is canceled.*
*The strike caused all trains to be canceled.*

**surrender** (v) to give up a weapon, position or cause to the opposing side
*They won't start negotiations until the rebels have renounced violence and surrendered their weapons.*
*The rebels surrendered and were taken to the capital.*

**surrounding** (adj) in the area, close to a location
*There are thousands of abused and abandoned animals in Pollville and surrounding Duxham county.*
*There are plenty of shops and services in the surrounding area.*

**tornado** (n) a very strong and dangerous wind in a twisting shape
*This year they hope to repair the damage caused...by the recent tornado.*
*The Midwest was hit by three tornadoes yesterday.*

**war-torn country** (n) a country experiencing a long and destructive period of war
*The minister of the war-torn country stated on TV that they won't start negotiations until the rebels have renounced violence.*
*The war-torn country is trying hard to rebuild itself.*

## Quiz 6.3

### 1 Use the words to complete the crossword.

> chairman damage dispute equipment foreign invoice loan rare retirement secure strikes tornado

**Clues**

**Across**
2 machinery
3 the period of time when you are able to stop working completely
6 bill
7 from a different country
9 argument
10 borrowed money
11 times when workers refuse to work because they are unhappy about something

**Down**
1 man in charge of a meeting, an organisation, etc
4 type of storm
5 to keep something safe
8 unusual
9 harm done to something so that it needs repair

### 2 Read the definitions and write *true* or *false*.

1 A *religious* person has a set of beliefs.
2 *Outlines* are basic descriptions.
3 An *abandoned* animal has been left on its own.
4 If you *raise* money you collect it.
5 *Closure* is the end of something.
6 A *facility* is a kind of university.
7 People have *protests* when they don't like something.
8 *Famed* means not very well-known.
9 *Negotiations* are discussions about a problem when people disagree.
10 When there is a *lack* of something, there's a lot of it.
11 *Fundraising* means increasing the profits of a company.
12 If you *renounce* something you give it up.
13 A *war-torn country* is still at war.
14 To *secure* something is to be certain that it's yours.
15 If you *repair* something you fix it.

16 If you *denounce* something you say that you believe in it.
17 If something has happened *recently* it was a long time ago.
18 An *opportunity* is a chance to do something.
19 *Extremely* means not very.
20 *Inconvenience* means something that's difficult to do.
21 *Livestock* is farm animals.
22 *Surrender* means to start a war.

### 3 Complete the sentences with the following words.

> abused accused claim employed originally pronounced refuse report rescued resolve situation social surrounding

1 The company is finding it very difficult to .................... the dispute.

2 Our .................... has changed, so we aren't going ahead with the takeover.
3 She had .................... planned to move into sales, but then found a better job in finance.
4 There are a number of different .................... groups in the city.
5 The company .................... twenty-five new people last year.
6 I .................... to do overtime at the weekend. I've already made plans.
7 While the boss is away I have to .................... that sales for this quarter are down.
8 Workers .................... that they aren't getting enough breaks.
9 I .................... Timothy of taking an important document from my desk.
10 Last week, the group .................... three dogs from bad treatment.
11 Many animals are .................... by their owners.
12 The hurricane damaged the coastal town and many houses in the .................... area.
13 I .................... the word badly so they didn't understand what I was talking about.

## Unit 7.3

**beverage** (n) a drink
*...the local New Year's Day tradition of warming up with home made...bean and bacon soup, good music and beverages.*
*The limit on importing alcoholic beverages was dropped.*

**complimentary** (adj) offered without charge
*We will shortly be serving complimentary tea.*
*Put a personalized message on your complimentary card.*

**culinary** (adj) associated with food and cooking
*One of the county's original culinary festivals.*
*His culinary expertise is evident.*

**the elderly** (n) old people
*Reduced price for the elderly...*

**ensure** (v) to make certain of something
*To ensure safety...*
*Please ensure that all arrangements are made at your end.*

**explorer** (n) a person who tries to go somewhere that others have not gone to before
*The celebration starts with a light-hearted re-enactment of the founding of the city by English explorer Francis Baker in 1879.*
*The first explorers were amazed to find buildings larger than anything in the civilized world.*

**festivities** (n) celebrations
*Festivities at this year's event will include over 25 local food vendors, a children's fair and more.*
*All guests are welcome to join in the festivities.*

**founding** (n) the starting of a town, company or nation
*The celebration starts with a light-hearted re-enactment of the founding of the city by English explorer Francis Baker in 1879.*
*The founding of the city is believed to have happened before the Romans arrived.*

**guarantee** (n) a promise to cover the quality of goods or services
*All products come with an unconditional money-back guarantee.*
*There is an option to purchase a five-year guarantee.*

**host** (v) to welcome guests or visitors to an event that the person is organizing
*The Bakerstown Polar Bear Club hosts this popular, annual...*
*The Giants host the Cougars in tonight's big game.*

**itinerary** (n) a schedule or plan, usually written in the form of a list
*As promised, here's the revised itinerary for next week's activities.*
*What is next on the itinerary?*

**orienteering** (n) a sport involving following a map to a series of locations as quickly as possible
*Canoeing will take place after orienteering.*
*A good brain is as important as strong muscles in the sport of orienteering.*

**personalized** (adj) made different to suit each individual
*Put a personalized message on your complimentary card.*

**prohibit** (v) to not allow or to stop something according to a rule
*Animals prohibited from entry.*
*It is prohibited to take any dangerous items on board.*

**re-enactment** (n) the recreation of a historical scene by modern actors or performers
*The celebration starts with a light-hearted re-enactment of the founding of the city by English explorer Francis Baker in 1879.*
*The Sealed Knot are famous for their re-enactments of British Civil War battles.*

**revised** (adj) done again, altered
*As promised, here's the revised itinerary for next week's activities.*
*The revised edition contains fewer errors than the original.*

**senior citizens** (n) old people, a more polite way to describing the aged
*Senior citizens get special rates.*
*The number of senior citizens taking up sports is on the increase.*

**tradition** (n) a custom or habit usually associated with a particular country, region or group
*...the local New Year's Day tradition of warming up with home made...bean and bacon soup, good music and beverages.*
*Going to church on Christmas Eve is a family tradition.*

**unconditional** (adj) without any conditions
*All products come with an unconditional money-back guarantee.*
*The unconditional surrender of arms was a key aspect of the peace process.*

**vendor** (n) a person selling goods, often from temporary shops or stalls
*Festivities at this year's event will include over 25 local food vendors, a children's fair and more.*
*Market vendors have a reputation for honesty.*

## Quiz 7.3

### 1 Choose the correct word.

1 Children under 12 are ................... entry.
(A) prohibited from
(B) prohibited to
(C) prohiibited

2 ................... get a discount on their tickets.
(A) Explorers
(B) Vendors
(C) Senior citizens

3 I'd like to see the ................... for tomorrow's course.
(A) tradition
(B) itinerary
(C) beverages

4 This product still has a ................... so I'd like my money back.
(A) vendor
(B) founding
(C) guarantee

5 There isn't going to be any food, but there will be ................... .
(A) traditions
(B) re-enactment
(C) beverages

6 The show will start with a(n) ................... of the climbing of Everest.
(A) re-enactment
(B) orienteering
(C) guarantee

7 The ................... of the city was an important historical event.
(A) elderly
(B) founding
(C) re-enactment

8 The offer is ................... so they do not need to get any licenses.
(A) personalized
(B) unconditional
(C) culinary

9 The food is expensive, but there's a ................... drink with every meal.
(A) complimentary
(B) unconditional
(C) culinary

### 2 Find eleven words in the puzzle. Then match them with their definitions.

| O | R | I | E | N | T | E | E | R | I | N | G | G |
|---|---|---|---|---|---|---|---|---|---|---|---|---|
| M | E | K | S | U | R | V | N | B | D | C | H | F |
| T | L | E | M | R | S | E | J | E | L | A | R | E |
| U | D | N | F | L | T | G | V | P | O | K | A | S |
| X | E | P | A | S | D | U | W | I | C | E | V | T |
| P | R | T | O | E | M | R | O | Z | S | H | I | I |
| L | L | H | E | N | S | U | R | E | X | E | J | V |
| O | Y | V | R | B | F | E | N | H | R | L | D | I |
| D | U | T | R | A | D | I | T | I | O | N | E | T |
| I | C | M | A | E | X | P | L | O | R | E | R | I |
| Z | E | P | C | Y | V | H | E | D | S | I | A | E |
| A | C | U | L | I | N | A | R | Y | O | F | R | S |
| P | E | R | S | O | N | A | L | I | Z | E | D | A |
| K | O | J | V | E | N | D | O | R | T | G | N | H |

1 cooking
2 a person who sells things
3 make certain
4 fun events
5 customs and beliefs
6 somebody who discovers new places
7 racing across the countryside
8 old people
9 made for a particular person
10 changed
11 the person holding a party or an event

## Unit 1.4

**bride** (n) a woman on her wedding day
*The bride is on the sidewalk.*
*The bride arrived late for the wedding ceremony.*

**commuter** (n) a person traveling to work
*The commuters are between the buses.*
*The train is full of commuters this morning.*

**control panel** (n) a part of a machine that allows the operator to use it, or that shows whether it is functioning correctly or not
*The man is sitting next to the control panel.*
*The warning light on the control panel lit up.*

**counter** (n) a flat, raised surface on which to place items, e.g. in a shop
*The woman is at the counter.*
*You can leave your bags behind the counter.*

**crash** (v) of computers, to stop working suddenly without warning, often temporarily
*The computer is going to crash.*
*My laptop crashed and I lost all the data I was working on.*

**customer** (n) a person paying for goods or services
*The customer is shopping for food.*
*The shop assistant is helping the customer.*

**cycle** (v) to ride a bicycle
*The woman is cycling through the city.*
*He used to cycle to work.*

**decorate** (v) to make something beautiful by placing colorful items, flowers, etc. on or around it
*The student decorates the cakes.*
*We decorated the hall for the farewell party.*

**deserted** (adj) having no people present
*The room is deserted.*
*The beach is usually deserted until 10 a.m.*

**display** (n) an arrangement of goods in a shop designed to attract customers
*The guitars are on display.*
*The Christmas display was particularly beautiful this year.*

**flight attendant** (n) an airline employee that takes care of passengers on board an airplane
*The flight attendant is wearing a red jacket.*
*Your flight attendant will demonstrate the safety procedures.*

**handle** (n) a lever that can be turned to either open something or operate a machine
*The woman is turning the handle.*
*He can't open the door as the handle is stuck.*

**harbor** (n) the place where boats are kept when not in use
*The ship is in the harbor.*
*We can catch the ferry at the harbor.*

**hide** (v) to place an item or yourself, so that it cannot easily be found
*The woman is hiding some clothes.*
*The children are hiding from their parents.*

**keyboard** (n) an input device for entering letters and numbers into a computer
*The keyboard is on the desk.*
*Type your name using the attached keyboard.*

**lean** (v) to stand at an angle
*The man is leaning against the car.*
*The Tower of Pisa leans slightly to one side.*

**locker** (n) a container for personal items that can be fastened with a key or other kind of lock
*The student is looking inside her locker.*
*He lost the key to his locker.*

**outfit** (n) a set of clothes, usually for a woman
*The woman is looking at the outfit.*
*She wore her new outfit to the interview.*

**point** (v) to indicate towards something usually using the index finger
*The man is pointing at something.*
*Several signs point the way to the gate.*

**raise** (v) to lift something
*The couple raise their glasses.*
*The crane raises the crate high above the ship.*

**resign** (v) to quit a job
*The man is going to resign.*
*He resigned when he was offered a better job.*

**set** (v) to place an item in a particular position
*The people are setting the table.*
*He set the glass on the counter.*

**sweep** (v) to clean the floor, using a broom or brush
*The man is sweeping the street.*
*The woman uses the broom to sweep the kitchen.*

**tool** (n) an item used to make completing a job simpler
*The girl is using a tool.*
*A screwdriver is an essential tool for an electrician.*

**tray** (n) a wide, flat carrying device
*The CD tray is open.*
*He carried a tray with tea and cookies into the living room.*

**walkway** (n) a passage or path only used by pedestrians
*A moving walkway connects the station to the shopping center.*
*Take the pedestrian walkway to get to the mall.*

## Quiz 1.4

### 1 Complete the sentences with the following words.

> bride  control panel  counter
> cycling  decorate  deserted
> display  handle  harbor  keyboard
> outfit  pointed  raise  set  tool

1  The ................... is next to the computer.
2  I need a new ................... for my cousin's wedding next month.
3  Please pay for your goods at the ................... .
4  Dinner is nearly ready – could you ................... the table, please?
5  When the World Cup final was showing on television, the shops were ................... .
6  Children always get excited when they ................... the Christmas tree.
7  Let's go down to the ................... , and we can watch all the boats come in.
8  ................... is good exercise.
9  Without the right ................... it's impossible to complete the job.
10  The art projects were put on ................... in the main hall.
11  If there's a problem, the ................... lights up and shows you what's wrong.
12  The ................... was led into church by her father.
13  Pulling the ................... opens the fire door – only use it in case of emergencies.
14  Do you think they will ever ................... the *Titanic* from the sea bed?
15  The teacher ................... to the capital cities on the map.

### 2 Choose the correct word to complete the definition.

1  A *customer / commuter* travels to work everyday.
2  A *flight attendant / control panel* works on board a plane.
3  To *resign / crash* means to quit your job.

4  To *decorate / sweep* means to clean the floor with a broom.
5  When a computer *crashes / leans* it stops working.
6  You can keep your personal items in a *locker / counter*.
7  You can carry things on a *tray / handle*.
8  A person paying for goods is a *customer / counter*.
9  A *walkway / harbor* is used by pedestrians.
10  When you are *pointing / hiding* no-one can see you.
11  To *lean / resign* means to stand at an angle.

## Unit 2.4

**amusing** (adj) funny, likely to make people laugh
*He really is an amusing speaker.*
*I saw an amusing program on the television last night.*

**appreciate** (v) to feel grateful to somebody because of what they have done for you
*Yes, I really appreciated all your help yesterday.*
*I would appreciate it if you could turn the volume down.*

**book** (v) to arrange to have something for a particular time. Similar to reserve
*Sorry, we are fully booked for this evening.*
*Can I book a table for three for nine o'clock?*

**borrow** (v) to take something with permission, and then return it later
*Can I borrow your pen for a moment?*
*My sister borrowed the car for the weekend.*

**calculator** (n) an electronic device used for mathematical functions
*Do you have a calculator I could borrow?*
*We'll need a calculator to work out the bill.*

**chair** (v) to be in charge of a meeting
*I have to chair a meeting.*
*He has chaired that committee for years.*

**committee** (n) a group that meets to discuss issues and to make decisions
*He has chaired that committee for years.*
*She is a member of the committee.*

**deliver** (v) to take something to give to someone
*The package was delivered to the wrong address.*
*My paper wasn't delivered this morning.*

**expect** (v) to imagine something, to believe that something will happen
*Harder than I expected.*
*I was expecting to be met at the airport.*

**fill out** (v) to write in all the details of a form or questionnaire
*Can you show me how to fill out this card?*
*All passengers have to fill out an immigration form.*

**frankly** (adv) honestly, truthfully
*Frankly, our sales staff isn't motivated.*
*He spoke frankly and told us exactly what he felt.*

**license** (n) a document that allows the owner to do something otherwise restricted or controlled by law
*You have to pass the test to get a license.*
*The shop has a license to sell alcohol.*

**maintenance** (n) work done to keep something in good working condition
*You have to take it to the maintenance section.*
*The machines need regular maintenance.*

**make sense** (v)  be easy to understand
*I don't think it makes much sense.*
*The instruction manual made perfect sense to me.*

**motivate** (v)  to make others want to try harder to do something
*Frankly, our sales staff isn't motivated.*
*The management try hard to motivate their workers.*

**opinion** (n)  a person's beliefs or feelings about a subject
*What's your opinion of the price quote?*
*I don't have a strong opinion about the issue.*

**policy** (n)  an idea or set of ideas used to make decisions, usually decided by politics or business management
*What is your opinion of the new policy?*
*That goes against company policy.*

**prefer** (v)  to like one thing more than another
*I prefer pop music.*
*Actually, I would prefer if you didn't smoke.*

**quote** (n)  the price someone says they will charge to do a job
*What's your opinion of the price quote?*
*We chose the company that gave us the lowest quote.*

**reserve** (v)  to arrange to keep something (e.g. a room at a hotel) for yourself and nobody else
*Can I reserve a table for 8:00?*
*I reserved the room two months ago.*

**retirement** (n)  the period of life after someone has stopped working, usually from around 60 years old
*What do you think about the changes to the retirement plan?*
*I am looking forward to my retirement.*

**terrific** (adj)  very good
*Terrific! It was really well done.*
*That was a terrific speech you gave last night.*

**the night is young** (expression)  it is still early
*Don't worry, the night is young.*
*The night is young, we can still go to the restaurant.*

**upset** (adj)  to feel unhappy or angry about something
*I'm sure a lot of people will be upset.*
*What are you upset about?*

## Quiz 2.4

### 1  Choose the correct word.

1  I'd like to .................... a table for four at 8.00 p.m.
(A)  borrow
(B)  quote
(C)  reserve

2  We're .................... the shipment to arrive on Friday.
(A)  delivering
(B)  expecting
(C)  motivating

3  They were very .................... when they heard the bad news.
(A)  amusing
(B)  terrific
(C)  upset

4  First you need to .................... this form and attach a photograph.
(A)  fill
(B)  fill out
(C)  fill up

5  He spent more time with his grandchildren after his .................... .
(A)  license
(B)  maintenance
(C)  retirement

6  The .................... agreed to introduce a new company dress policy.
(A)  attitude
(B)  calculator
(C)  committee

7  Actually, I'd .................... if we discussed the matter in private.
(A)  expect
(B)  motivate
(C)  prefer

8  I need someone to .................... the up-date meeting this afternoon.
(A)  borrow
(B)  chair
(C)  appreciate

9  I've changed my .................... about the new manager; he's not as efficient as I thought.
(A)  opinion
(B)  policy
(C)  quote

10  Please send this by courier and have it .................... by hand.
(A)  booked
(B)  chaired
(C)  delivered

11  Students are not be allowed to use a .................... in the maths exam.
(A)  calculator
(B)  committee
(C)  license

12  Who calculated these figures? They really don't .................... to me.
(A)  borrow
(B)  make sense
(C)  expect

13  Let's go for a drink after the show. The night is ....................!
(A)  early
(B)  new
(C)  young

### 2  Find eleven words in the puzzle. Then match them with their definitions.

| R | T | F | R | A | N | K | L | Y | L | R |
|---|---|---|---|---|---|---|---|---|---|---|
| A | W | E | R | T | Y | M | G | D | I | E |
| M | A | I | N | T | E | N | A | N | C | E |
| U | P | A | S | I | D | F | G | H | E | P |
| S | P | E | T | T | O | H | A | I | N | O |
| I | R | O | Q | U | O | T | E | K | S | L |
| N | E | I | A | D | K | Q | U | I | E | I |
| G | C | U | T | E | R | R | I | F | I | C |
| R | I | Y | T | B | D | S | E | R | T | Y |
| O | A | T | B | O | R | R | O | W | Y | U |
| A | T | G | M | O | T | I | V | A | T | E |
| T | E | B | U | K | I | O | P | S | E | T |

1  a proposed price
2  to reserve a room or a table
3  a set of ideas used to make a decision
4  a document that allows you to do something
5  funny
6  honestly
7  to feel grateful
8  to take something and return it later
9  to make people want to try harder
10  very good
11  work done to keep something in good condition

## Unit 3.4

**a cut above** (adj)  better than, usually by a large amount
*It was a cut above the competition.*
*This meal is a cut above what we usually have at home.*

**allow** (v)  give permission for somebody to do a particular thing
*I'm sure they wouldn't allow it.*
*We are not allowed to smoke anywhere inside the building.*

**arrange** (v)  organize or make plans for something
*Could you arrange my hotel for me?*
*I've already arranged to take Mr. Wong to play golf tomorrow.*

**awkward** (adj)  feeling uncomfortable or embarrassed
*I'd feel a little awkward asking him to borrow money.*
*It is an awkward situation.*

**cancel** (v)  to request that an order or reservation be stopped
*He worries he can't cancel his flight.*
*I canceled my subscription to the newspaper as I didn't have enough time to read it.*

**carousel** (n)  a moving conveyor belt in an airport where passengers collect their luggage
*All the luggage came off the carousel but my case wasn't amongst the bags.*
*Passengers on flight 301 should go to carousel F to collect their bags.*

**commendable** (adj)  worthy of praise, done well
*It was commendable.*
*He made a commendable effort.*

**expectations** (n)  what someone thought would happen in a particular situation
*It met his expectations.*
*Although we had low expectations of the hotel, it was actually quite pleasant.*

**ineffective** (adj)  not working well, or not good at doing a particular job
*It is noisy and ineffective.*
*He was an ineffective manager.*

**postpone** (v)  delay a function or event until a later time or date
*I am thinking of postponing the meeting.*
*The seminar will be postponed until next week.*

**prefer** (v)  to like one thing more than another
*I prefer pop music.*
*I would prefer if we could put it off till this evening.*

**press** (v)  to use an iron to remove creases or wrinkles from clothing and get them ready to wear
*Could you clean and press these two shirts?*
*The hotel staff can press your suit pants if required.*

**racket** (n) a loud and unpleasant noise
*It makes a terrible racket whenever I use it.*
*He makes a real racket when he practices the drums.*

**recline** (v) to lie back, or adjust a seat to be closer to horizontal position
*They didn't fully recline.*
*Always ask the person sitting behind you before reclining your seat.*

**recommend** (v) to make a suggestion as to a particular choice
*Would you recommend it?*
*I recommend the fish—it is very fresh and delicious.*

**representative** (n) a person who has been chosen to speak for a company
*I suggest you talk to an airline representative.*
*I work as a sales representative for a medical supply firm.*

**response** (n) an answer or reaction to an inquiry or question
*What is the man's response?*
*I haven't heard his response yet.*

**suggest** (v) to offer your idea on how to do something
*I suggest we wait.*
*What does the man suggest?*

**suitable** (adj) a good match for the person concerned, acceptable for the purpose
*There are no suitable places left.*
*I don't know of any suitable hotels that the president can stay at.*

## Quiz 3.4

**1 Read the definitions and write *true* or *false*.**

1 A *racket* is a loud and pleasant noise.
2 To *allow* someone to do something means to give them permission.
3 If you *arrange* a meeting you decide the time and place.
4 A *carousel* can be found at an airport.
5 To *recline* means to sit up straight.
6 If something is *ineffective* it works very well.
7 An *awkward* situation makes you feel amused.
8 A *cut above* means better than usual.
9 If something is *commendable* it means that it was done too quickly.

**2 Complete the sentences with the following words.**

canceled   expectations   postpone
prefer   pressed   recommended
representative   response   suggest
suitable

1 There has been a very positive ................... to the new retirement policy.
2 The conference suite is already booked. Can you ................... an alternative venue?
3 The order was ................. because the company could not guarantee the delivery date.
4 We chose a local company to do the work because they were ................... by a neighbor.
5 The picture is not ................... for the brochure; we need something more colorful.

6 The elections for the union ................... will be held next week.
7 I can't wear this shirt – it hasn't been ................... .
8 They are going to ................... the soccer match until next week due to bad weather.
9 Which wine do you ................... ? Red or white?
10 They had very high ................... of the new manager.

## Unit 4.4

**affordable** (adj) not too expensive, at a price that the customer can pay
*We are focused on keeping prices affordable.*
*The property in that area is generally quite affordable.*

**attendee** (n) a person that is joining an event, usually having been invited to do so
*Why must attendees wear their identification tags?*
*All attendees must register at the entrance.*

**constant** (adj) not changing, staying the same over time
*The price has remained constant despite tax rises.*
*He is the only constant member of the team.*

**ensure** (v) to make certain of something
*To ensure safety...*
*Keep wallets hidden to ensure they are not stolen.*

**evacuation** (n) leaving a building or area due to a disaster
*Check the fire evacuation notice posted on your door.*
*In the event of evacuation, please leave all belongings behind.*

**impression** (n) how something makes you feel, your initial feeling about it
*They can create the right impression.*
*I get the impression he is not interested in the project.*

**kiosk** (n) a small shop, usually selling newspapers, magazines and refreshments
*At the platform kiosks sandwiches and other refreshments are available.*
*There's a kiosk outside the office where I often get my snacks.*

**layer** (n) a (usually thin) amount of a material or substance that covers another, or is between two other amounts
*There is a special inner layer.*
*A layer of snow covers the ground.*

**organize** (v) to make plans for an event, or be responsible for its completion
*I'm helping to organize the shareholders' meeting.*
*Can you organize the food for the party?*

**outlook** (n) a prediction for how the future is likely to be
*The outlook for the weekend, cold, with showers...*
*The outlook for this project is not so good.*

**overrun** (v) to go over the allotted time, to continue too long
*The last speaker overran.*
*We were late for the train as the concert overran by about twenty minutes.*

**patented** (adj) an idea or invention protected from being copied by government recognition
*You know it's a Seymour suit by the patented breathable lining.*
*It has a patented anti-lock braking system.*

**reasonably** (adv) fairly, at an acceptable level; or to some extent, quite
*They are reasonably priced.*
*It is a reasonably long walk.*

**remind** (v) to help someone else to remember something
*The organizers would like to remind attendees...*
*She reminded me to bring my laptop to the presentation.*

**revolutionary** (adj) new and different to anything that was previously available
*A revolutionary new factory.*
*It is a revolutionary idea.*

**shower** (n) a short period of rain
*The outlook for the weekend, cold, with showers...*
*The forecast says there will be showers this afternoon, so take an umbrella.*

**slump** (v) of people, to lie or fall to the ground because you are very tired or fell ill; of prices, to drop suddenly
*Sales have slumped in the last year.*
*He slumped to the floor.*

**stable** (adj) not likely to break, fail to operate, fall over or have any other problems
*The new software is much more stable than the previous version.*
*Make sure the ladder is stable before you climb up it.*

**suspicious** (adj) appearing to be dangerous or illegal
*To report a suspicious package.*
*A suspicious looking man has been waiting near the bank all day.*

**toiletries** (n) products used for personal cleaning or making the user look beautiful
*To purchase toiletries...*
*I get all my toiletries at the drugstore around the corner.*

**(in) transit** (n) when traveling, changing from one plane to another to continue a journey
*We were in transit to Paris.*
*The goods are currently in transit.*

**unattended** (adj) left without an owner present
*To collect his unattended bag...*
*Unattended bags will be taken away and destroyed.*

## Quiz 4.4

**1 Complete the sentences with the following words.**

evacuation   impression   patented
reasonably   suspicious   toiletries
transit   unattended

1 The staff are required to train for an emergency ................... of the building once a year.
2 Passengers flying on to other destinations please make your way to the ................... lounge.
3 Essential ................. are provided and can be found in the bathroom of your hotel room.
4 Passengers are reminded not to leave their baggage ................... at any time.

5 Did you notice anything ................... last night? Our neighbor's car was stolen.
6 Products that are ................... cannot be produced or sold by other companies.
7 The price slump has resulted in more ................... priced electronic goods.
8 At an interview, the candidates clothing gives an initial ................... of the type of person he or she is.

## 2 Use the definitions to find the words to complete the puzzle.

1 to make certain
2 a person joining an event
3 to continue more than the allotted time
4 a short period of rain
5 a prediction about the future
6 to drop suddenly
7 regular, without changing
8 to make people remember
9 a small shop
10 to be responsible for arranging an event
11 unlikely to have any problems
12 reasonably priced
13 a thin amount of material

## Unit 5.4

**attend** (v)  to go to or be present at a function (usually formal)
*I attended my sister's wedding.*
*Jane and her new assistant attended the conference.*
**capital** (n)  money used to start a business, buy a house, etc.
*The failed project has left us without working capital.*
*Selling the property will help to release some capital.*
**debt** (n)  money that is owed to another person or, often, a bank or other financial institution
*He was unable to pay his debts.*
*The bank has requested immediate repayment of all outstanding debt.*
**(high) demand** (n)  very popular, wanted by many people
*The things the local people make are in high demand.*
*The latest games consoles are in high demand just before Christmas.*
**dent** (n)  a mark in a metal object made by hitting it
*The customer is liable for any dents found on the vehicle.*
*The car has a large dent in the fender.*
**ensure** (v)  to make certain of something
*To ensure safety...*

*Management has tried to ensure a low-stress working environment.*
**function** (n)  a large formal dinner or other party
*Ms. Smithers will attend the function.*
*All guests at the function were given a gift.*
**immediate** (adj)  without hesitation, connected to now
*The bank has requested immediate repayment of all outstanding debt.*
*Is there any immediate action to be taken?*
**liable** (adj)  responsible for, the person that has to take charge of or pay for something
*The customer is liable for any dents found on the vehicle.*
*The insurance company is not liable for any damage caused by improper use.*
**particularly** (adv)  specially, more so than others
*The candidate is particularly suitable for the position.*
*He is a particularly interesting man.*
**pretend** (v)  to act as though something is different to how it really is
*We pretended not to notice their argument.*
*He pretended not to see me.*
**properly** (adv)  correctly, done the right way
*The watch didn't fit properly.*
*Be sure to fasten your seatbelt properly to avoid injury.*
**realize** (v)  to understand something (often suddenly)
*I realize that this is a non-working day.*
*The staff realized the amount of time that had gone into the job.*
**receptacle** (n)  a container, something to put items into
*Place all items into the receptacle.*
*Leave your keys in the receptacle on the desk when checking out.*
**reception** (n)  the place in a company where guests are greeted
*You have to sign in at the reception.*
*I'll come down and meet you at the reception.*
**receptive** (adj)  open and willing to listen to something
*The director was very receptive to your ideas.*
*The marketing section is always receptive to suggestions.*
**renew** (v)  to do something again, or extend a contract
*We will not be renewing your contract this year.*
*If you need to renew a library book, you can now do this online.*
**repayment** (n)  paying money back that was previously borrowed
*The bank has requested immediate repayment of all outstanding debt.*
*It is possible to spread repayments over two years.*
**submit** (v)  to give a required document to the person that needs it
*I had to submit the request three weeks in advance.*
*Please submit three photographs with each application.*
**(in) transit** (n)  when traveling, changing from one plane to another to continue a journey
*We were in transit to Paris.*
*The containers were damaged in transit.*
**upset** (adj)  to feel unhappy or angry about something
*The members were upset that dinner hadn't been arranged.*
*I think he was very upset by the news.*

### 1 Complete the sentences with the following words.

> capital  demand  dent  ensure
> immediate  particularly  pretended
> properly  realize  reception
> submitted

1 The company needs more ................... to be able to complete the project successfully.
2 All guests will be met by the manager at the ................... .
3 I ................... not to hear Paul when he said hello to me because I didn't want to talk to him.
4 Experienced engineers are in high ................... .
5 Three applications for the post of manager have been ................... already.
6 I like to ................... that all the employees in my department are happy.
7 I ................... it's a good promotion, but I don't want to live abroad right now.
8 We had to pay the company some money because there was a(n) ................... on the car.
9 The new employee is going to make a(n) ................... start.
10 I didn't do the report ................... so I had to do it again.
11 I think Tina is ................... suitable for the job because she is so experienced.

### 2 Read the definitions and write *true* or *false*.

1 A *function* is an event.
2 If you are *upset* you are feeling very happy.
3 A *debt* is an amount of money owed to somebody.
4 A *repayment* is the return of an amount of money.
5 If something is in *transit* it's moving.
6 A *receptacle* is part of an office.
7 If you *attend* an event you don't go to it.
8 If you *renew* something you start again.
9 A *receptive* person listens to new ideas.
10 If you are *liable* for something you are responsible for it.

## Unit 6.4

**agriculture** (n)  farming
*The agriculture of this area is mainly devoted to raising livestock.*
*The agriculture minister promised to support the farmers in their troubles.*
**alternative** (adj)  being a further choice, or a different option
*We need to find an alternative route.*
*We are currently seeking an alternative supplier.*
**apology** (n)  the act of saying sorry for one's actions
*Please accept my apology.*
*I demand an apology.*

**confirm** (v) to state that something is definitely correct
*I'm writing to confirm...*
*We will be happy to notify you as soon as we receive information to confirm this.*

**critical** (adj) absolutely essential, very very important
*Having a clear job description is critical.*
*This is a critical period for the company.*

**deficit** (n) not enough, the difference between what is available and what is required
*A fire damaged one of their main manufacturing plants, and this has left us with a deficit of replacement parts.*
*The federal budget deficit was cut by half last year.*

**delivery** (n) carrying or transporting something, by mail or courier
*We are currently unable to offer a clear date for delivery.*
*The delivery was delayed due to a fire in the warehouse.*

**developer** (n) the person that comes up with an idea and produces it
*We are all excited to hear about your proposals for the solar electric generator at the developers' conference on the 25th.*
*The site was bought by a property developer.*

**dissatisfaction** (n) being unhappy or not content with something
*Ineffective hiring practises lead to customer dissatisfaction.*
*He expressed his dissatisfaction most strongly.*

**environment** (n) the world around us
*Pollution has done irreparable damage to the local environment.*
*If you care about the environment, then choose one of our hybrid engine vehicles.*

**fail** (v) to not succeed to do something
*He passed the initial interview but failed the second interview.*
*Only 5 percent of test-takers fail to reach the required level.*

**hesitate** (v) to pause or stop before doing something
*Don't hesitate to contact me.*
*Customers are hesitating to buy the new model.*

**industry** (n) the production of goods on a large scale
*Industry provides the majority of jobs in the area.*
*The town became a center of industry in the late nineteenth century.*

**ineffective** (adj) not working well, or not good at doing a particular job
*It is noisy and ineffective.*
*Ineffective hiring practises lead to customer dissatisfaction.*

**initial** (adj) coming first before other events
*He passed the initial interview but failed the second interview.*
*My initial thought was that it must have been a spaceship.*

**investment** (n) money used to make a profit in the future
*We bought the house as an investment.*
*Small companies are sometimes a risky investment.*

**keen** (adj) interested and excited, very much wanting to do something
*I'm sure you will be keen to attend.*
*We are keen to show him the new production line.*

**luxury** (n) an expensive an high quality item, not usually something needed
*We have the service to suit you if you want to travel in luxury...*
*Enjoy the luxury of real silk next to your skin.*

**manufacture** (v) to produce a large number or amount of something, usually in a factory or plant
*There was a fire at one of their main manufacturing plants.*
*The parts are manufactured overseas, but assembled in our factory here in the US.*

**plant** (n) a factory, or the place where goods are manufactured
*A fire damaged one of their main manufacturing plants, and this has left us with a deficit of replacement parts.*
*The shoes are made at our Asian plant.*

**seek** (v) to look for someone or something very carefully
*We are currently seeking an alternative supplier, and hope to be able to confirm a deal by the end of the month.*
*The Giants are seeking a new player, after Robinson broke his ankle in training.*

**solar** (adj) powered by sunlight
*We are all excited to hear about your proposals for the solar electric generator at the developers' conference on the 25th.*
*The calculator operates on a solar cell, so no batteries are required.*

**suit** (v) to match or fit somebody well
*We have the service to suit you...*
*That new hairstyle really suits you.*

## Quiz 6.4

**1 Use the definitions to find the words in the puzzle.**

1  look for
2  make certain
3  savings and assets
4  the opposite of pass
5  farming
6  of the sun
7  first
8  produce
9  a shortage
10  production of goods
11  a different option

**2 Choose the correct word.**

1  I'm very upset and I want a(n) .................... .
(A) apology
(B) dissatisfaction
(C) luxury

2  There should be a(n) .................... of parts to the factory this Friday.
(A) delivery
(B) developer
(C) industry

3  There is .................... amongst the workers about the low wage increase.
(A) deficit
(B) dissatisfaction
(C) investment

4  There are several .................... who have new plans and ideas for the company.
(A) plants
(B) industries
(C) developers

5  A job as a receptionist would really .................... me right now.
(A) confirm
(B) fail
(C) suit

6  I'm not so .................... going to the movies; I prefer going to the theatre.
(A) keen
(B) keen on
(C) keen to

7  It's .................... that the company increases its profits next year.
(A) critical
(B) ineffective
(C) keen

8  We assemble the monitors at this .................... .
(A) environment
(B) investment
(C) plant

9  The prize is a fourteen-day .................... cruise around the Mediterranean.
(A) deficit
(B) luxury
(C) solar

10  Please don't .................... to ask me any questions.
(A) hesitate
(B) seek
(C) suit

11  I think Mr Harris is .................... as a manager and should leave the company.
(A) alternative
(B) ineffective
(C) keen

## Unit 7.4

**appreciate** (n) to feel grateful to somebody because of what they have done for you
*I really appreciated your help.*
*I would appreciate some compensation.*

**compensation** (n) money paid to apologize for disappointment with goods or services
*I would appreciate some compensation.*
*We demanded compensation for our lost luggage.*

**confirm** (n) to state that something is definitely correct
*I am just writing to confirm...*
*I've received replies from almost all of you confirming attendance, but...*

**constant** (adj) not changing, staying the same over time
*He was the only constant member of the team.*
*The number or rehires remained constant.*

**enthusiastic** (adj) very interested, keen and excited about something
*You should be enthusiastic and knowledgeable about the movie business.*
*Enthusiastic students can hope to learn in as little as four weeks.*

**immensely** (adv) very much
*I was looking forward to the holiday immensely.*
*I enjoyed the party immensely.*

**knowledgeable** (adj) understanding something to a great degree
*You should be enthusiastic and knowledgeable about the movie business.*
*He is very knowledgeable about cars.*

**(be) led** (v) caused to think something, persuaded
*Firstly, I was led to believe that all rooms in the hotel...*
*I was led to think that there was no future for me in the business.*

**mere** (adj) only, a smaller than expected amount
*...a mere five minutes from the beautiful blue waters of the Aegean.*
*He wrote his first piece when he was a mere seven years old.*

**overall** (adj) total, complete, related to the whole thing
*It has the best overall features.*
*Which model sold the greatest number overall?*

**period** (n) an amount of time
*In which sales period was the smallest number of Townstars sold?*
*The period is best known for the Battle of Crecy.*

**recruit** (n) a person hired by a company to do a job
*Recruits from other companies.*
*The number of recruits fell last year.*

**rehire** (n) a person hired again to do the same job
*The number of rehires remained constant.*
*Rehires are often sought after, as they require less training.*

**renovate** (n) to repair something to a condition as good as new
*The house really needs to be renovated.*
*Stay at the recently renovated Casa Stanoupolos Hotel.*

**represent** (n) show, or indicate
*What does the chart represent?*
*This represents three years of hard work.*

**secretarial** (adj) associated with the work of secretaries, administrative work
*Secretarial position available starting March.*
*Secretarial skills are essential in this line of work.*

**unspoiled** (adj) not damaged, altered or affected (especially by tourists)
*...visit the unspoiled island of Kefalonia.*
*It is an unspoiled area with few hotels.*

## Quiz 7.4

**1 Complete the sentences with the following words.**

> confirm   knowledgeable   led
> mere   rehires   renovated
> represent   secretarial

1 I'd like to apply for the .................... position. I have good computer skills and can communicate well.
2 The farm buildings have been .................... at last.
3 We were all .................... to believe that there would be an increase in our salaries this year.
4 The hotel is a .................... five minute walk from the beach.
5 There have been several .................... of experienced people this month.
6 Helen is very .................... . She has researched the company well.
7 These figures .................... sales last year.
8 Can you .................... that the order will arrive on Friday?

**2 Find nine words in the puzzle. Then match them with their meanings.**

| C | O | M | P | E | N | S | A | T | I | O | N | L |
|---|---|---|---|---|---|---|---|---|---|---|---|---|
| T | A | P | P | R | E | C | I | A | T | E | W | E |
| M | N | S | E | U | D | B | Y | W | D | F | U | P |
| A | E | J | R | S | G | W | A | E | O | Y | M | O |
| B | K | I | Z | W | A | N | L | P | L | Q | E | V |
| R | D | H | N | E | P | I | F | E | P | S | L | E |
| E | A | F | T | K | O | B | S | V | E | C | O | R |
| C | O | L | J | P | N | N | I | J | R | U | L | A |
| R | V | G | S | C | E | T | V | A | I | S | M | L |
| U | C | N | O | M | A | B | T | Z | O | G | A | L |
| I | U | X | M | V | F | O | R | F | D | A | B | M |
| T | B | I | H | A | E | W | O | D | R | C | S | E |
| A | C | O | N | S | T | A | N | T | O | F | Y | A |
| E | N | T | H | U | S | I | A | S | T | I | C | X |

1 payment
2 new employee
3 an amount of time
4 keen
5 be thankful for
6 related to the whole thing
7 untouched, perfect
8 regular
9 greatly

# Quizzes key

## 1.1
1 keyboard   2 green   3 oar   4 discuss
5 tied   6 waved   7 covered   8 incredible

## 2.1
1
1 B, 2 C, 3 B, 4 C, 5 A, 6 A, 7 C, 8 B

2
1 goods   2 vacation   3 parcel   4 customer
5 notice   6 overtime   7 repairs   8 recently
9 cheap   10 terrible   11 decide   12 arrange

## 3.1
1
1 loan   2 plug   3 purchase   4 courier
5 improvement   6 branch   7 stock
8 replacement   9 appreciate
10 participant   11 auction

2
1 included   2 socket   3 label   4 block
5 buckle   6 feedback   7 company
8 adaptor   9 appreciation   10 pleased
11 criticized   12 practical   13 previous
14 theoretical

## 4.1
1
1 C, 2 B, 3 C, 4 B, 5 B, 6 B, 7 C, 8 B, 9 A, 10 C,
11 A, 12 B

2
1 false   2 true   3 false   4 false   5 true
6 true   7 true   8 true   9 false   10 true
11 false   12 false   13 true   14 true   15 true
16 false   17 false   18 true

## 5.1
1
1 considered   2 welfare   3 credit   4 downturn
5 impact   6 margin   7 complexity   8 distribution
9 immediate   10 accommodation
11 recommendations   12 advantage

2
1 false   2 false   3 true   4 false   5 true
6 true   7 true   8 true   9 false   10 false
11 false   12 true

## 6.1
1
1 B, 2 C, 3 A, 4 A, 5 A, 6 A, 7 B, 8 C, 9 C

2
1 audit   2 penalty   3 consignment   4 on behalf
5 specification   6 customer   7 invention
8 monument   9 thief   10 foreman

## 7.1
1
1 recipient   2 facility   3 termination   4 failure
5 barcode   6 nonpayment   7 reservation
8 certification   9 inquiry   10 intend

2
1 nominate   2 applicants   3 intention
4 benefit   5 enable   6 anticipate   7 assist
8 potential   9 intended   10 responsible
11 promptly   12 tag   13 consignment
14 complaint   15 appropriately   16 suitably
17 administrative

## 1.2
1
1 overpass   2 skyscraper   3 passenger   4 dock
5 collect   6 pour   7 revise

2
1 withdraw   2 guardrail   3 lie   4 monitor
5 freeway   6 customer   7 shining   8 holding
9 tent

## 2.2
1
1 A, 2 A, 3 C, 4 B, 5 B, 6 C, 7 B, 8 B, 9 A, 10 B,
11 A, 12 B

2
1 depart   2 drive   3 upstairs   4 invite
5 probably   6 handy   7 member   8 detailed
9 venue

## 3.2
1
1 refund   2 attend   3 file   4 inquire   5 relative
6 pushy   7 discount   8 content   9 cover
10 receipt

2
1 seminar   2 disagreement   3 shipping
4 turnover   5 document   6 suggest   7 recent
8 exceed   9 satisfied

3
1 situation   2 inexperienced   3 argument
4 carelessness   5 definitely   6 shortcut
7 graduated   8 mileage   9 unappreciated
10 demanding   11 drastically

## 4.2
1
1 B, 2 C, 3 A, 4 B, 5 A, 6 B, 7 A, 8 C, 9 A, 10 C,
11 A, 12 B

2
1 true   2 false   3 true   4 false   5 true   6 true
7 false   8 true   9 true   10 true   11 false
12 true   13 true   14 true   15 false   16 true

## 5.2
1
1 B, 2 C, 3 A, 4 B, 5 A, 6 C, 7 A, 8 C, 9 A, 10 C

2
1 false   2 false   3 true   4 true   5 true   6 false
7 true   8 true   9 true   10 false   11 false
12 true   13 false

## 6.2
1
1 meticulously   2 eager   3 enforced   4 serious
5 comfortable   6 consistently   7 grueling
8 timely   9 restored   10 emerged

## 2
1 C, 2 A, 3 B, 4 B, 5 A, 6 C, 7 A

## 7.2
1
1 driftwood   2 pier   3 predict   4 improper
5 freak   6 forecaster   7 refund
8 memorandum   9 fail   10 strategy   11 yacht

2
1 campaign   2 withdrawal   3 cancellation
4 participants   5 complaints   6 remittance
7 alumni   8 bulletin   9 applications
10 cardiovascular   11 criticism   12 swathe
13 occurrences

3
1 false   2 false   3 true   4 true   5 true   6 true
7 false   8 true   9 true   10 true   11 false
12 true   13 false   14 true   15 true   16 false

## 1.3
1
1 C, 2 B, 3 A, 4 A, 5 A, 6 A, 7 B, 8 C, 9 C

2
1 chef   2 valley   3 grill   4 ruin   5 bored   6 draw
7 plow   8 kneel   9 tie

3
1 plain   2 wooden   3 fixed   4 backpack   5 yard
6 forest   7 weight   8 figurine   9 trawler   10 cry
11 pier   12 scene

## 2.3
1
1 blocks   2 drawer   3 cupboard   4 bank
5 ordered   6 cafeteria   7 kept   8 several
9 actually   10 polite

2
1 false   2 true   3 false   4 true   5 false   6 true
7 false   8 true   9 false   10 false

## 3.3
1
1 A, 2 B, 3 B, 4 C, 5 C, 6 A, 7 B, 8 A, 9 A, 10 A,
11 C

2
1 calculations   2 catch   3 right away
4 amusing   5 stadium   6 initially   7 withdrawal
8 unreasonable   9 reservation   10 heel

## 4.3
1
1 keen   2 optimistic   3 spectator   4 vigilant
5 innovation   6 schedule   7 delighted
8 salvage   9 realize   10 feature

2
1 vicinity   2 particular   3 lookout   4 ambitious
5 latecomers   6 support   7 hand over   8 adjust
9 impact   10 background

**5.3**

1

1 investigation  2 repetitiveness  3 intercom
4 document  5 bankrupt  6 impatient
7 non-refundable  8 internship  9 dependence
10 criticize

2

1 C, 2 B, 3 C, 4 A, 5 A, 6 C, 7 B, 8 A, 9 B, 10 C,
11 A

**6.3**

1

1 chairman  2 equipment  3 retirement
4 tornado  5 secure  6 invoice  7 foreign
8 rare  9 damage  10 loan  11 strikes

2

1 true  2 true  3 true  4 true  5 true  6 false
7 true  8 false  9 true  10 false  11 false
12 true  13 true  14 true  15 true  16 false
17 false  18 true  19 false  20 false  21 true
22 true

3

1 resolve  2 situation  3 originally  4 social
5 employed  6 refuse  7 report  8 claim
9 accused  10 rescued  11 abused
12 surrounding  13 pronounced

**7.3**

1

1 A, 2 C, 3 B, 4 C, 5 C, 6 A, 7 B, 8 B, 9 A

2

1 culinary  2 vendor  3 ensure  4 festivities
5 tradition  6 explorer  7 orienteering  8 elderly
9 personalized  10 revised  11 host

**1.4**

1

1 keyboard  2 outfit  3 counter  4 set
5 deserted  6 decorate  7 harbor  8 Cycling
9 tool  10 display  11 control panel  12 bride
13 handle  14 raise  15 pointed

2

1 commuter  2 flight attendant  3 resign
4 sweep  5 crashes  6 locker  7 tray
8 customer  9 walkway  10 hiding  11 lean

**2.4**

1

1 C, 2 B, 3 C, 4 B, 5 C, 6 C, 7 C, 8 B, 9 A, 10 C,
11 A, 12 B, 13 C

2

1 quote  2 book  3 policy  4 license  5 amusing
6 frankly  7 appreciate  8 borrow  9 attitude
10 motivate  11 terrific  12 maintenance

**3.4**

1

1 false  2 true  3 true  4 true  5 false  6 false
7 false  8 true  9 false

2

1 response  2 suggest  3 canceled
4 recommended  5 suitable  6 representative
7 pressed  8 postpone  9 prefer
10 expectations

**4.4**

1

1 evacuation  2 transit  3 toiletries
4 unattended  5 suspicious  6 patented
7 reasonably  8 impression

2

1 ensure  2 attendee  3 overrun  4 shower
5 outlook  6 slump  7 constant  8 remind
9 kiosk  10 organize  11 stable  12 affordable
13 layer
Mystery word: revolutionary

**5.4**

1

1 capital  2 reception  3 pretended  4 demand
5 submitted  6 ensure  7 realize  8 dent
9 immediate  10 properly  11 particularly

2

1 true  2 false  3 true  4 true  5 true  6 false
7 false  8 true  9 true  10 true

**6.4**

1

1 seek  2 confirm  3 investment  4 fail
5 agriculture  6 solar  7 initial  8 manufacture
9 deficit  10 industry  11 alternative]

2

1 A, 2 A, 3 B, 4 C, 5 C, 6 B, 7 A, 8 C, 9 B, 10 A,
11 B

**7.4**

1

1 secretarial  2 renovated  3 led  4 mere
5 rehires  6 knowledgeable  7 represent
8 confirm

2

1 compensation  2 recruit  3 period
4 enthusiastic  5 appreciate  6 overall
7 unspoiled  8 constant  9 immensely

# Alphabetical Word list

**Unit**

## A

| | |
|---|---|
| a cut above (adj) | 3.4 |
| abandoned (adj) | 6.3 |
| abused (adj) | 6.3 |
| accommodation (n) | 5.1 |
| accuse (v) | 6.3 |
| actually (adv) | 2.3 |
| adapter (n) | 3.1 |
| adjust (v) | 4.3 |
| administrative (adj) | 7.1 |
| advanced (adj) | 5.2 |
| advantage (n) | 5.1 |
| advise (v) | 5.2 |
| affordable (adj) | 4.4 |
| agriculture (n) | 6.4 |
| aid (v) | 5.1 |
| allow (v) | 3.4 |
| alternative (adj) | 5.2, 6.4 |
| alumnus (plural alumni) (n) | 7.2 |
| ambitious (adj) | 4.3 |
| amusing (adj) | 3.3, 2.4 |
| anticipate (v) | 7.1, 7.2 |
| apologize (v) | 4.1 |
| apology (n) | 6.4 |
| applicant (n) | 7.1, 5.2 |
| application (n) | 7.2 |
| appointment (n) | 3.1 |
| appreciate (v) | 3.1, 2.4, 7.4 |
| appreciation (n) | 3.1 |
| appropriately (adv) | 7.1 |
| argument (n) | 3.2 |
| arrange (v) | 2.1, 3.4 |
| arrangement (n) | 2.1 |
| assist (v) | 4.1, 7.1 |
| attend (v) | 3.2, 5.4 |
| attendee (n) | 4.4 |
| attentively (adv) | 6.2 |
| attorney (n) | 5.1 |
| auction (n) | 3.1 |
| audit (n) | 6.1 |
| available (adj) | 2.2, 3.3 |
| awkward (adj) | 3.4 |

## B

| | |
|---|---|
| background (n) | 4.3 |
| backpack (n) | 1.3 |
| bank (n) | 2.3 |
| bankrupt (adj) | 4.2, 5.3 |
| bankruptcy (n) | 5.1 |
| barcode (n) | 7.1 |

| | |
|---|---|
| behalf (n) | 6.1 |
| benefit (v) | 7.1 |
| beverage (n) | 7.3 |
| block (n) | 2.3 |
| block (v) | 3.1 |
| boardroom (n) | 2.3 |
| boast (v) | 4.2 |
| book (v) | 2.4 |
| boost (v) | 4.1 |
| bored (adj) | 1.3 |
| borrow (v) | 2.4 |
| bother (v) | 2.1 |
| branch (n) | 3.1 |
| bride (n) | 1.4 |
| briefcase (n) | 2.2 |
| buckle (n) | 3.1 |
| bulletin (n) | 7.2 |

## C

| | |
|---|---|
| cafeteria (n) | 2.3 |
| calculations (n) | 3.3 |
| calculator (n) | 2.4 |
| camp (v) | 1.2 |
| campaign (n) | 7.2 |
| cancel (v) | 4.1, 3.4 |
| cancellation (n) | 7.2 |
| capital (n) | 5.4 |
| cardiovascular (adj) | 7.2 |
| careless (adj) | 5.2 |
| carelessness (n) | 3.2 |
| carousel (n) | 3.4 |
| catch (v) | 3.3 |
| cautiously (adv) | 6.2 |
| certain (adj) | 2.2 |
| certification (n) | 7.1 |
| chair (v) | 2.3, 2.4 |
| chairman (n) | 6.3 |
| cheap (adj) | 2.1 |
| chef (n) | 1.3 |
| circumstance (n) | 4.1 |
| claim (v) | 6.3 |
| closure (n) | 4.2, 6.3 |
| coach (adj) | 3.3 |
| collect (v) | 1.2 |
| comfortable (adj) | 6.2 |
| commendable (adj) | 3.4 |
| commercial (adj) | 5.2 |
| committee (n) | 2.4 |
| commuter (n) | 1.4 |
| company (n) | 3.1 |

| | |
|---|---|
| compensation (n) | 7.4 |
| complain (v) | 6.1 |
| complaint (n) | 2.1, 7.1, 7.2 |
| complexity (n) | 5.1 |
| complimentary (adj) | 4.1, 7.3 |
| comprehensive (adj) | 7.2 |
| confirm (v) | 6.1, 6.4, 7.4 |
| considered (be) (v) | 5.1 |
| consignment (n) | 6.1, 7.1 |
| consistently (adv) | 6.2 |
| constant (adj) | 4.4, 7.4 |
| content (adj) | 3.2 |
| control panel (n) | 1.4 |
| cordless (adj) | 4.2 |
| co-supervise (v) | 5.3 |
| counter (n) | 1.4 |
| courier (n) | 3.1, 5.1 |
| cover (v) | 3.2 |
| covered (adj) | 1.1 |
| crash (v) | 2.3, 1.4 |
| credit (n) | 5.1 |
| critical (adj) | 6.4 |
| criticism (n) | 7.2 |
| criticize (v) | 3.1, 5.3 |
| cry (v) | 1.3 |
| culinary (adj) | 7.3 |
| cupboard (n) | 2.3 |
| custom (n) | 2.2 |
| customer (n) | 2.1, 6.1, 1.2, 1.4, |
| cycle (v) | 1.4 |

## D

| | |
|---|---|
| damage (n) | 6.3 |
| deadline (n) | 4.1 |
| debt (n) | 4.2, 5.4 |
| decide (v) | 2.1 |
| decorate (v) | 1.4 |
| deficit (n) | 6.4 |
| definitely (adv) | 3.2 |
| delighted (adj) | 4.2 |
| delighted (adj) | 4.3 |
| deliver (v) | 2.3, 2.4 |
| delivery (n) | 6.4 |
| demand (high) (n) | 5.4 |
| demand (v) | 5.2 |
| demanding (adj) | 3.2 |
| denounce (v) | 6.3 |
| dent (n) | 5.4 |
| depart (v) | 2.2 |
| dependence (n) | 5.3 |

deposit (n)   3.3
depressing (adj)   4.2
deserted (adj)   1.4
desperate (adj)   3.3
detailed (adj)   2.2
deter (v)   4.1
devastate (v)   5.3
developer (n)   6.4
diagram (n)   1.3
disagreement (n)   3.2
disconnect (v)   5.3
discount (n)   3.2
discuss (v)   1.1, 2.1, 1.3
display (n)   1.4
disposal (n)   4.1, 7.2
dispute (n)   6.3
dissatisfaction (n)   6.4
distribution (n)   5.1
dock (n)   1.2
document (n)   3.2, 5.3
double (v)   4.2
downturn (n)   5.1
drastically (adv)   3.2
draw (v)   1.3
drawer (n)   2.3
driftwood (n)   7.2
drive (v)   2.2

**E**

eager (adj)   6.2
elderly (n)   7.3
elderly (people) (adj)   4.2
emerge (v)   6.2
emergency (n)   5.1
employ (v)   6.3
enable (v)   7.1
endurance (n)   6.2
enforced (adj)   6.2
ensure (v)   7.3, 4.4, 5.4
enter (v)   2.3
enthusiastic (adj)   7.4
entrée (n)   5.2
environment (n)   6.4
equipment (n)   6.3
evacuation (n)   4.4
evaluate (v)   6.1
evidence (n)   5.2
exceed (v)   3.2
expand (v)   4.2
expect (v)   2.4
expectations (n)   3.4
explorer (n)   7.3
extensive (adj)   7.2
extremely (adv)   6.3

**F**

facility (n)   7.1, 6.3
fail (v)   7.2, 6.4
failure (n)   7.1
famed (adj)   6.3
feature (v)   7.2, 4.3
feedback (n)   3.1
festivities (n)   7.3
figurine (n)   1.3
file (v)   3.2
fill out (v)   2.4
fix (v)   1.3
flight attendant (n)   1.4
focus (v)   1.1
focused (adj)   1.3
forecaster (n)   7.2
foreign (adj)   6.3
foreman (n)   6.1
foremost (adj)   4.1
forest (n)   1.3
forget (v)   2.2
founding (n)   7.3
frankly (adv)   2.4
freak (adj)   7.2
freeway (n)   1.2
function (n)   5.4
fundraising (n)   6.3
further (adv)   7.2

**G**

gains (n)   4.1
gesture (n)   4.2
get along (with) (v)   2.1
getaway (n)   4.1
goods (n)   2.1
gradually (adv)   5.2
graduate (v)   3.2
green (n)   1.1
grill (n)   1.3
grueling (adj)   6.2
guarantee (n)   7.3
guardrail (n)   1.2

**H**

hand you over (v)   4.3
handle (n)   1.4
handling (n)   4.3
handy (adj)   2.2
hang (v)   1.3
harbor (n)   1.4
harshness (n)   6.2
hazardous (adj)   4.1
heel (n)   3.3
hesitate (v)   6.4
hide (v)   1.4
hiker (n)   1.3

hold (v)   1.2
hospital (n)   2.3
host (v)   7.3

**I**

identify (v)   5.3
illegal (adj)   5.2
immediate (adj)   5.1, 5.4
immensely (adv)   7.4
impact (n)   5.1, 4.3
impatient (adj)   5.3
impending (adj)   7.2
impression (n)   5.2, 4.4
improper (adj)   7.2
improvement (n)   3.1
in the meantime (expression)   4.1
inaccuracy (n)   7.2
included (adj)   3.1
inconvenience (n)   4.1, 6.3
incredible (adj)   1.1
industry (n)   6.4
ineffective (adj)   3.4, 6.4
inexperienced (adj)   3.2
infer (v)   7.2
influential (adj)   6.1
initial (adj)   6.4
initially (adv)   3.3
injuries (n)   4.1
innovation (n)   4.3
inquire (v)   3.2
inquiry (n)   7.1
install (v)   6.1
intend (v)   7.1
intended (adj)   7.1
intention (n)   7.1
intercom (n)   5.3
internship (n)   5.3
interrupt (v)   4.1
invention (n)   6.1
investigation (n)   5.3
investment (n)   6.4
invite (v)   2.2
invoice (n)   6.3
involve (v)   4.1
isolate (v)   4.1
itinerary (n)   7.3

**J**

journey (n)   2.3

**K**

keen (adj)   4.3, 6.4
kept (be) (v)   2.3
keyboard (n)   1.1, 1.4
kiosk (n)   4.4
kneel (v)   1.3
knowledgeable (adj)   7.4

## L

| | |
|---|---|
| label (n) | 3.1 |
| lack (n) | 6.3 |
| laden (adj) | 4.2 |
| landscape (n) | 4.1 |
| landslide (n) | 4.2 |
| latecomers (n) | 4.3 |
| layer (n) | 4.4 |
| lean (v) | 1.4 |
| led (adj) | 7.4 |
| liable (adj) | 5.4 |
| license (n) | 3.3, 2.4 |
| licensing (n) | 6.1 |
| lie (on something) (v) | 1.2 |
| lift (give someone a) (n) | 2.1 |
| limousine (n) | 5.2 |
| livestock (n) | 6.3 |
| loan (n) | 6.3 |
| loan (v) | 3.1 |
| locker (n) | 1.4 |
| luxury (n) | 6.4 |

## M

| | |
|---|---|
| maintenance (n) | 2.4 |
| make sense (v) | 2.4 |
| manufacture (v) | 6.4 |
| margin (n) | 5.1 |
| medical (adj) | 7.2 |
| member (n) | 2.2 |
| memorandum (n) | 7.2 |
| mention (v) | 4.2 |
| mere (adj) | 7.4 |
| meticulously (adv) | 6.2 |
| mileage (n) | 3.2 |
| mind (v) | 2.2 |
| mishear (v) | 5.3 |
| monitor (n) | 1.2 |
| monument (n) | 6.1 |
| motivate (v) | 2.4 |

## N

| | |
|---|---|
| negotiation (n) | 6.3 |
| nominate (v) | 7.1 |
| nonpayment (n) | 7.1 |
| non-refundable. (adj) | 5.3 |
| notice (n) | 2.1 |
| nuisance (n) | 3.3 |

## O

| | |
|---|---|
| oar (n) | 1.1 |
| occurrence (n) | 7.2 |
| on the lookout for (expression) | 4.3 |
| onwards (adv) | 7.2 |
| opinion (n) | 2.4 |
| opportunity (n) | 7.2, 6.3 |
| optimistic (adj) | 5.1, 4.3 |
| ordered (be ... to do something) (v) | 2.3 |

| | |
|---|---|
| organic (adj) | 4.1 |
| organize (v) | 4.4 |
| orienteering (n) | 7.3 |
| originally (adv) | 6.3 |
| outfit (n) | 1.4 |
| outline (n) | 6.3 |
| outlook (n) | 4.4 |
| outraged (adj) | 5.1 |
| overall (adj) | 4.2, 7.4 |
| overpaid (adj) | 5.3 |
| overpass (n) | 1.2 |
| overrun (v) | 4.4 |
| overtime (n) | 2.1 |

## P

| | |
|---|---|
| package (n) | 2.3, 3.3 |
| parcel (n) | 2.1 |
| participant (n) | 3.1, 7.2 |
| particular (adj) | 4.3 |
| particularly (adv) | 5.4 |
| passenger (n) | 1.2 |
| patented (adj) | 4.4 |
| patience (n) | 4.1 |
| penalty (n) | 6.1 |
| period (n) | 7.4 |
| personalized (adj) | 7.3 |
| philosopher (n) | 5.1 |
| pier (n) | 7.2, 1.3 |
| plain (view) | 1.3 |
| plant (n) | 6.4 |
| pleasantly (adv) | 4.1 |
| pleased (adj) | 3.1 |
| plow (v) | 1.3 |
| plug (it) into/in (v) | 3.1 |
| point (v) | 1.4 |
| policy (n) | 2.4 |
| polite (adj) | 2.3 |
| politician (n) | 4.2 |
| popular (adj) | 1.3 |
| postpone (v) | 3.4 |
| potential (adj) | 7.1 |
| pour (v) | 1.2 |
| practical (adj) | 3.1 |
| predict (v) | 7.2 |
| prefer (v) | 2.2, 2.4, 3.4 |
| prepare (v) | 2.2 |
| press (v) | 3.4 |
| pretend (v) | 5.4 |
| previous (adj) | 3.1 |
| principal (adj) | 5.2 |
| prior to (adj) | 5.2 |
| probably (adv) | 2.2 |
| profit (n) | 2.1 |
| prohibit (v) | 7.3 |
| prompt (adj) | 6.1 |

| | |
|---|---|
| promptly (adv) | 7.1 |
| pronounce (v) | 6.3 |
| properly (adv) | 5.4 |
| protection (n) | 5.2 |
| protest (n) | 6.3 |
| purchase (v) | 3.1 |
| pushy (adj) | 3.2 |

## Q

| | |
|---|---|
| questionnaire (n) | 5.2 |
| quote (n) | 2.4 |

## R

| | |
|---|---|
| racket (n) | 3.4 |
| raise (v) | 6.3, 1.4 |
| rare (adj) | 3.3, 6.3 |
| reach (v) | 5.1 |
| realize (v) | 4.3, 5.4 |
| rearrange (v) | 2.2 |
| reasonably (adv) | 4.4 |
| receipt (n) | 3.2 |
| receive(d) (be) (v) | 2.1 |
| recent (adj) | 3.2 |
| recently (adv) | 2.1, 6.3 |
| receptacle (n) | 5.4 |
| reception (n) | 5.4 |
| receptionist (n) | 5.2 |
| receptive (adj) | 5.4 |
| recipient (n) | 7.1 |
| recline (v) | 3.4 |
| recommend (v) | 3.4 |
| recommendation (n) | 5.1 |
| recruit (n) | 7.4 |
| reduction (n) | 4.1 |
| re-enactment (n) | 7.3 |
| refrigerator (n) | 2.3 |
| refund (n) | 4.1, 3.2, 7.2 |
| refuse (v) | 4.1, 6.3 |
| regardless (adv) | 7.2 |
| regret (v) | 5.2 |
| rehire (n) | 7.4 |
| relative (n) | 3.2 |
| religious (adj) | 6.3 |
| remarkable (adj) | 4.2, 3.3 |
| remind (v) | 4.4 |
| remittance (n) | 7.2 |
| renew (v) | 5.4 |
| renounce (v) | 6.3 |
| renovate (v) | 4.2 |
| renovate (v) | 5.3, 7.4 |
| repair (v) | 6.3 |
| repairs (n) | 2.1 |
| repayment (n) | 5.4 |
| repetitiveness (n) | 5.3 |
| replacement (adj) | 3.1 |
| report (v) | 6.3 |

| | | | | | | |
|---|---|---|---|---|---|---|
| represent (v) | 7.4 | spacious (adj) | 4.2 | **U** | |
| representative (n) | 3.4 | specification (n) | 6.1 | unappreciated (adj) | 3.2 |
| rescue (v) | 6.3 | spectator (n) | 4.3 | unattended (adj) | 7.2, 4.4 |
| resent (v) | 5.2 | stable (adj) | 4.4 | unconditional (adj) | 7.3 |
| reservation (n) | 7.1, 3.3 | stack (v) | 1.3 | underprivileged (adj) | 5.1 |
| reserve (v) | 2.4 | stadium (n) | 3.3 | understand (v) | 2.2 |
| resign (v) | 1.4 | stare (v) | 2.3 | unfavorable (adj) | 4.2 |
| resolve (v) | 6.3 | steep (adj) | 1.3 | unfortunately (adv) | 2.2 |
| respond (v) | 4.2 | stock (n) | 3.1 | unprecedented (adj) | 7.2 |
| response (n) | 3.4 | strategy (n) | 7.2 | unreasonable (adj) | 3.3 |
| responsible (for) (adj) | 7.1, 4.2 | streamline (v) | 5.1 | unspoiled (adj) | 7.4 |
| restore (v) | 6.2 | strictly (adv) | 6.2 | unwrap (v) | 5.3 |
| resurface (v) | 5.3 | strike (n) | 6.3 | upset (adj) | 2.4, 5.4 |
| retirement (n) | 6.3, 2.4 | struggle (n) | 4.2, 6.2 | upstairs (n) | 2.2 |
| retirement fund (n) | 5.1 | subdivided (v) | 5.3 | **V** | |
| revise (v) | 1.2 | submit (v) | 5.4 | vacancies (n) | 3.3 |
| revised (adj) | 7.3 | suggest (v) | 3.2, 3.4 | vacation (n) | 2.1 |
| revolutionary (adj) | 4.4 | suit (v) | 6.4 | valley (n) | 1.3 |
| right away (adv) | 3.3 | suitable (adj) | 3.4 | variety (n) | 5.2 |
| rivals (n) | 5.2 | suitably (adv) | 7.1 | vendor (n) | 7.3 |
| rugged (adj) | 4.1 | support (v) | 4.3 | venture (n) | 4.2 |
| ruin (v) | 1.3 | surrender (v) | 6.3 | venture capitalist (n) | 4.2 |
| runner up (n) | 4.2 | surrounding (adj) | 6.3 | venue (n) | 2.2 |
| **S** | | suspicious (adj) | 4.4 | vicinity (n) | 4.3 |
| salvage (v) | 4.3 | swathe (n) | 7.2 | vigilant (adj) | 4.3 |
| satisfied (adj) | 3.2 | sweep (v) | 1.4 | vital (adj) | 6.1 |
| scene (n) | 1.3 | **T** | | **W** | |
| schedule (v) | 4.3 | tag (v) | 7.1 | walkway (n) | 1.4 |
| seaside (n) | 1.3 | takeover (n) | 5.2 | war-torn country (n) | 6.3 |
| secluded (adj) | 4.1 | tent (n) | 1.2 | wave (v) | 1.1 |
| secretarial (adj) | 7.4 | termination (n) | 7.1 | weight (n) | 1.3 |
| secure (adj) | 6.3 | terrible (adj) | 2.1 | welfare (n) | 5.1 |
| secure (v) | 6.3 | terrific (adj) | 2.4 | withdraw (v) | 1.2 |
| seek (v) | 6.4 | the night is young (expression) | 2.4 | withdrawal (n) | 7.2, 3.3 |
| seminar (n) | 3.2 | theoretical (adj) | 3.1 | wooden (adj) | 1.3 |
| senior citizens (n) | 7.3 | thief (n) | 6.1 | **Y** | |
| serious (adj) | 6.2 | through (read/go) (adv) | 2.2 | yacht (n) | 7.2 |
| set (v) | 1.4 | tidy (adj) | 6.1 | yard (n) | 1.3 |
| several (adj) | 2.3 | tie (v) | 1.1, 1.3 | | |
| severity (n) | 7.2 | timely (adj) | 6.2 | | |
| shareholders (n) | 4.2 | toiletries (n) | 4.4 | | |
| shine (v) | 1.2 | tool (n) | 1.4 | | |
| shipping (n) | 3.2 | top (n) | 2.2 | | |
| shortcut (n) | 3.2 | tornado (n) | 6.3 | | |
| shower (n) | 4.4 | tradition (n) | 7.3 | | |
| situation (n) | 3.2, 6.3 | transit (in) (n) | 4.4, 5.4 | | |
| skyscraper (n) | 1.2 | trawler (n) | 1.3 | | |
| sleeves (n) | 3.3 | tray (n) | 1.4 | | |
| slump (v) | 4.4 | tremendous (adj) | 4.1 | | |
| social (adj) | 6.3 | tremor (n) | 4.2 | | |
| socket (n) | 3.1 | triumph (n) | 6.2 | | |
| soften (v) | 5.3 | turnover (n) | 3.2 | | |
| solar (adj) | 6.4 | typos (n) | 4.1 | | |

# OXFORD
UNIVERSITY PRESS

Great Clarendon Street, Oxford OX2 6DP

Oxford University Press is a department of the University of Oxford.
It furthers the University's objective of excellence in research, scholarship,
and education by publishing worldwide in

Oxford  New York

Auckland  Cape Town  Dar es Salaam  Hong Kong  Karachi
Kuala Lumpur  Madrid  Melbourne  Mexico City  Nairobi
New Delhi  Shanghai  Taipei  Toronto

With offices in

Argentina  Austria  Brazil  Chile  Czech Republic  France  Greece
Guatemala  Hungary  Italy  Japan  Poland  Portugal  Singapore
South Korea  Switzerland  Thailand  Turkey  Ukraine  Vietnam

OXFORD and OXFORD ENGLISH are registered trade marks of
Oxford University Press in the UK and in certain other countries

ISBN-13: 978 0 19 456428 1
ISBN-10: 0 19 456428 2

Printed in China

Design and typesetting by Oxford Designers & Illustrators

ACKNOWLEDGEMENTS

*The publisher would like to thank the following for reviewing / piloting the material in
this course:* Mr JOE Dae-ho, Testwise SISA, Jongno, Seoul; Ms YANG Soh Jeong,
Korea University, Seoul; Ms SEO young-ja, Korea Foreign Language University,
Seoul; Ms. Jo Kirihara, Ritsumeikan University, Kyoto; Mr. Nobuo Tsuda,
Konan University, Hyogo; Ms. Rena Yoshida, Obirin University, Kanagawa; Ms.
Keiko Slaybaugh, Showa Ongaku Daigaku, Kanagawa; AIT Foreign Language
Center, Tokyo; Tsuda Jukukai Institute, Tokyo; Nichibei Kaiwa Gakuin, Tokyo;
International Language Centre, Tokyo; Graeme Petrie, Tokyo; Grant Trew,
Stephen Yoell, Mark Barrett, Osaka.

The TOEIC test directions are reprinted by permission of Educational Testing
Service, the copyright owner. However, the test questions and any other
testing information are provided in their entirety by Oxford University Press.
No endorsement of this publication by Educational Testing Service should be
inferred.